THE CLASSICS OF WESTERN SPIRITUALITY
A Library of the Great Spiritual Masters

Marguerite Porete
THE MIRROR OF SIMPLE SOULS

TRANSLATED AND INTRODUCED BY
ELLEN L. BABINSKY

PREFACE BY
ROBERT E. LERNER

PAULIST PRESS
NEW YORK • MAHWAH

Library of Congress Cataloging-in-Publication Data

Porete, Marguerite, ca. 1250-1310.
    [Miroir des simples âmes. English]
    The mirror of simple souls/Marguerite Porete: translated and
introduced by Ellen L. Babinsky: preface by Robert E. Lerner.
      p.   cm.—(The Classics of Western spirituality)
    Includes bibliographical references and indexes.
    ISBN 0-8091-0464-4: (cloth)—ISBN 0-8091-3427-6: (paper)
    1. Contemplation. 2. Spiritual life—Christianity—Early works to
1800. 3. Mysticism—France—History—Middle Ages, 600-1500. 4. Beguines—
France—History. I. Babinsky, Ellen L., 1944- . II. Title. III. Series.
BV5091.C7P6713   1993
248.2'2—dc20
                                        93-14479
                                          CIP

Published by Paulist Press
997 Macarthur Boulevard
Mahwah, New Jersey 07430

Printed and bound in the
United States of America

Contents

Translator of this Volume

ELLEN L. BABINSKY is currently Associate Professor of Church History at Austin Presbyterian Theological Seminary in Texas, where she has served on the faculty since 1988. Following in the footsteps of both her grandfathers and her father who were pastors in the Reformed Church in America, she was ordained a Presbyterian minister in 1976. She holds a B.A. in Philosophy from Earlham College in Richmond, Indiana, a Master of Divinity degree from McCormick Theological Seminary in Chicago, and a Master of Theology degree from Lutheran Northwestern Theological Seminary in St. Paul, Minnesota. She earned her Ph.D. in the history of Christianity from the University of Chicago, having written her dissertation entitled, "A Beguine in the Court of the King: Love and Knowledge in *The Mirror of Simple Souls* by Marguerite Porete." Future scholarly pursuits include continued study in the area of beguine life and spiritual practice.

Author of the Preface

ROBERT E. LERNER took his B.A. at the University of Chicago and his Ph.D. at Princeton University. He is Professor of History at Northwestern University, where he has served as Director of the Humanities Program. Professor Lerner has won awards from the National Endowment for the Humanities, the American Council of Learned Societies, the Guggenheim Foundation, the Rockefeller Foundation, and the Historisches Kolleg in Munich. He is a Fellow of the Medieval Academy of America and the American Academy in Rome. His books include *The Age of Adversity: The Fourteenth Century*; *The Heresy of the Free Spirit*; and *The Powers of Prophecy*.

For my mother,
Margaret Helen Voskuil Babinsky (1917–1973),
and
my father,
William Babinsky (1918–1989)

Preface

It is a privilege to introduce one of the greatest vernacular authors of the Middle Ages to the wider public she deserves. The occasion has been long overdue. Marguerite Porete, cruelly burned alive in the main public square of Paris in 1310, was virtually forgotten to posterity until 1965, when the publication of the original French version of her *Mirror of Simple Souls* became the basis for one of the most dramatic scholarly retrievals of the present century. Since then a growing number of specialists who can read Old French have come to appreciate how exciting a thinker and writer Marguerite was—how her *Mirror*, to quote Peter Dronke, stands as "a wonder and an inspiration." Now Ellen Babinsky offers English-language readers the first translation of the complete work so they may "taste and see" for themselves.

Although Marguerite Porete wrote during the high summer of Scholasticism, *The Mirror of Simple Souls* has little scholastic articulation. Sprawling and episodic, switching unpredictably from narrative to dialogue, it often seems less a treatise than a happening. Nevertheless, the work has great literary force. For one, it employs the device of direct discourse with consummate power. The main speakers, personifications of "Love," "Reason," and "the Soul," discuss sublime matters as one might hear lively discussions on the street: "Oh, for God's sake, Love, what are you saying?"; "Reason, you'll always be half-blind"; "Oh, you sheep, how crude is your understanding!" Had Erich Auerbach known of Marguerite's dialogue he could easily have used it to strengthen his arguments concerning high-medieval representations of reality in which *sublimitas* and *humilitas* are fused.

Equally compelling is Marguerite's use of lively imagery. The liberated soul is "parchment" on which the Holy Spirit writes its lessons; the soul, having lost its will, dwells in "the valley of humility,

1

the plain of truth, and the mountain of love"; once liberated, it loses its name and direction, just as rivers, be they Oise or Seine, lose their names and their courses when they join the sea. Startling imagery may be accompanied by startling paradox: the soul "swims in the sea of joy," yet "feels no joy since she herself is joy." Striking too is Marguerite's joining of the religious with the courtly-erotic. The soul longs for her far-off beloved just as a princess of legend once longed "to see and to have" Alexander; love tells the soul to express her desire "nakedly."

Perhaps the pinnacle of Marguerite's literary accomplishment is her lyricism. The princess who longed for Alexander sought to comfort herself by imagining his looks. Then she had an image painted that portrayed him the way she imagined him. And then "by the means of this image and her other practices she dreamt the king himself." Most of *The Mirror* is composed in rhythmic prose, but sometimes it breaks into full-fledged poetry. One example is a "rondeau" in which the refrain appears three times:

Thinking no longer matters
nor work, nor speech.
Love has brought me so high
(Thinking no longer matters)
with its divine regard
that I have no understanding.
Thinking no longer matters
nor work, nor speech.

Doubtless despite these protestations, Marguerite Porete had not lost her gift of speech.

Much as *The Mirror of Simple Souls* impresses as a vibrant work of literature, it is yet more impressive as a searching and daring work of mystical theology. Caroline Walker Bynum has observed that Marguerite stands apart from the main line of medieval women's spirituality insofar as she discounts "works" (not only fasting and prayers but also the sacraments) and pays no attention to the physicality of Christ. Marguerite also minimizes the usefulness of Scripture: "Love's" teachings surpass the Scriptures of "Holy Church." Hardly anything is predictable in *The Mirror of Simple Souls*. Instead the author offers "new perceptions of the divine realm" (Peter Dronke) in "a religious testimony of incomparable originality" (Kurt Ruh).

PREFACE

Her treatment of mystical union is frank and fearless, provocatively raising issues of autotheisim, quietism, and antinomianism. Her conception of the true church as a community of the spiritual elite is fearless too, and her discussion of the superiority of the true church to the "Little Church" governed by reason gives her mystical treatise an ideological scope of atypical breadth.

Marguerite Porete refused to apologize for being a woman. Because she was certain that her work was divinely inspired, she refused to apologize for having written it—or even to explain to her judges (inevitably male judges) how she had come to do so. As Bernard McGinn has observed, *The Mirror of Simple Souls* contains no hint of the conventional female apology for trespassing male terrain in writing about the highest things. Indeed, it even lacks any appeal to an authenticating visionary experience. Dante, rapt in Paradise, compares himself to St. Paul, but Marguerite exceeds even this amazing boldness by insisting that the soul's annihilation in divinity is more valuable than the vision of the Trinity granted to St. Paul in the third heaven!

Marguerite's characterization of the fabulous princess who longed for Alexander as a woman of "great heart" and "noble courage" can be applied easily to the author herself. Between 1296 and 1306 she was forced to watch the public burning of her book in Valenciennes and to listen to a formal warning that if she circulated it again she would suffer the direst penalties. Yet she did circulate it again and was rearrested. Once imprisoned, she refused steadfastly to cooperate with her jailers, even while knowing that death at the stake could be the only outcome. Marguerite calls the liberated soul a "phoenix," and that is another characterization that could apply equally well to the author of *The Mirror of Simple Souls*.

Introduction

On 1 June 1310 in Paris at the Place de Grève a beguine, referred to as a *"pseudo-mulier,"*[1] was burned at the stake as a relapsed heretic, having written a book "filled with errors and heresies." Her comportment to the last was such that many were moved to tears at the sight of such piety.[2] Her name was Marguerite Porete and her book, *The Mirror of Simple Souls*, written in Old French, had been condemned twice before she herself was committed to the flames.

Scholarly recognition of the importance of *The Mirror of Simple Souls* has been focused in several areas. Until recently, students of the heresy of the Free Spirit have regarded Marguerite Porete as "the first apostle in France of the German sect of Brethren of the Free Spirit."[3] More recently it has been proposed that some of the articles from the Council of Vienne, 1311–12, which condemned the Free Spirit heresy, were excerpted from Marguerite's book, and that very little evidence for the heresy's existence prior to this council can be found in Germany. As a result of these investigations, Marguerite Porete was called "one of the most important figures in the history of the heresy of the Free Spirit."[4] After Marguerite Porete's authorship of *The Mirror* was established in 1946 and a critical edition was published,[5] there were conflicting assessments of the beguine's orthodoxy.[6]

Scholars interested in medieval mysticism include Marguerite's *Mirror* in their studies of late medieval mysticism. In particular, students of Eckhart's thought have found the German Dominican's ideas about union with God, especially those in his vernacular sermons, to be strikingly similar to the French beguine's.[7] Others find Marguerite to be an important subject in their investigations of beguine mystical writing.[8] Scholars concerned to study medieval women's writing have found her text to be an intriguing contribution to their studies and anthologies.[9]

DEVELOPMENT OF BEGUINE COMMUNITIES

The twelfth-century prelude to the beguine story witnesses to an expansion of human possibilities that gave rise to what scholars have called an early "humanism," a veritable "renaissance," a sense of human consciousness that was not evident before.[10] For M.-D. Chenu, the twelfth-century awakening of human possibility was also reflected in, perhaps even grounded in, an evangelical revival in which some committed Christian people penetrated society as apostles of the gospel.[11] In contrast to a conception of the *vita apostolica* expressed in the stability of the common life of the older, more traditional monastic orders, the emerging forms of the apostolic life movement stressed the proselytizing activity of the apostles of the early church. For these evangelists the dominant guiding biblical image of the mission of the seventy in Luke 10:1–12 took precedence over the description of the communal life described in Acts 4:32. Preaching was the central activity for these new groups, specifically itinerant preaching, in contrast to monastic stability and episcopal preaching. Chenu notes that the profound shifts occurring in religious expression were indicated by Anselm of Havelburg when he classified different groups according to their penetration of worldly society, that is, their relative distance from centers of population. The twelfth-century religious awakening was marked by movement into the world, not withdrawal from it.

Women were found among those who responded enthusiastically to this religious awakening, and they developed forms of religious life in number and variety remarkable enough to be clearly identified as a women's movement.[12] In 1216, when Jacques de Vitry obtained verbal permission from the pope for groups of pious women in the Lowlands, France, and Germany to live together, the papacy had been confronted for the first time with a strong movement of feminine piety, which had been evolving since the mid-twelfth century. The women's religious movement in these lands had adapted itself to the orders and forms which had evolved from the itinerant evangelicals, specifically to the Premonstratensians, who early on had included women in their establishments. While it is true that by the end of the twelfth century the Premonstratensians had excluded women, they had still offered to religious women the opportunity to realize their commitment to poverty, continence, and contemplation in strict enclosure according to the Augustinian Rule.

The endurance of these convents beyond the time when the order was closed to women indicates that these houses were not merely a result of Premonstratensian propaganda but were the precipitate of a strong religious women's movement, which lived from an inner drive and need.

The feminine religious movement did not die out when the men closed themselves off from the women, but rather grew even stronger and sought new forms. While the Premonstratensians were receiving convents into their order, groups of women were also insinuating themselves into the Cistercian fold.[13] When Cistercian men along with their Premonstratensian brothers refused acceptance to additional convents, the time came when the female convents of the Premonstratensians and the Cistercians were no longer capable or willing to absorb additional women. Nonetheless, every community that had been newly formed and belonged to no order and followed no prescribed rule remained firmly committed to the precepts of feminine piety in poverty, chastity, fasting, and prayers. This "extra-cloistral form of feminine religiosity" was evident all over the northern European area.[14]

In the late-twelfth and early-thirteenth centuries, these women were called beguines, initially as a derisive, negative term intended to convey the suspicious, even heretical, character of their piety in the judgment of their social peers and the ecclesiastical authorities.[15] By the second half of the thirteenth century, however, the term was used in a more general sense. The name "beguine" applied to all sorts of persons who lived a religious life outside the ecclesiastical norms of regular orders. The term was ordinarily applied to women, both to those who lived together in a house called a beguinage and to women who lived as religious solitaries. The solitary beguine could live as a recluse, or as a mendicant, itinerant teacher, or preacher. The name was also still given to those suspected of heresy. Because the name "beguine" referred to such a wide variety of expressions of piety, the name itself has a large role to play in the story of these women.

The beguine life evolved into a variety of patterns depending on many circumstances. Despite the absence of an overall pattern, historians have attempted to offer descriptions of beguine development.[16] Herbert Grundmann's careful analysis stresses the importance of viewing the emergence of the beguines within the context of the relation of the religious women's movement as a whole to the papacy. The basic presupposition of the papacy had always been that the "religious life," to be truly in service to the church, must be bound to particular regulations and secured through established order. Every ecclesiastically recognized religious way of life had to be based on established rules, norms, and disciplines, for without clear and strong regulation of communities, all religious life would be in danger of losing the right way and the sure foundation. The papacy, therefore, held the conviction that the religious life achieved its true worth and constancy only if it could conform to the existing religious order. When the Fourth Lateran Council of 1216 forbade the founding of new religious orders, however, there was no particular form which was suitable for absorbing the beguine pattern as a form in itself. The *vita religiosa* of the women could be regulated only with reference to male orders and could be achieved only if the women were treated as an annex to them.[17] Therefore, the organizational life and development of the beguine movement is best understood in the context of the perspective of the papacy, of the male religious orders, and of the communities of women themselves.[18]

The convents related to the Cistercians, Dominicans, and Franciscans reached the point where they could not absorb any more women because of overcrowding. At the same time the male orders would accept only those communities of women who could support all their members in strict enclosure out of their own resources, without depending on alms. The options for the unrelated communities were either to find a founder who would furnish an adequate endowment or to accept only wealthy women who would bring their assets with them. There were some men, such as Jacques de Vitry and Lambert le Begue of Liège, who had supported particular religious communities of women outside of established orders, but their efforts never extended beyond the geographical boundaries under their jurisdiction. Grundmann notes that they neither had created an organizational structure with a common rule for all beguines at large, nor had they provided them with the opportunity for ecclesiastical recognition as a kind of independent order. Consequently, beguines formed a sort of middle way between ecclesiastical orders and lay status, living the religious life in chastity and in communities organized by house rules to which members vowed obedience.

The "between status" of the beguines was to be their undoing. Around the middle of the thirteenth century, public opinion took on hostile overtones regarding the beguines, related in large part to polemics against the newer forms of religious life advanced by William of St. Amour, among others. After William had been severely reprimanded by the papacy for his attacks on the mendicant orders, he turned his attention to the beguines, who were an easy and open target for his invectives.[19] He remained on conservative ecclesiastical ground: since they were not an established ecclesiastical order, beguines ought not to live as if they were. They ought not to wear special dress, and they ought not to cut their hair. Since they are only worldly types, such behavior is a violation against the order of the church and therefore is sin deserving excommunication. Beguines are young and able to work, William continued, but they do not; instead they live from alms. They are too young to carry out their vow of chastity without strict discipline. They remain in too close contact with the Dominicans, who also impinge on the rights of the parish clergy. The Dominicans hear beguines' confessions, they preach to them, and they care for them with alms. The Dominicans even converse with them and write letters to them.

William of St. Amour is only one example of rising public suspicion about the beguines. The dangers and problems attendant to the beguine way of life were recognized by detractors, ecclesiastical authorities, and the beguines themselves. The implementation of ecclesiastical regulations was frustrated because there was no unanimous agreement as to who should have the responsibility for oversight and pastoral care of the beguines. On the one hand, the parish clergy claimed authority for the guidance and care of beguines as their parishioners. On the other hand, the beguines, attempting to avoid being bound to the parish, allowed themselves to be given special privileges from papal legates or attached themselves to a wealthy founder. Many beguines tried to place themselves under the pastoral care of the mendicant orders. From the start beguines felt free to confess to the mendicants, and they made use of this possibility to such a great extent that the mendicants were widely employed as special confessors for the beguines. Officially, the leadership of the orders had expressly forbidden their members to administer the sacraments of communion and extreme unction to beguines and to undertake their pastoral care. They neither arranged for the relationships which emerged between the beguines and the Franciscans and the Dominicans, nor were they favorably disposed toward these relationships, but they seemed to be unable to do anything about it.[20] The beguines themselves preferred the Franciscans and Dominicans to parish clergy and often settled near mendicant houses, where individual members of the orders made themselves available for the guidance of beguine communities. In the latter part of the thirteenth century, bishops and/or founders gave oversight and pastoral care of beguines to the mendicants, although general authority remained with the parish clergy.[21]

The confusion about how to order the beguine life becomes even more clear in light of the decisions of the Second Council of Lyons in 1274, which was guided by the decrees of the Fourth Lateran Council in 1215. The Fourth Lateran Council under Innocent III expressed a strong reaction against the proliferation of new monastic orders in the wake of the apostolic life movement, declaring that any new religious groups had to order themselves according to an already existing, established rule, instead of submitting a new rule for approval. In effect, no new orders could be established. The Second Council of Lyons reiterated the prohibition of the Fourth Lateran Council that no new orders be established.[22] The declaration included a supplementary statement that any new orders founded since 1215 without papal approval were forbidden and dissolved. Doubtless the beguines were meant, and the council must have believed that with this proclamation the dangers and disgraces of the beguines could be erased.

In Grundmann's view, the council was ignorant of the fact that the beguine way had evolved into two basic forms so that no general overall order for all beguines could be implemented.[23] On the one hand, there were beguines, by far the majority, who led a stable life in beguine houses, in many cases in close connection with the mendicant orders, supporting themselves with their incomes or with the work of their hands. On the other hand, there were the few who triggered the complaints that the beguines remained in no cloister but wandered without discipline, living off alms instead of working. Such a separation became, as Grundmann sees it, of disastrous significance for the later history of the beguines. The lack of organizational distinctions between the two groups made the measures against the unregulated wandering beguines unworkable, because the same name for so vastly different outward forms of life had mixed the regulated innocent beguines into the catastrophe. Grundmann closes his discussion of the beguines by noting that local statutes which committed the beguine communities to a kind of enclosure were neither uniformly nor completely carried out. There were religious women who remained outside the beguine communities, wandering and begging; these solitary beguines, according to Grundmann, became adherents of the heresy of the Free Spirit. Since both groups were called beguines, the repression of the Free Spirit put all beguines in danger, orthodox as well as heretical.[24]

The growing suspicion led to a major attack on beguines with two decrees from the ecumenical Council of Vienne held from 1311 to 1312. These decrees, far from clarifying the situation for beguines and ecclesiastical authorities, only contributed to the confusion and had dire consequences for the women.[25] One decree, *Cum de quibusdam mulieribus,* explicitly condemned the status of beguine, citing beguines as being in violation of the Fourth Lateran ban on new orders.[26] The condemnation also included a very general judgment concerning doctrinal aberrations of the beguines, terming their theological attempts as "madness." The decree maintained the confusion about beguines, however, for the document closed with an "escape clause" which conceded that truly pious women might be allowed to live penitently, with or without vows of chastity, in communal houses.[27] The decree gave no criteria as to how one was to make the distinction between those who were to be suppressed and those who were to be protected. If the distinction was between the solitary, itinerant beguines and the stable women in community, the document did not say so.[28]

The other decree, *Ad nostrum,* was concerned with doctrine and listed eight errors of "an abominable sect of malignant men known as beghards and faithless women known as beguines," which have been generally considered to be the fundamental tenets of the heresy of the Free Spirit.[29] The articles of *Ad nostrum* accused these heretics of claiming that they could attain such perfection in the present life that they were incapable of sin. In addition, because of this supposed perfection, the Vienne articles charged that these heretics claimed they were not subject to obedience to human laws or to the laws of the church. In effect, the Free Spirit heretics were accused of a radical mysticism and antinomianism. It is important to note that if the first decree perpetuated confusion by offering no criterion by which to discern the "good" beguines from the "bad," the second decree in catastrophic fashion identified beguines and their male counterparts, beghards, as one organized heretical sect, namely, the heretics of the Free Spirit. The Vienne decree *Ad nostrum* used "beguine" as a technical term for adherents of the Free Spirit heresy, as if beguines were by definition heretical. The failure of the council to develop a workable distinction between pious and impious beguines, and its legal definition of beguine as an adherent of the Free Spirit heresy, resulted in what was tantamount to "a hundred years' war" against beguines and beghards in Germany, ending with the Council of Constance in 1417.[30] Many women lost their lives to inquisitorial condemnation; on the other hand, many beguines were protected from inquisitors by advocates from the mendicant orders, by bishops, and by civil magistrates.[31] The threat to beguine communities came not from the poor reputation and heretical tendency of the solitary beguines, as Grundmann argued, but from the inherent ambiguity of the decrees from the Council of Vienne.

The beguine/Free Spirit ambiguity becomes even more apparent in the important work by Robert E. Lerner.[32] Through meticulous research and analysis, he has determined that the data do not support the assumptions of *Ad nostrum*. He found that the Free Spirits were not a sect in the sense of an organization with institutionalized forms of practice and government in communication with other adherents. Instead, they were individuals who held Free Spirit doctrines and who did not form like-minded groups in any formalized way. Not all Free Spirits were beguines and beghards. The heresy was found mainly in urban centers and middle-sized towns. While statistics are not available, the evidence for Free Spirits suggests to Lerner that they were from the more prosperous classes in that they were literate, "a near monopoly of the well-off."[33] Lerner notes that some of the heretics found in the sources were authors, and those that were not writers could still read. Many had a well-developed theological vocabulary. They were not school-trained Latinists, however, which would account for the negative judgment of these persons as "unlearned idiots."[34]

The Free Spirits were committed to poverty and mendicancy as an outgrowth of the *vita apostolica* movement. The centerpiece of the Free Spirit perspective seems to be that arduous ascetic practice was necessary to attain the divine life of union with God. In this view, only through extreme purgation could one divest the self of all will and desire in order to attain perfection. The motivation for the Free Spirits was the search for spiritual perfection, not a revolutionary antipathy to the church, as some scholars have thought.[35]

Lerner's work shows that those independent beguines who were Free Spirits were mostly educated and literate, and therefore presumably from wealthier backgrounds. Such evidence would indicate that the solitary, itinerant, begging beguines probably chose their mode of life as a continuation of the apostolic ideal, in which case their mendicancy would have religious and not merely economic significance. Not every solitary beguine was a Free Spirit, but they were all suspected of being such. As Lerner shows, the evidence from the protocols indicates that such women were viewed as heretical probably because they were solitaries, and because they were visible and did not conform to the prescribed order.[36] Again, according to Lerner's findings, not all female Free Spirits were beguines. Some were laywomen who had been disciples of male Free Spirit teachers. Also, some beguine Free Spirits belonged to a community, and therefore were not the independents who were led into the heresy as Grundmann supposed.[37]

These considerations indicate that generalizations are hard to come by in the study of both the beguines and the adherents of Free Spirit ideas. The Free Spirit heresy is related to the beguines, but not so clearly as was supposed either by the Council of Vienne or later scholarship. What is clear, however, is that economic and social issues do not define the limits for the discussion of the beguine movement, nor does the study of beguines exhaust our understanding about the contours of the Free Spirit heresy.

BEGUINES IN FRANCE

Beginning around 1230 in the French kingdom, beguine houses of various types and sizes were founded, and they flourished particularly in the north.[38] These French beguine houses received powerful protection from individual clergy who were favorably impressed with the piety of the women, and from wealthy persons, often women from either the nobility or upperclass bourgeois, who furnished lands and buildings and convinced local magistrates to support these houses.[39] Some French beguine houses were founded and supported by the French crown, a phenomenon which certainly would have served to legitimate the beguine way of life and may have contributed to the circumstances surrounding the death of Marguerite Porete. Of the houses founded by the Capetians, we have available the statutes for the great beguinage in Paris founded in 1264 by Louis IX.[40] According to the confessor of Louis IX, who took an active interest in their welfare, the Paris beguines numbered close to four hundred. Louis IX's heirs continued the support of beguine houses with royal revenues. During the reign of Philip IV, the crown made certain that papal privileges, exemptions, and indulgences continued to the benefit of the Paris beguinage, and ensured the construction of a chapel for them in which a priest was to celebrate mass once a year.[41] However much beguines suffered from inquisitorial proceedings in Germany, they remained quite undisturbed in France owing to the esteem in which they were held by their powerful patrons.

This support was especially strong from the crown, as the preamble to the rule given to the Paris beguines in 1327 by Charles IV shows:

> Since . . . our holy father the Pope, by a council which was held at Vienne, because certain beguines outside our realm comported themselves badly and because of certain excesses and evildoing which they committed, had struck down and abolished all those in that estate; and because, as much as through inquiry as by common acclaim and renown, the beguines living in the said house were found innocent and not blameable of the above stated misdeeds, it pleased our Holy Father to reinstate them in their estate and their place.[42]

Made confident by the tacit papal approval, the beguines apparently had submitted to Charles IV for review the statutes they had received from the prior of the Dominicans, to whose direction they had been committed by Philip IV, Louis X, and Philip V. These regulations were promulgated in 1327.[43] Fourteen years later, in 1341, these same statutes were added to and confirmed anew by Philip VI. They give a good picture of what sort of structure guided the life of the beguines in the great beguinage in Paris from the time of Philip IV.[44] The regulations contained in the statutes for the Great Beguinage exhibit what I call *moderate* enclosure, and this moderate enclosure was enforced by regulations of the beguines' property.

The beguinage was surrounded by a large wall, which effectively shielded the beguines from the outside world. A woman could choose to live either in community or alone in her own small cottage. The mistress of the beguinage lived in her own house, which was probably larger and better furnished than the other cottages. Apparently a large building housed those who preferred communal living, and it contained a dormitory and a refectory. Other buildings included an infirmary, a place to teach children, and the chapel constructed during the time of Louis IX. In the center of the courtyard was a well to meet the water needs of the beguinage.[45]

The governance of the beguinage was entrusted to the mistress, named by the almoner of the king, who had final jurisdiction over the beguinage. The mistress was placed under the immediate supervision of the prior of the Dominicans of Paris, whose role established by the king was that of guardian and governor of the beguinage. The mistress was obligated both to seek the advice of the prior in all important matters and to report all financial transactions to him. With the counsel of the Dominican prior, the mistress was to appoint three or four elder beguines as her council to assist her in the administration of the beguinage.[46]

The pattern of responsibility for management provides important data for understanding the regulations of the beguinage. All of the original residences, private and communal, were retained by the crown but managed by the mistress and the council under the guidance of the Dominican prior.[47] The original residences built by the crown could be purchased or rented if the beguine had the resources. A beguine also could choose to build her own house, presumably within the surrounding wall. The picture seems to be a sort of fourteenth-century condominium community.

The beguines certainly were allowed to have commerce with the outside world, and the principles of enclosure to which they were subject were of a modified sort; there were times when the women could leave the beguinage, in contrast to their cloistered sisters in regular orders.[48] Four articles of the *Statuts* of 1341 demonstrate enclosure themes and delineate clearly the circumstances under which beguines were permitted to leave the beguinage. Beguines were allowed to leave their precincts only with permission of the mistress and in the company of a companion approved by the mistress. Failure to comply meant immediate dismissal.[49] That the circumstances under which the Paris beguines could leave the beguinage were strictly regulated is clear. Three of the articles indicate that the first infraction of those regulations was cause for punishment only; in the first article, however, should a beguine leave the beguinage without approval or without an approved companion, the first infraction was grounds for immediate dismissal.

Moderate enclosure was also maintained by carefully regulating entry into the beguinage. Four articles deal with who may enter the beguinage and when. No man, secular or religious, regardless of class or station, could take any meal within the beguinage without the expressed permission of the mistress.[50] A beguine who lived "en couvent" could not receive any man in her room but could speak with him in the refectory or in the chapel.[51] The infraction of this regulation had immediate consequences: if a beguine were found alone with a man, and if there were any suspicion of malfeasance, she would be dismissed, apparently on the first infraction.[52] Finally, no man could sleep overnight in the beguinage, nor could any male child, no matter how young. The beguine in whose room such a male was found would be dismissed immediately.[53] It is clear that the moderate enclosure principles held for entry as well as exit. Apparently there was no prohibition of female acquaintances of beguines from entering the beguinage; only male presence was curtailed.

The property regulations of the *Statuts* pertain to real estate, and there are two general classifications: the disposition of the houses of those beguines who were dismissed from the beguinage for infractions of the rules noted above, and the regulations pertaining to the houses of the resident beguines. The article pertaining to the first category is straightforward: if a beguine was dismissed from the beguinage for any of the reasons noted above, she lost her house and its value no matter what repairs she might have made, or even if she had built her own house.[54] Such a house, along with houses vacated because of death or voluntary withdrawal from the community, could be either sold for profit to the community or maintained as "freely managed" houses. The decision was made according to the judgment of the Dominican guardian, the mistress, and the council of elder beguines.[55]

The second category has several subcategories. Resident beguines were of two kinds: those who entered the beguinage with no income with which to purchase or rent their living space, and those who had sufficient income to purchase, rent, or build their living space. The poorer beguines were welcomed and given a "freely managed" residence rent-free.[56]

Other beguines apparently had the economic resources to purchase their residence or to build a house within the beguinage. A clear set of regulations applied to these wealthier beguines as well. A beguine of this type could rent her house to another, but only with permission and for an amount to be determined by the Dominican guardian, the mistress, and her council of elder beguines.[57] A beguine who wished to sell or rent her house was required to sell or rent only to a beguine. Failure to comply meant return of the house to the beguinage, which could sell the house for common profit.[58]

A beguine could choose to leave the beguinage to marry or simply to return to the outside world with very little loss of the property she brought with her to the beguine house. As long as she had been in good standing, an exiting beguine could rent her house, or presumably also sell it, under the conditions listed above, for an amount to be determined by the Dominican guardian, mistress, and beguine council. As with any sale or rental, one third of the income was to be handed over to the beguinage "for the purpose of maintaining the other houses and meeting other needs."[59]

The property regulations referred only to the management of real estate, and they performed two functions. The regulations clearly protected the assets of the beguinage and facilitated its maintenance. From this examination, however, it is also clear that the property regulations functioned as the means to enforce moderate enclosure. A beguine very likely would think twice before she took the risk of disobeying the regulations, particularly those regulations which carried the penalty of immediate dismissal upon the first infraction. A beguine who risked dismissal from the royal beguinages might risk disapproval from the royal functionaries related to them. Moreover, it is likely that a beguine who was not a member of a beguine house, whether she was dismissed or chose to be solitary, would be subject to public criticism, if not harassment, because of positive royal and perhaps general approval directed toward those beguines who submitted to the sort of enclosure we have examined. We shall return to this possibility with the story of the trial of Marguerite Porete.

The situation of beguines in France, given the royal connections, was very likely dependent on ecclesiastical-political developments, especially during the reign of Philip the Fair (1285–1314). While it is not my intention to discuss in detail the major issues of the reign of Philip IV, we must review some aspects of it, including a general review of his suppression of the Templars, to provide insight into the dynamics surrounding the trial and death in 1310 of Marguerite Porete.

Philip IV was a pious leader who was genuinely concerned about the fate of the church and who took seriously his title as "Most Christian King." Philip's political goals included the church, and his view of himself as a faithful son of the church informed his policies for his kingdom. The overall program of Philip the Fair was the centralization of authority in France, and one of the primary tasks of centralization was to garner loyalty to the king.[60] As long as loyalties were divided between papal authority and secular authority, such centralization could not take place. The union of the idea of sacred king with the idea of the holy country facilitated the emergence of the French state.[61]

Royal propaganda programs were effectively developed under Philip as a way to engender loyalty to the crown. The basic themes were that the kings of France had always been defenders of the faith, that the people of France are devout and pious, and that the kingdom of France is so specially favored by God that it is the most important pillar of the church. The logical conclusion was that any attack on the rights of the king or the integrity of the kingdom was to be under-stood as an attack on the faith. Conversely, any steps the king took to defend his kingdom were for the good of the faith and Christendom: what was good for France was good for the church, and what injured France injured the church. People's loyalties were subtly rearranged without any sense of contradiction between their duties to the church and duties to the state as Philip garnered more power to the crown.[62]

The developments of Philip's administration had important im-plications for the church. Philip IV and the church leadership in France were mutually dependent, and Philip had no desire to abolish the special status of clergy in his realm.[63] While royal centralizing efforts caused some problems for the clergy, the disputes were set-tled by negotiation and compromise on both sides. In fact, the French secular clergy "seem to have had more confidence in the royal gov-ernment than in the papal Curia. The price of papal intervention was papal interference in local affairs, which was always expensive and not always helpful. . . . Decisions made by outsiders might be impar-tial; they might also be ill-informed."[64] In short, the leaders of the church in France seem to have concluded that their welfare could be best served by working with and through royal officials and friends of the king. Forces of centralization thus included the French clergy, and if one ought not to speak of a French church per se, one can speak of clergy more loyal to the king than to the pope. Conflicts between the crown and the clergy had more to do with the negotiation of the limits of temporal and spiritual powers *within* the realm. This shift of clergy loyalty to the king and away from the pope played a large role in the events surrounding the suppression of the Templars, an objective unattainable without the cooperation of the clergy.[65]

The Templars were a military religious order founded in the early twelfth century as a part of the Christian effort to reclaim the Holy Land from Muslim hands. Templar involvement in the crusades netted them extensive land holdings both in Palestine and Syria as well as in the West, especially in France. They bore the bulk of responsibility for the defense of the crusader states in the East, which served to augment their power and influence.[66] Their international organization facilitated their gradual emergence as bankers on a large scale for the papacy and for French monarchs. By 1291, however, Christians were driven out of Palestine, and the Templars were cut off from the mainstay of their existence. In the first months of 1307 Templars living in France were suddenly arrested by the officials of Philip IV, and their property was confiscated. They were charged with a variety of heresies, from denial of Christ to homosexuality and idol worship. Pope Clement V at first viewed the arrests as a direct affront to papal authority, since the Templars were directly responsible to the papacy. Instead of resisting Philip, however, he bent his efforts to maintain his authority over the inquisitorial proceedings.[67] When almost six hundred Templars attempted to mount a defense of their order, Philip arranged for drastic action, which resulted in fifty-four Templars being burned at the stake in a field outside Paris in May of 1310. By 1312 the papacy officially suppressed the Templars.

Much scholarly ink has been spilled as to the reasons why Philip IV sought the repression of the Templars.[68] The question remains a difficult one, and it influences one's decision regarding the forces behind the trial and death of Marguerite Porete, as we shall see. The most obvious motive for Philip's action against the Templars was financial.[69] A second obvious answer is that Philip was a pious king, and he took the charges of heresy against the Templars very seriously.[70] However, the real coup for Philip was related to the success of the royal propaganda of Philip as a loyal defender of the faith. The king was portrayed as the champion of orthodoxy, a faithful guardian of the church, quicker than the pope to detect heresy and zealous to suppress it. Throughout the entire process a close alliance between the king and the leadership of the French church was forged, as indicated by the fact that William of Paris, the confessor of the king, had been made inquisitor for France in 1305, and in 1307 skillfully directed the campaign against the Templars. "Instead of the pope having a right to intervene in secular affairs to preserve justice and peace, the king of France was praised for intervening in ecclesiastical affairs to preserve the faith."[71]

Promotion of the theme of sacred king and holy country, centralization of authority in the crown, loyalty to the king on the part of the clergy, and the image of the king as tireless defender of the faith in opposition to heresy: all these factors came together in the trial of Marguerite Porete.

THE TRIAL OF MARGUERITE PORETE

The narrative of Marguerite's trial can be pieced together with the help of the recent work of Robert Lerner and Paul Verdeyen.[72] These scholars indicate that we must consider all the relevant manuscripts pertaining both to the trial of Marguerite and to the trial of one Guiard de Cressonessart, a self-appointed defender of Marguerite. In this way we can have a better picture of the chronology of Marguerite's trial and therefore also a clearer idea of the influences that were at work in the background, which both scholars perceive as having everything to do with the suppression of the Templars. The documents of both trials were found in the collected papers of William of Nogaret and William of Plaisians, who were not mentioned in any part of the documents themselves, but were confidantes of the king and played a large role in the procedures against the Templars. The fact that these royal ministers had kept the documents pertaining to both processes allows the presumption that there is some connection between the trials of Marguerite and Guiard and the actions against the Templars.[73]

In March of 1310, William of Paris gathered five professors of law along with eleven theologians to receive advice about the cases against Marguerite and Guiard.[74] It seems that in the latter part of 1308, both Marguerite and a certain beghard from Beauvais, Guiard de Cressonessart, had been arrested by the order of the Dominican inquisitor, William of Paris.[75] Guiard had declared himself publicly as a defender of Marguerite even though she had been suspected of heresy herself. By March of 1310 both Marguerite and Guiard had been held in prison for approximately a year and a half.[76] The point of this preliminary gathering was to decide in which direction to proceed, whether the theologians or the lawyers should be in charge of the trial of the two suspects. The canonists were given the job of overseeing the trial of both prisoners.

The first deliberations against Marguerite and Guiard were held 3 April 1310. Prior to the first consultation against Marguerite, the inquisitor had commanded Marguerite numerous times to appear before the inquisitorial commission, but she had refused persistently to appear in court. He personally had brought her before him, and even though she was fully aware that she was before the inquisitor himself, she contumaciously refused to swear the oath according to the regulations of the inquisitor's office. For this reason he had imprisoned Marguerite under major excommunication, which she had endured nearly a year and a half with a kind of toughness. During this time she had been frequently exhorted to swear and to respond, the inquisitor himself offering her the benefits of absolution, but Marguerite did not care either to ask for or to accept this absolution.[77] Given these circumstances, William of Paris gathered the canonists for this first consultation for counsel as to how to proceed. The canonists judged her to be contumacious, rebellious, and deserving to be condemned as a heretic and to be given over to the secular authorities unless she should repent immediately before or after the sentence. In the latter case, they judged that she should be perpetually imprisoned.[78] The document regarding the first consultation against Guiard on the same day shows that he, like Marguerite, also had refused to take the oath required by the inquisition, and he, too, had submitted to excommunication for one and a half years. The canonists rendered the same judgment about his behavior.[79]

The first consultations were held not only to guide the inquisitor, but also as an ultimate threat of death to the prisoners. The second consultations indicate that the threat had worked in the case of Guiard, but it had no effect on the intrepid beguine. At the second consultation against Guiard, held 9 April 1310, Guiard confessed, giving the inquisitor all the details of his mission as the Angel of Philadelphia.[80] The canonists declared Guiard a heretic, not because he wanted to found a new order or because he wore a religious habit without ecclesiastical authorization, but because he maintained a

21

theory of two churches and did not recognize the total supremacy of the pope in the universal church.[81]

The most current interpretation of the condemnation of Guiard is that in the procedure against the Templars, Clement V and Philip IV had disputed with each other concerning who had the jurisdiction to judge the order and dispose of its goods. The condemnation of Guiard underscores the supreme authority of the papacy concerning any action against heresy.[82] According to this view, the condemnation would serve as legitimation for Philip's suppression of the Templars.

This interpretation needs to be qualified in that Philip and his ministers were not so much anti-papal as pro-crown. The canonists and theological faculty were in agreement with the centralizing efforts of Philip's administration, which included the portrait of Philip as the loyal defender of the faith and the church in France as the most important pillar of Christendom. The pope was held to be the supreme authority of the church universal as an article of true faith, but this affirmation was to be understood as no infringement on the legitimate rights of the French crown. Guiard's condemnation indeed conformed to royal policy, but for more simple reasons, which do not necessarily include the disenfranchisement of the Templars.

Events regarding Marguerite's status transpired quickly. On 11 April 1310 William of Paris gathered twenty-one theologians to pass judgment on Marguerite's book, from which fifteen suspect articles had been excerpted.[83] After deliberation, the theologians declared that the book should be condemned as heretical. Verdeyen raises the question of why so many theologians would be required to decide about this book, especially since it already had been condemned sometime between 1296 and 1306 by Guy of Colmieu, bishop of Cambrai, who had it publicly burned at Valenciennes in Marguerite's presence.[84]

Marguerite states that she had sent her book to three authorities, who had all approved of it. The first two are unknown to us except for their names: a Franciscan named John of Quaregnon, and a Cistercian named Dom Franco from the Abbey of Villers.[85] A troubling fact for the Paris theologians was that the third authority was Godfrey of Fontaines, a renowned and highly respected doctor of the University of Paris, who had approved the book prior to the condemnation of the bishop. Godfrey's approval was not without qualification, however. He was concerned that if some weaker souls read it they would attempt to attain a level of perfection which would not be possible for them and thus be deceived. Godfrey's view, according to Marguerite, was that the book required a strong and fearless spirit to attain to such practices.[86] Verdeyen observed that with such theological expertise favorable to the book, additional scholarly weight would be needed to countermand it.[87] With the condemnation of the book, the inquisitor could continue the proceedings against Marguerite.

The second deliberation against Marguerite Porete was held 9 May 1310, in which the canonists determined that the beguine had refused to take the oath and respond to the inquisitor's questions. Furthermore, they judged that she had not submitted to the injunction of the bishop of Cambrai forbidding her to speak again of her book. Therefore, she deserved to be condemned as a relapsed heretic and to be given over to the secular authorities. The accusations against her were as follows:

> The case is as follows. From the time that Marguerite called Porete was suspected of heresy, in rebellion and insubordination, she would not respond nor swear before the inquisitor to those things pertaining to the office of inquisitor. The inquisitor set up a case against her nevertheless, and by the deposition of many witnesses he found that the said Marguerite had composed a certain book containing heresies and errors, which had been publicly condemned and solemnly burned as such on the order of the Reverend Father Lord Guy, formerly bishop of Cambrai. The abovesaid bishop had ordered in a letter that if she attempted again to propagate by word or writing such things as were contained in this book, he would condemn her and give her over to the judgment of the secular court. The inquisitor learned next that she had acknowledged, once before the inquisitor of Lorraine, and once before Reverend Father Lord Philip, the next bishop of Cambrai, that she still had in her possession, even after the condemnation mentioned above, the said book and others. The inquisitor learned also

that the said Marguerite, after the condemnation of the book, had sent the said book containing the same errors to the Reverend Father Lord John, by the grace of God bishop of Châlons-sur-Marne. And she had not only sent this book to this Lord, but also to many other simple persons, beghards and others, as if it were good.[88]

According to this document, Marguerite had been judged by three bishops and the inquisitor from Lorraine. While there is no reason to raise any question about Guy of Colmieu, the witness of Philip of Marigny is not a source of confidence in terms of his integrity.[89] Philip of Marigny was the brother of Enguerrand, who was guardian of the treasury and a confidant of Philip IV. Philip of Marigny became bishop of Cambrai after Guy, and in 1309 he was promoted to archbishop of Sens by the demand of the king as a first step in the process against the Templars. Once again, the case of the Templars appears alongside Marguerite's case.

The official condemnation of Marguerite and Guiard was pronounced on 31 May 1310 by the inquisitor, William of Paris. Marguerite remained silent, and the next day, 1 June 1310, she was given over to the flames. Guiard, having renounced his errors, was imprisoned for life.

Why was so much official interest and energy expended on one beguine? Verdeyen suggests two reasons. First, the inquisitor was anxious to demonstrate that the inquisition maintained tight control over correct doctrine and ecclesiastical discipline, and he was unwilling to allow any questioning of his authority by secular power. Second, Philip the Fair was interested in obtaining support from the mendicant orders in the actions taken against the Templars. Many Franciscans and Dominicans made no secret of their contempt for beguines and beghards, and, in return for their support of royal activity, they may have demanded exemplary action against them—in which case Marguerite and Guiard would simply have been caught between the parties to a political deal.[90]

The official interest in Marguerite may be explained another way, however. The likelihood of mutual cooperation of church leadership in France and royal administrators in the disenfranchisement of the Templars has already been discussed. This cooperation may help us to understand why Marguerite Porete died in the flames that fateful first day of June 1310. In addition, we can perhaps abandon the attempt to explain Marguerite's death in terms of the effort to suppress the Templars. Marguerite was put to death because she was a symbol of a threat, real or perceived, to the established order intimately connected with the strengthening of royal power.

The established order certainly would have included royal patronage of beguine houses in France, and we have seen that a moderate enclosure of beguines was very likely in force during the reign of Philip IV. It may be that the primary fault of Marguerite was that she was solitary and itinerant.[91] The charges against Marguerite in the second consultation give a sense that she moved among the towns in the northern area. Verdeyen's notion that mendicants despised beguines needs to be qualified, because although the leadership of the mendicant orders resisted pastoral care of beguines, individual priests of the orders seem to have continued their pastoral efforts nonetheless. But the positive view of particular members of the mendicant orders toward beguines seems to have been directed toward beguines regulated in moderate enclosure, in which case mendicant antipathy would have been directed toward a solitary beguine. These two aspects, that "true" beguines lived in moderate enclosure, and that these beguines, and not the solitaries and wanderers, were supported by the mendicants, may be reflected in Marguerite's writings themselves:

O my Lover, what will beguines say and religious types,
When they hear the excellence of your divine song?
Beguines say I err, priests, clerics and Preachers,
Augustinians, Carmelites, and the Friars Minor,
Because I wrote about the being of the one purified by Love.[92]

Marguerite refers to beguines as opponents perhaps because by "beguine" she meant the so-called true beguines who had consented to the official statutes requiring moderate enclosure regulations.

A second reason for her death may have been the fact that she wrote her book in vernacular French, a factor which church leadership in France had already found to be disquieting. The chronicle of Jean d'Outremeuse, *Ly Myreur des Histors*, includes a note about Marguerite Porete to the effect that she had translated the Holy Scriptures, expressed errors against the articles of faith and against the eucharist.[93] While there is no evidence of Marguerite's having translated Scripture, her vernacular treatise contains clear scriptural references.

A third threat to the established order may relate to her book's popularity and notoriety. It is likely that Marguerite did not submit to Guy's episcopal condemnation, and that she kept *The Mirror* in her possession. She may have taken confidence in the prior approval by such a renowned theologian as Godfrey of Fontaines. She was accused of distributing copies of her work; perhaps her writing had already enjoyed a certain popularity: it was highly unlikely that she could have removed a text which was already in people's possession. Moreover, her silence throughout the whole trial period, her refusal to explain or elaborate anything, shows clearly that she had no wish to deny her teachings.[94] That Marguerite's book may have been popular is born out by the manuscript evidence. While the original text is no longer extant, there are presumably three copies in Old French, though only one is accessible. There were many translations—four Latin, two Italian, and three Middle English. Of the Italian translations, it is possible that thirty-six copies were circulating in the fifteenth century. The three Middle English translations are fifteenth-century manuscripts and were probably done by Carthusians. A Carthusian monk, Richard Methley (1451–1528), translated the text from Middle English to Latin.[95] The bishop of Cambrai did not burn the only existing book; in fact, his warning to Marguerite could indicate that he knew there were additional copies, and the details of the report of the second consultation indicate that the book was in the possession of many "simple persons, beghards and others." If so, both the burning of the book and Marguerite's condemnation to the flames could be interpreted as a symbolic public warning against theological views which were becoming widespread. Such views, understood to be antinomian, would be in official eyes a threat to the order that both the crown and the French ecclesiastical leadership had worked together to establish.

The historical setting of Marguerite Porete's *The Mirror of Simple Souls* is the maelstrom of political and ecclesiastical tensions and conflicts. Having told as much as possible of the story of these women called beguines, as well as the possible circumstances surrounding the death of our intrepid French beguine Marguerite Porete, we are now ready to undertake a theological analysis of *The Mirror* itself.

MARGUERITE ON THE NATURE OF THE SOUL AND ITS SPIRITUAL PROGRESS

The Mirror of Simple Souls would be correctly viewed as both a treatise and a kind of handbook designed to assist believers with their spiritual quest. As a treatise, *The Mirror* is written in the format of a dialog in the Boethian tradition among the allegorical figures of Reason, Love, and the Soul.[96] These figures debate with one another about the proper relation of the human and the divine and how this relation allows the spiritual ascent of the soul to God. The discourses, along with poetry interspersed among the arguments of the debaters, are articulated by means of expressions from the French courtly tradition.[97] *The Mirror* is also a spiritual handbook in that it helps believers discern what is necessary to live a spiritually successful life. With Marguerite Porete's *Mirror* we find a daring attempt by a beguine author to penetrate the relation of the discursive and affective capacities of the soul in her portrayal of the nature of the soul and in her outline of spiritual progress. Her views about how these relations effect transformation and union of the soul with God will be given our attention below.

First we shall examine what for Marguerite is the nature of spiritual progress by reviewing the seven stages she uses to sketch this itinerary. In order to comprehend this itinerary fully, two other critical factors, namely, her notions of three deaths and two kinds of souls, must also be considered. This examination will set the framework within which her view of the nature of the soul is to be understood. Such an analysis will show that Marguerite makes important distinctions in a faculty psychology, which enable her to delineate the relation of love and knowledge in the spiritual progress of the soul. Since the soul received the image of the Trinity at creation, we must grasp the beguine's understanding of the three Persons in order to comprehend her teaching on how the distinctions among the faculties of the soul form the image of the Trinity. In this way we shall see how the relation of love and knowledge within the faculties is the means by which the soul can make spiritual progress toward the divine life.

We begin with a brief overview of Marguerite's outline of the seven stages of the process of ascent; this will help us to analyse two important components of spiritual progress, namely, three kinds of death and two kinds of souls.[98] Marguerite's distinction between desirous love and *Fine Amour* or divine love is especially important for understanding her outline, since divine love does not act directly upon the soul until the transition from the fourth stage to the fifth.

In the first stage, the soul is touched by grace, stripped of her capacity for mortal sin, and commanded by God to love him with all her heart and her neighbor as herself.[99] The soul moves to the second stage when she abandons self in the mortification of nature to accomplish the counsels of evangelical perfection.[100] The third stage is marked by an abundance of love for the works of perfection which sharpens the spirit of the soul and boils up in her, creating a desire to multiply her good works. Since what is most prized in love is to offer what is most loved, the soul sacrifices her good works, which she loves, pulverizing her spirit, and beating and bruising herself in order to enlarge the place where her love would want to be. She relinquishes the works which give her such delight, and she submits in obedience to the will of another, all in the effort to put the will to death.[101] The point seems to be that the submission of the soul to another and the desired destruction of the will is accomplished by the strength of the soul's will so that the soul's own love is enlarged. The contradictory nature of the statement indicates that the soul is still willing with her own will.

In the fourth stage the soul is consumed in an ecstasy of love in which she is deceived into thinking that God has no greater gift in store for her. But divine love carries her higher, outside herself.[102] At the fifth stage the soul ponders interiorly two considerations: that God is Who is, from whom everything is, and that she is not, from whom no thing is.[103] She sees that free will has been placed in her from the being of God who is Being, and that the will ought to be placed in its source. Thus the will departs from its own will and renders itself back to God without retaining anything of its own. The will which gave her the feeling of love in the fourth stage of contemplation has departed from her.[104] In the sixth stage the soul no longer sees herself because of the abyss of humility into which she has fallen. Neither does she see God because of his highest goodness. Instead God sees himself in her by his divine majesty, which makes the soul transparent.[105] The seventh stage cannot be described, and it will be known only when the soul has left the body.[106]

There are two critical ingredients within the framework of

these stages of spiritual progress. One is Marguerite's description of the three kinds of death along the path. The other is her distinction between the two kinds of souls who practice the virtues in the second stage.

Three transitions or "deaths," which give birth successively to three higher kinds of life, move the soul toward spiritual perfection. Marguerite calls these deaths death to sin, death to nature, and death to the spirit.[107] The first death, to mortal sin, births the life of grace in the first stage. At the first stage one begins with the commandments of the church and the help of God, who commands that one love him with all one's heart, soul, and virtue, loving self as one ought, and neighbor as self, all of which is necessary for salvation.[108] The life of grace is the life of ordinary believers.[109] Compared to those who live the noble divine life, however, these folk are like peasants. They are coarse and without refined graces. They therefore are kept outside, apart from the noble ones and away from the secrets of the court of the most high King.[110]

The life of the spirit, lived by those who pursue the counsels of evangelical perfection, is born from the death to nature, corresponding to the second stage. This life is lived in obedience to the virtues according to Reason.[111] Marguerite asserts that this life, too, must die before one can live the divine life.[112] The life of the spirit (Rachel) must die before the divine life (Benjamin) is born, because the life of the spirit is filled with will, however spiritual it might be.[113] Even though the will in the life of the spirit is spiritual, nonetheless it still wills itself. The death of the spirit and the departure of the will in the fifth stage are absolutely necessary. Only at this point is it possible for the Divine Will alone to will in the annihilated, perfect soul.[114]

The second element of spiritual progress toward perfection is the distinction between the two types of souls who live the life of the spirit: the lost and the sad. The lost are in the second stage and remain there, obedient to Reason and the virtues. Of course they will be saved, but they will never live the divine life in this world.[115] These souls do not heed the call of divine love despite their practice of the virtues. They do not understand that the virtues are the messengers of divine love, and therefore they do not understand that the virtues call them to a higher, better life. They remain encumbered with themselves, and they will never live the divine life in this world to which Love calls them.[116]

The sad souls also remain in desire and will, and they practice the virtues in the life of the spirit; in fact, they are identical to the lost, but with one distinguishing mark: they understand that there is more to be accomplished in their spiritual life.[117] Divine love calls the sad ones wise because they understand that there is a better way, and they understand that they do not possess understanding. The lost do not understand either of these things.[118]

This basic structure of spiritual progress will be a useful reference as we now direct our attention to the beguine's perspective on the nature of the soul. Because the soul received the image of the Trinity at creation,[119] spiritual progress is grounded in that image within the soul. In order to see how this is so, however, first we must consider Marguerite's understanding of the inner relation of the divine Persons.

The beguine's references to the Trinity are not located in one section, but are scattered throughout the treatise so that what follows is a reconstruction. Early on she affirms the traditional attributes of God as Power, Wisdom, and Goodness, "one Power, one Wisdom, one Will. One God alone in three persons, three persons and one God alone."[120] Marguerite elaborates on the traditional notion of the procession of the Persons, and she includes the concept of the Father as the source of the Trinity.[121] She draws upon the familiar Augustinian concept of God as Lover, Loved, Love,[122] and expands it into an expression of divine goodness as self-diffusive.[123] She asserts the unity of the Trinity in one divine will,[124] which generates eternal substance, pleasing fruition, and loving conjunction, which seems to be Marguerite's peculiar interpretation of the appropriated names for the three Persons.[125] The unity of the Trinity consists in the mode of the procession of the persons so that "the Holy Spirit possesses in Him this same divine nature which the Father and the Son possess."[126] When the Holy Spirit draws the soul into the divine life in the fifth and sixth stages, the fullness of divinity is given to the perfect, annihilated soul.[127]

Marguerite has outlined traditional doctrine regarding the nature of the Trinity. However, we shall see that her interpretation of these teachings, particularly the Person of the Father as source without source of the Trinity, and the Holy Spirit as possessing entirely what the other two Persons possess, will allow her to make radical statements about the kind of union with God which can be experienced by the soul in this life. For our purposes at this point, however, this outline of Marguerite's trinitarian theology serves as the basis for our exploration of her understanding of the nature of the soul.

Marguerite's complex analysis of the nature of the soul is based on important distinctions in her faculty psychology. The beguine's perceptions regarding the faculties in the soul and how the will affects them are crucial to her notions of transformation and union. Marguerite uses precise terminology to describe the discursive capacity of the soul, which in turn is qualified by the object of the will, either enabling spiritual progress or impeding it. We shall first examine her analysis of the discursive faculties as the image of the Trinity and delineate the specifics of her terminology. We will then be in a position to discuss Marguerite's notion of the will and its relation to the discursive capacity. Finally, we will be able to discern how, for the beguine, the relation of love and knowledge is the means by which the soul can progress spiritually toward the divine life.

Marguerite Porete distinguishes between ability (*engin*), intellect (*entendement*), and understanding (*cognoissance*) in a precise manner. Her precision is crucial to her program. These distinctions occur specifically in one chapter where she defines the nature of a "skill" (*art*) in a creature.[128] For our beguine the discursive capacity of the soul is trinitarian in nature and as such is the image of God. Natural ability (*engin*) is the substance of the soul, understanding (*cognoissance*) is generated from both ability and intellect (*entendement*), while intellect is generated from ability alone. Understanding is at once the height of the soul and the most inward part. In Marguerite's view, the natural tendency of ability is to attain the completion and perfection of its enterprise, which is the will of God, and therefore is the driving force behind whatever spiritual progress occurs. From this outline we can see that the trinitarian image within the soul mirrors the procession of the Persons, and this is the framework within which the relation of love and knowledge is to be understood.

Marguerite uses three different terms that describe three kinds of knowledge of which the intellect of the soul is capable. In the world of created beings, the intellect is able to know (*savoir*) about the world of things, and to perceive or grasp (*entendre*) their meanings by means of reasoning activity. "To understand" (*connaistre*), and "understanding" (*cognoissance*), however, seem for Marguerite to be technical terms referring to things pertaining to the divine realm.

The terms *connaistre* and *cognoissance* refer both to mental content and mental capacity as demonstrated by Marguerite's description of the sad soul. Marguerite states that the sad soul *understands* that she lacks the *understanding* which comes from the divine life, something that the lost soul does not understand.[129] The first use, the verb, would appear to indicate the content, what is understood, namely, that the capacity is lacking. The second use, the noun, would appear to indicate the capacity that the sad soul lacks. However, the fact that the soul understands that she lacks the capacity paradoxically gives to the soul a kind of capacity, an *understanding* which contributes to spiritual progress. Thus Divine Love calls the sad souls wise.[130] The lost soul lacks content and therefore the capacity as well. In the sixth stage, both the capacity of the understanding in the sad soul and the content of what is understood are transformed and subsumed by divine knowing which Marguerite also calls "understanding." This dynamic of transformation will receive full attention below. All three kinds of knowledge, *savoir, entendre*, and *connaistre*, depend upon the object of the will, which governs the intellect generated by ability. In the beguine's structure of the movement toward perfection, ability, intellect, and will, while differentiated, work very closely together.

In the fifth stage, the will must "depart its own will" and "render itself back to God." Although free will has been placed in the soul by the goodness of God, with the power of the free will, the soul freely removed her will from the will of God.[131] Having removed the will from God, who properly possesses free will, the soul separated herself from God, willing independently from the divine will. To will the divine will is the proper activity of the human will; to will independently of the divine will is what constitutes the separation of humanity from God. To will independently of God is even to *steal* the will from God, who is the proper locus of the human will.[132] The removal of the will from the divine will does not therefore render the will unfree however. For Marguerite, as for Augustine, Bernard, and their successors, the will is still free either to wander into perdition, or, through grace, to replace itself where it belongs, in the divine will.[133]

Sin, then, is the freely chosen removal of the will from Divine Being.[134] Therefore, virtue is the freely chosen returning of the will to God, for God has freely given the gift of free will to the soul, "without a why," simply out of the fullness of God's goodness.[135]

Precisely because of the nature of the gift, the will cannot be taken away without the soul's willing of it, for to take the will from the soul would contradict the goodness of God in giving free will in the first place. The will, then, can only be placed where it belongs by the will itself. The will must be rendered back to God in the same way and as freely as it was first given.[136] The free rendering of the will back to God, where it belongs, is the goal of the spiritual path and is the particular task of the fifth stage. The soul who has rendered her will freely to God is the annihilated, perfect soul.

In this state of annihilation the soul finds her perfection; she no longer has a will with which to will or desire, but rather God's will alone wills in her.[137] If the soul freely wills anything independently of God, she separates herself from the divine will.[138] Thus the will, for Marguerite, is the locus either of separation from God or of spiritual perfection; if perfection is attained, then the soul wills not her own will, but only the will of God wills in her.

The trinitarian character of the soul, ability-intellect-understanding, is the created nature of the sad soul alone. The free will of the soul, freely given by divine gift, can turn itself toward created things or toward divine things. If the soul remains in her own will, she is turned toward created things, and ability is limited insofar as it is impeded from carrying out its enterprise which is the will of God. The intellect is limited thereby also since intellect comes from ability, and therefore it will be limited in its knowledge. As long as the will wills something other than the will of God, it remains in an existence independent of God. Intellect, generated by ability and controlled by the will, gives only as much knowledge as the will allows. As long as the will remains in the world of createdness, of things, the intellect will be limited to that realm, and therefore knowledge will be of a particular kind. Therefore the lost soul does not possess understanding, which is related to divine things, because the will of the lost soul is oriented toward created things, thereby impeding ability and limiting intellect. Only the sad soul has the capacity for understanding, because the will of this soul is oriented toward divine things. Thus the object of the will sets the limits for the enterprise of ability and the function of the intellect, and therefore also the kind or level of knowledge.

For Marguerite, Reason and Love are personified acts, and each has an intellect appropriate to its function, which allows to each its own kind of knowledge. Reason has a specific and positive role in the quest for spiritual perfection; namely, that reasoning activity guides the will with a particular kind of perceptiveness, a particular way of grasping what is before the mind.[139] Reason, through the virtues, teaches the will the important preliminary steps of evangelical perfection in the first four stages. The soul would make no progress toward perfection without this guidance.[140] Reason and the virtues carefully teach a particular kind of knowledge to the soul, molding her ability and thus producing the sort of intellect that can allow the soul to make further progress. The will, in order to be what it ought to be, must first be guided by Reason to learn its proper object, the will of God, so that ability may fulfill its enterprise and generate the intellect by which the soul may progress along the path toward perfection.

Reason's intellect is limited, however, because it is part of created being and cannot grasp the teachings of the intellect of divine love and Reason is thus servant to her mistress, Divine Love.[141] Once Reason has fulfilled her function of teaching the preliminary steps to the soul, she must assume her proper role of servant to the annihilated soul. She cannot accompany the soul into the splendid palace of divine understanding but must remain outside the gate.[142]

Thus, for Marguerite, in the first two stages of spiritual progress the affective power is first guided by the kind of knowing afforded by reasoning activity. Then the affective power takes the lead in the third and fourth stages, so that ability can fulfill its enterprise and generate the sort of intellect from which understanding comes. At the opening of the fifth stage the understanding is expanded by divine illumination. At the height of the fifth the affective power is subsumed or absorbed by divine love when the will is annihilated. When the soul is in the height of the fifth stage, reasoning activity is left behind.

> *Love:* Thought has no more lordship in her [the soul]. She has lost the use of her senses—not her senses, but the use. For Love has carried her from the place where she was, in leaving her senses in peace, and so has seized their use. This is the completion of her pilgrimage, and the annihilation by her rendering of her will which is dissolved in [Love].[143]

The use of the term "senses" (*sens*) here is somewhat reminiscent of William of St-Thierry's theory of human knowledge, where he defined the inward *sensus* as intellect.[144] Marguerite seems to use this term in a similar way to refer to the given created intellectual nature of the sad soul, ability-intellect-understanding. The faculties remain, but the transformation of the soul's affective power into divine love means that the soul no longer makes use of the faculties in a human way. This aspect of Marguerite's thought will receive attention below.

The sad soul, for Marguerite, is the one in whom understanding comes from both intellect and ability. We recall that, according to Marguerite, intellect is generated by ability, which is controlled by the object of the will, which in the early stages is governed by Reason and the virtues. The object of the will in the sad soul is that better being which is desired because it is lacking. In a way reminiscent of Richard of St. Victor,[145] the desire for the better being engages the enterprise of ability, which is the will of God, thereby generating the good intellect by a kind of "sharpening."[146] When the sad soul heeds Love's call, her will is oriented toward the gifts of divine love, which orients ability toward its true goal and generates her intellect. From this ability and this intellect comes her understanding, which understands that she does not possess the understanding divine love gives. The sad soul understands that there must be a better life, senses her wretchedness because she lacks it, and yearns for that life. The capacity for this understanding of the sad soul is directly related to the strength of her yearning desire, and the more the soul yearns, the more she will be able to understand.[147] Ardor and desire draw the soul by means of the dream of glory in the third stage and move the soul into the ecstasy of ardent love in the fourth where divine love comes to do her work.[148] This ardent love and desire of the will in the life of the spirit of the sad soul are necessary, although this kind of love is not sufficient for the beguine's agenda. Ardent desire is the servant of spiritual progress and ensures the rightful inheritance of the soul.

Marguerite's distinctions among the faculties of the soul allow her to offer some insights about what in her view is the nature of the relation of love and knowledge in spiritual progress. For Marguerite, spiritual progress occurs as love and knowledge grow together in mutual and reciprocal relation. Reasoning activity teaches the will what it must love so that the will is oriented toward the truth. What one loves is what one knows, however, and therefore the object of the will in turn governs the knowing faculty. Marguerite asserts that the natural tendency of ability is to undertake the enterprise of the will of God. It is apparent, however, that for the beguine this enterprise is available to the ability only when the will is rightly directed. If the will is oriented to created things, ability is impeded, and what sort of intellect operates within the soul is impeded as well, since ability generates intellect in Marguerite's outline.

The beguine theologian uses a number of terms for different kinds of knowing. The knowing available to the soul oriented only toward created things is termed *savoir* (which I translate *to know*), and the knowing related to the meanings of created things is termed *entendre* (which I translate *to perceive* or *grasp*). Marguerite reserves her terms *connaistre* and *cognoissance* (which I translate *to understand*, and *understanding*, respectively) for the knowing which is related to divine things, and which refers both to mental content and mental capacity. On the one hand, the terms refer to the understanding in the sad soul for which ardent love and desire are absolutely necessary. On the other hand, the terms are used to refer to the divine knowing, which subsumes and transforms the understanding of the sad soul. That the mental content and mental capacity of understanding are one allows the transformation in the sixth stage to take place. Ardent love and desire for divine things in the sad soul frees the ability for its true enterprise, generating the sort of intellect from which a particular sort of understanding emerges in the soul. How this understanding is transformed and the nature of the divine life of the soul in union with God is our next subject.

MARGUERITE ON TRANSFORMATION AND UNION

If Marguerite's distinctions of faculties enabled her to make important statements about the relation of love and knowledge in spiritual progress, the same distinctions also continued to serve her purposes as she explored the dynamics of the soul's transformation and union with God. For Marguerite, love and knowledge remain in tension with each other on the path to spiritual perfection so that as one expands or progresses, so does the other. In the beguine's view, love and knowledge each increase the capacity for the other both in spiritual progress and in the goal of transformation and union.

Therefore, first we shall analyze how the understanding of the sad soul is expanded at the opening of the fifth stage. Next, we will observe how the transformation of desirous love into divine love places the soul in the abyss of humility, the height of the fifth stage. We shall then be able to see how the soul is lifted into the sixth stage, where her understanding is transformed into divine understanding. Finally, when we examine the beguine's images of union, we shall see that Marguerite intends a union of identity between the soul and God which has two moments, both grounded in her theology of the Trinity.

We have seen that the sad soul possesses the kind of understanding from her intellect and her ability which understands that there must be a better life, senses her wretchedness because she lacks it, and so yearns for that life. This mutual interaction of the sad soul's understanding and yearning moved the soul through the first four stages. Marguerite makes use of the traditional threefold pattern of spiritual growth as she describes the illuminative fifth stage, which occurs by divine initiative alone. At the opening of the fifth stage, the sad soul receives from the movement of divine light some considerations by which her understanding is to be expanded.[149] These considerations reveal to the soul her true nature and the manner of her relation to God. By the teachings of faith the soul knows that God is Power, Wisdom, and Goodness.[150] The expansion of the understanding begins when she understands that she knows nothing about herself or about God, and that what she understands about herself is what she understands about God.

At this juncture it is well to pause to consider briefly Marguerite's use of the term "nothing" or "nothingness," which is important for the following discussion. Marguerite employs the term in two ways to indicate the relation of God and the soul. Most often "nothing" or "nothingness" designates the soul's state in the fifth stage, where she remains in extreme humility without any will of her own and only the divine will wills in her. "Nothing" in this case refers to the nothing from which God created all things. This sort of "nothing" is thus related to the soul's virtual existence in God before she was created.[151] At the moment of creation, when God created from nothing, the soul was this nothing but lost this nothingness when she willed independently from God.[152] The soul lost her "nothingness" and became "another thing" in the sense that created beings are distinct from God and from one another.

The other meaning of "nothing" is apparent also in the sense of something less than God.[153] God is true Being or Existence, the one who truly is. Compared with the divine nature, the created nature of the soul is nothing. The beguine theologian moves between these two perspectives with little warning, something which can make her writing difficult to follow for her twentieth-century reader.

Because of her view of the absolute distinction between the divine nature and the nature of the soul, the beguine theologian sets up a dialectic in order to describe the relation between God and the soul. What is predicated of the soul is therefore negated of God, and what is predicated of God is negated of the soul.

> Lord, you are One Goodness, through overflowing goodness, and all in yourself. And I am One Wretchedness, through overflowing wretchedness, and all in myself.
>
> Lord you are, and thus everything is perfected through you, and nothing is made without you. And I am not, and thus everything is made without me, and nothing is made through me.
>
> Lord, you are all power, all wisdom, and all goodness, without beginning, without being contained, and without end. And I am all weakness, all ignorance, and all wretchedness, without beginning, without being contained, and without end.[154]

Given this dialectic, the soul can understand her wretchedness only insofar as she can understand God's goodness, and what the soul understands of God's goodness is what she understands of her own wretchedness. The soul's understanding of this dialectical relation brings her to the understanding of herself and of God where the soul understands nothing if she does not understand her wretchedness, and the soul now has the ability to understand divine goodness by means of her wretchedness.[155] We should note here that the soul has not been given a new ability. Rather, the understanding has been expanded to include the dialectical relation, and now the ability, already strengthened by the ardor of the sad soul, is further empowered and expanded to complete the perfection of its enterprise, which is to attain the will of God. This expanded understanding will in turn enlarge her love and make it ready for transformation.

Once the soul begins to understand the nature of the God-soul relation by means of the dialectic, her understanding grows by means of illumination as she begins to comprehend the intimate relation between her own wretchedness and God's goodness: she cannot have his goodness except through her wretchedness, and since the soul cannot lose her wretchedness she cannot lose his goodness.[156] This understanding moves the soul along to even greater understanding.

The soul is given to understand by divine light that she has been accorded a free will in order to will the divine will alone. In addition, she understands that her will has separated itself from the divine will to will independently of God and that her will must now depart from itself in order for her to return to her true home. In this showing from divine light, the soul understands where she was when God made all things from nothing, and so she is certain that her true nature is nothing, "no-thingness." At the same time she sees that she removed her will from God in one sole moment of consent to sin. In this sense she understands who she is by nature, and who she has become through sin. By nature the soul is "nothing" in the sense of having been created by God from nothing. Through sin, by willing independently from God, the soul has become "another thing," one being among other beings.[157] The soul, by removing, or as Marguerite says, "stealing" her will from God, is now in debt to God. But she cannot pay the debt, for she has nothing with which to pay except her own wretchedness, which of course will not suffice. God can be satisfied only by the power of divine goodness.

With her understanding expanded, the soul's desire to please God becomes the focus of the transformation process. Having understood her wretchedness and the consequence of her independent will, the soul understands that she must empty herself of her own will. And she must be willingly so emptied in order for her to be true emptiness, or nothingness, which can be filled only with divine will and understanding. The soul proceeds to ponder how her will might please God, and she considers the things her will would consent to in order for her never to have willed anything other than God's will or pleasure.

(1) If she could have existed as long as God has and without any deficiency, she would be willing to suffer as much poverty, rejection, and torment as God has goodness, wisdom, and power.

(2) Even if she possessed as much worthiness as God himself has, she would place everything which she possessed in God, and

return to nothingness, rather than keep back from God anything which came from him.

(3) If God gave to her as much goodness as he had worthiness, she would not love the goodness except for his sake. And if she should lose this gift, it would not matter to her except for his sake.

(4) If it would please him, she would be willing to return to nothingness and no longer have any being.[158]

In all these considerations, however, the soul still wills her own will, although it may be true that she wills what God wills. She has not reached the point of having no will of her own, where God alone wills his will in her.

At this point the soul in her yearning love despairs that she will ever be able to please her beloved. Her own ardor is pressed to its limits when she ponders the possibilities which will ultimately cause her desire to be annihilated. As if God himself were pressing these hard questions, the soul considers that God might be better pleased if she should love another more than him; that he might love another more than her; that he might will that another might love her more than he.[159] The soul's senses fail,[160] and in abandoning her ardor by means of her ardor, the soul's desirous love is emptied of all self-will, all desire, and her will is annihilated. In this moment of abandoning her ardor, the soul freely annihilates her will, and her ardor is transformed into overflowing, outpouring divine love itself, which loves for the sake of love alone. In this transformation the soul's love is absorbed or subsumed into divine love by the power of the Holy Spirit.[161] Like air rushing in to fill a vacuum, the soul is now filled with the Holy Spirit. She is submerged in pure divine love, no longer willing anything of her own.

The transformation of the soul's love creates true emptiness and places the soul in an abyss of humility of the highest and purest kind, humility which constitutes the height of the fifth stage.[162] In this pure humility the soul understands only her wretchedness and her nothingness in relation to God. In the soul's self-understanding, she has no goodness whatsoever in herself and this very self-understanding constitutes the purity of her humility. In this abyss of her humility, the annihilated soul understands that only the total goodness of God filling her completely can overcome the poverty of her wretchedness and nothingness. Therefore divine goodness belongs to her by reason of her necessity and God's righteousness.[163]

The soul emptied of all will requires the divine filling because of the nature of the abyss of humility on the one hand, and because of the nature of divine goodness on the other.[164] The annihilated soul has fallen so far down into the nothingness of humility that she cannot raise herself, for to raise herself would require some self-will on the part of the soul which she does not have.[165] Instead, she remains in the lowest depths of pure humility from which she can see clearly "the true Sun of the Highest Goodness, for she has nothing which would impede the vision."[166]

Through the annihilation of the will, this soul has become supreme humility, which has its source in divinity,[167] and at this point the Holy Spirit fills the soul and generates the Trinity within her.[168] Thus Marguerite can assert that the soul has "the treasure of the Trinity, hidden and enclosed within her."[169] The generation of the Trinity within the soul takes place within the trinitarian relation of the faculties in the sad soul, which are the image of the divine Trinity. This "treasure" of the Trinity comes only to the annihilated soul in the height of the fifth stage. Prior to this moment the sad soul has the image but not the "treasure" of the Trinity itself. According to Marguerite's theology of the procession of the Persons within the Trinity, the sad soul receives the whole Trinity when the Holy Spirit enters because the Holy Spirit possesses completely what the other two Persons possess.[170] This filling by the Holy Spirit occurs in the understanding or height of the sad soul.[171] We recall that this faculty is the "wisdom" of the sad soul in that the sad soul understands that she lacks the understanding of the divine life. When the sad soul comes to understand her wretchedness, and therefore God's goodness, her ability is also enlarged so that ultimately her understanding can be transformed into divine understanding.[172] At this point the Holy Spirit transforms the understanding of the sad soul and "takes away," or absorbs the annihilated soul's expanded understanding.[173] The annihilated soul is thus united by the power of the Holy Spirit to the Trinity, in whom she is dissolved and melted so that the one divine will of the Trinity wills in her.[174] When the Holy Spirit fills the soul, she receives the fullness of divinity and at that moment is lifted into divine existence in union with the Trinity. By this melting and joining of the soul to the Trinity, the soul is made completely transparent, so that God sees only Godself, which is, for Marguerite, the goal and limit of spiritual perfection that can be attained in this life.[175]

Marguerite calls the divine seeing of the divine self in the soul the spark, the flash of light through an aperture which signals the brief arrival of the sixth stage and quickly passes away. Even when the spark passes away, however, the soul remains in a union of identity with God before and after the opening of the aperture.[176] When the aperture opens, the soul is lifted to the sixth stage, which Marguerite calls the showing from the glory of the soul.[177] At this moment the soul is lifted to her virtual existence, to where she was in the source of all being before she was given being. The beguine theologian grounds this moment in her understanding of the unity of the Trinity, who enters the annihilated soul through the power of the Holy Spirit. The logic of the procession of the Persons allows the soul to receive the whole Trinity, because the Holy Spirit possesses completely what the Father and Son possess. The unity of the Trinity permits Marguerite to assert that the soul is in the Father, the source of the Trinity and of all things.[178] The classic description of the Father as source of the Trinity grounds Marguerite's assertion that through the work of the Holy Spirit the soul is necessarily conformable to the Godhead, and therefore the soul receives her virtual existence in this gift.[179] The soul, carried into the unity of the Trinity, is moved to the source of the Trinity, the Father, so that she knows all things and knows nothing, which is superior, divine understanding. At this point God has taken understanding from the soul and keeps what the soul understands.[180] The movement of the Trinity transforms the soul's understanding of herself and of God in the fifth stage into divine understanding itself in the sixth stage. This flash of divine understanding moves the soul from the fifth stage to the sixth when the aperture opens.[181] The opening does not last long, and when it closes the soul drops back to the fifth stage, but not to the fourth because she has been established in the divine life.[182] From now on the soul is moved from the fifth to the sixth and back again as often as the Trinity moves within her.

When the soul drops back to the fifth stage, she remains in the annihilated state, without any will of her own, in deepest, supreme humility. The whole Trinity has filled the soul and the divine will alone wills in her. Submerged in the divine life, the soul cannot be touched by any sense of shame or honor, poverty or wealth, not even by a fear of hell or desire for paradise.[183] The fifth stage is the supreme peace of the soul, in which nothing can be given to her nor taken away from her.[184] The soul could be called both impassible and audacious. In her impassibility, she not only takes no account of things which might please or harm, but she also audaciously neither desires nor despises the practices of the church and she seeks nothing.

> This Soul . . . no longer seeks God through penitence, nor through any sacrament of Holy Church; not through thoughts, nor through words, nor through works; not through creature here below, nor through creature above; not through justice, nor through mercy; not through glory of glory; not through divine understanding, nor through divine love, nor through divine praise.

> . . . Such a Soul neither desires nor despises poverty nor tribulation, neither mass nor sermon, neither fast nor prayer, and gives to Nature all that is necessary, without remorse of conscience. But such nature is so well ordered through the transformation by unity of Love, to whom the will of this Soul is conjoined, that nature demands nothing which is prohibited.[185]

This soul has taken leave of the virtues, and now they serve her. Nature has been so well ordered within her that she can give to nature what nature demands, unlike those who still remain in the life of the spirit, in desire and will.

> (It is the contrary in the case of the Unencumbered Soul.) The life . . . which we call the life of the spirit, cannot have peace unless the body always does the contrary of its own will; that is, that such folk do the contrary of sensuality, or else they would fall into perdition from such a life, if they do not live contrary to their pleasure.
>
> Those who are unencumbered do the opposite. For insofar as it is necessary that in the life of the spirit they do the contrary of their own will if they wish not to lose peace, so likewise in an opposite way, the unencumbered ones do everything that pleases them if they wish not to lose peace, since they have arrived in the stage of freeness, that is, since they have fallen from the Virtues into Love, and from Love into Nothingness.[186]

These daring statements about the spiritual perfection of the soul in the fifth stage were the source of the condemnation of Marguerite's theology. At this point, however, we can say that Marguerite's intention is to describe a spiritual life totally given over to the divine will, without any regard whatsoever for the ordinary cares and concerns of creaturehood. The divine life of the soul in the fifth stage renders the soul impervious to anything that would disturb her supreme peace. She has attained the perfection of which she is capable in this life: perfect charity, the gift of the Trinity.

For the beguine theologian, love and knowledge, while distinct, grow together mutually in a creative tension. The increase of one prepares the soul for the expansion of the other. We now turn to her use of three images, which deepen the expression of the creative tension between love and knowledge in a union of identity between the soul and God.

Marguerite's images reflect two closely related though distinct moments of a union of identity. Marguerite shows us that she is aware of the traditional notion of union, in which the soul though united with the divine remains distinct from it, for she freely admits that a difference of natures remains in the union between the soul and God.

> This Soul . . . has entered into the abundances and the flowings of divine love, not, says Love, by the attainment of divine understanding; for it could not be that any intellect, however enlightened, could attain any of the flowings of divine Love. But the love of such a Soul is so conjoined to the flowings of the greater part of this absolute divine Love (not by attainment of the Intellect of Love, but by attainment of her absolute love), that the Soul is adorned with the adornments of this absolute peace in which she lives, and endures, and is and was and will be without being.[187]

In this passage, although the soul's love is transformed into divine love, her intellect has not been replaced with divine intellect; instead, her intellect no longer functions in a human way. The soul in union with the divine retains her created faculties but abandons her human use of them.[188] The soul's created faculties have been filled with the divine nature, however.[189] That the faculties remain human even though they are filled with the divine maintains the distinction of natures in Marguerite's notion of union. Despite the beguine's affirmation of the difference in natures, however, she gives this difference little weight in her schema. The annihilated soul remains in the fifth stage, in union with the Trinity, without an independent will, in a state of nothingness, having abandoned the mode of willing which kept her separate from God.

When Marguerite employs the image of the inebriation of the soul, she indicates that if there is any difference of natures it does not make any difference because of the transforming power of divine love.[190] This difference of natures is the difference between what the soul has become by grace and who God is by nature.[191] For Marguerite this difference is a difference which makes no difference because the soul's union with God is a union of identity between the soul and God, as she makes clear with her use of two other images.

When the beguine refers to the traditional iron in fire, she insists that the iron *becomes* fire itself by virtue of the strength of the fire.[192] The soul, Marguerite says, is completely enflamed in the furnace of the fire of Love. Union of identity is clearly intended by the beguine as she insists that the soul becomes *properly* fire itself because the soul is transformed into the fire of divine love.[193]

When she uses the traditional image of water, it is of a river that loses its name when it flows into the sea.[194] The soul no longer has the name soul, but the name of the one into whom she has been melted and dissolved. It is difficult to see how Marguerite could be any more clear about the nature of the union as identity.

A close reading of her use of the images of iron in fire and of water indicates that for Marguerite there are two moments of union, intimately connected yet distinct, which reflect the relation of love and knowledge. With the iron-fire image, Marguerite insists that the iron loses its own semblance because fire is stronger and transforms the iron into itself. The same principle holds for the transforming power of the divine love of the Trinity, for it "takes no account" of the lesser part as it absorbs or subsumes the desirous love in the soul in the fifth stage. The understanding of the dialectical relation of God and the soul in the fifth stage is transformed by the unity of the Trinity in the sixth stage.

In her image of a river flowing into the sea and losing its name, Marguerite is pointing to the moment when the unity of the Trinity drives the soul into the Father, the source without source of the Trinity, where she receives her virtual existence, losing her "name," which denotes distinct being. The soul's virtual existence is given explicit attention toward the end of her book.

> His farness is greater nearness, because, from nearby, in itself, it better knows what is far which [knowing] always makes her [the Soul] to be in union by his will, without the interference of any other thing which may happen to her. All things are one for her, without a why, and she is nothing in a One of this sort. . . . Then is she stripped of all things because she is without existence, where she was before she was. . . . Thus she has from God what He has, and she is what God is through the transformation of love, in that point in which she was, before she flowed from the Goodness of God.[195]

This is the moment of the flash of light of the sixth stage, which shines from the seventh stage, giving the being of the sixth to the soul; the soul receives a kind of supra-conscious awareness of the glory she will have in the next life, which will be her virtual existence.[196] It cannot last very long because the soul has not left her body; nonetheless, the unity of the Trinity lifts the soul into her virtual existence as often as the Trinity moves within her.[197] This fluidity between the fifth and sixth stages is the key to the two moments in Marguerite's notion of a union of identity. The annihilated soul remains in a union with the Trinity in the fifth stage and from time to time is lifted into her virtual existence in the sixth.

Marguerite's two-moment union is a union of identity of the soul with God in the divine threeness and oneness. Love is the divine relation of the three Persons: Lover, Loved, Love.[198] The divine oneness is in the Father, the source without source of the Trinity, true being itself from whom all things are. The unity of the Trinity is one divine will and consists in the procession of the Persons, so that the Holy Spirit "possesses in Him this *same divine nature* which the Father and the Son possess."[199] When the soul is in the fifth stage, she is transformed into the divine love of the Holy Spirit, who is the love of the Father and of the Son. Thus she becomes God who is three. The movement of the Trinity, the power of the unifying oneness of the Persons, lifts the soul into the sixth stage, into her virtual existence in the Father, the One who is true being, the source of all existence. Hence, for the beguine theologian, the fluidity between the fifth and sixth stages reflects the ebb and flow of divinity as Trinity and unity.

Throughout her book Marguerite consistently maintains the creative tension between love and knowledge. We have seen how each enlarges the capacity for the other in the spiritual progress and transformation of the soul. At the level of union, this creative tension is reflected in the fluidity between stages five and six. We have already noted that divine love has an intellect, which would indicate that for Marguerite, as for so many others, love is a kind of knowing. However, our beguine does not suggest a simple identity of love and knowledge within the divine realm. On the contrary, she seems to be advocating an intimate relation between love and knowledge that maintains their creative tension. For Marguerite, the transformation into divine understanding comes from the transformation of the soul into divine love. In this sense, loving and understanding generate each other in mutuality, and this mutuality of generation is represented in the fluidity between stages five and six. Love and knowledge while closely bound together remain distinct.

Marguerite grounds the mutuality in the distinction of love and knowledge on the divine level in her view of the dynamic of the Trinity. We should observe here that the beguine does not seem to be interested in the traditional role of the second Person as the Wisdom of the Father. When she mentions the Son as Wisdom, her expressions seem to be more formulaic without any development or connection to her larger program. For example, we noted that for Marguerite the faculties of the soul are filled with the Trinity at the fifth stage, and the soul's intellect possesses the wisdom of the Son.[200] Her focus is not the role of the Son in the process of transformation, however, but the Holy Spirit and the unitive power of the divine love of the Trinity. Thus unity is generated by the love relation of the three Persons and the divine unitive love in turn generates the Three. When the soul therefore is transformed into divine love, that is, the Holy Spirit who is the love of the Father and the Son, she is driven by the unity of this love into the Father, the One who is, the source without source of the Trinity, true Being from whom all existence comes. Her understanding of the dialectical relation between divine nature and created nature is thus transformed into divine understanding, which is divine nature itself.

The rich and complex, and therefore also sometimes baffling, character of the beguine's thought is apparent. Marguerite makes finely nuanced distinctions that allow her to penetrate deeply into the mysteries of the relation of love and knowledge where she strives to show how love and knowledge grow together. Marguerite's two moments of union point to this truth, so that the intimate relation remains at the furthest reach of the spiritual life. Marguerite also insists that this high point of spiritual perfection is attainable only by the power of the Holy Spirit, who has the primary role in the dynamic of spiritual growth. With Marguerite's absolute insistence on a union of identity grounded in the annihilation of the will, she posits a humility in the soul of an extraordinary kind, an emptiness, a vacuum which requires divine filling by the Holy Spirit. In Marguerite's schema, the work of the Holy Spirit is the means by which the soul is transformed in a radical way. The soul, for our beguine, does not become merely one spirit with God; the soul becomes God who is, three and one.

THE TRANSLATION

This translation is based on the full critical edition of the Old French and Latin with Middle English notes and supplements published in *Corpus Christianorum: Continuatio Mediaevalis* 69, edited by Romana Guarnieri and Paul Verdeyen (Turnhout, Belgium: Brepols, 1986). The text presented in this volume is the only accessible manuscript, Chantilly, *Musée Condé*, XIV F 26, Catalog 157, a copy produced toward the end of the fifteenth century. The original is not extant, and this manuscript has several problems, most notably that several chapters are missing. In light of these difficulties, the editors of the volume present the Latin and some supplements in Middle English. In translating I have attempted to stay as close to the Old French text as possible, taking particular care to preserve all personifications and literary stylizations as far as possible. Where the Old French was not clear or missing, I turned to the Latin text for clarity or to supply the lacuna. Sometimes only the Middle English was available. I have indicated where I have made use of a text other than the Old French. In many cases delightful word plays in the text are not apparent in English. Despite this limitation, I hope that Marguerite Porete's facility with language will be apparent to her modern reader.

NOTES TO THE INTRODUCTION

1. *Pseudo-mulier* means, literally, "fake woman."

2. *Continuatio chronici Guillelmi de Nangiaco* in *Recueil des historiens des Gaules et de la France* (Paris: Welter, 1894), 20:601. The text also appears in the article by Paul Verdeyen, "Le Procès d'inquisition contre Marguerite Porete et Guiard de Cressonessart (1309–1310)," *Revue d'histoire ecclésiastique* 81 (1986), pp. 88, 89.

3. Henry C. Lea, *A History of the Inquisition in the Middle Ages,* 3 vols. (New York: n.p., 1888), 2:122–23. See also Gordon Leff, *Heresy in the Later Middle Ages: The Relation of Heterodoxy to Dissent, c. 1250-c. 1450,* 2 vols. (New York: Barnes & Noble, Inc., 1967), 1:308–407.

4. Robert E. Lerner, *The Heresy of the Free Spirit in the Later Middle Ages* (Los Angeles: University of California Press, 1972), p. 71. Malcolm Lambert, *Medieval Heresy: Popular Movements from Bogomil to Hus* (New York: Holmes & Meier Publishers, Inc., 1977) follows Lerner.

5. Romana Guarnieri established Marguerite's authorship in an article published in *Osservatore Romano,* June 1946; see Lerner, *Heresy of the Free Spirit,* p. 73, n. 32. The first critical edition of the Old French text appeared in 1965, ed. Romana Guarnieri, *Archivio Italiano per la Storia della Pietà,* 5 vols. (Rome: n.p., 1965), 4:513–635. A full critical edition of the Old French and Latin with Middle English notes and supplements has been published in *Corpus Christianorum: Continuatio Mediaevalis* 69, ed. Romana Guarnieri and Paul Verdeyen (Turnhout, Belgium: Brepols, 1986), hereafter cited as *CCCM.*

6. Before Marguerite Porete's authorship was recognized, an English translation was published under the auspices of the Downside Benedictines, Clare Kirchberger, trans., *The Mirror of Simple Souls* (London: n.p., 1927). The view that the text is heretical is maintained by Edmund Colledge, "Liberty of Spirit: 'The Mirror of Simple Souls'," *Theology of Renewal* 2 vols. (Montreal: n.p., 1968), 2:100–17; Edmund Colledge and Romana Guarnieri, "The Glosses by 'M.N.' and Richard Methley to 'The Mirror of Simple Souls,' " *Archivio Italiano per la storia della pietà,* 5 vols. (Rome: n.p., 1968) 5:381–82. J. Orcibal believes it is orthodox, "Le 'Miroir des simples âmes' et la 'secte' du Libre Esprit," *Revue de l'histoire des religions* 175 (Paris, 1969):35–60.

7. Kurt Ruh, *Meister Eckhart: Theologe, Prediger, Mystiker* (Munich: C.H. Beck, 1985), chapter 6, "Meister Eckhart und die Beginenspiritualität;" Edmund Colledge and J. C. Marler, " 'Poverty

of the Will': Ruusbroec, Eckhart and *The Mirror of Simple Souls*," *Jan van Ruusbroec: The Sources, Content and Sequels of His Mysticism*, ed. P. Mommaers and N. de Paepe (Leuven: Leuven University Press, 1984). For instance, Eckhart's favorite description of the spiritual life as living "without a why" is also employed by Marguerite Porete in *The Mirror of Simple Souls*. See pp. 157, 161, 165, 167, 168, 174, 183, 217, 218.

8. Kurt Ruh has contributed extensively to these studies: "Beginenmystik: Hadewijch, Mechthild von Magdeburg, Marguerite Porete," *Zeitschrift für deutsches Altertum und deutsche Literatur* 106 (1977):265–77; " 'Le Miroir des Simples Ames' der Marguerite Porete," *Verbum et Signum*, ed. H. Fromm, W. Harms, and U. Ruberg (Munich: W. Fink, 1975), pp. 365–87.

9. Peter Dronke, *Women Writers of the Middle Ages: A Critical Study of Texts from Perpetua (d. 203) to Marguerite Porete (d. 1310)* (New York: Cambridge University Press, 1985); *Medieval Women's Visionary Literature*, ed. Elizabeth A. Petroff (New York: Oxford University Press, 1986); *Medieval Women Writers*, ed. Katharina M. Wilson (Athens, Ga.: The University of Georgia Press, 1984). The last two volumes contain English translations of selections.

10. For a review of the literature see Carolyn Walker Bynum, "Did the Twelfth Century Discover the Individual?" *Jesus as Mother: Studies in the Spirituality of the High Middle Ages* (Los Angeles: University of California Press, 1984), pp. 82–109.

11. The following discussion is a distillation from M.-D. Chenu, "Monks, Canons, and Laymen in Search of the Apostolic Life" and "The Evangelical Awakening," *Nature, Man, and Society in the Twelfth Century: Essays on New Theological Perspectives in the Latin West*, ed. Jerome Taylor and Lester K. Little (Chicago: University of Chicago Press, 1968).

12. Herbert Grundmann, *Religiöse Bewegungen im Mittelalter: Untersuchungen über die geschichtlichen Zusammenhange zwischen der Ketzerei, den Bettelorden und der religiösen Frauenbewegung im 12. und 13. Jahrhundert und die geschichtlichen Grundlagen der deutschen Mystik* (Berlin, 1935; reprint, Hildesheim, 1961), chapter 4, "Die Anfänge der religiösen Frauenbewegung."

13. See Janet I. Summers, " 'The Violent Shall Take It by Force': The First Century of Cistercian Nuns, 1125–1228" (Unpublished Ph.D. dissertation, University of Chicago, 1986).

14. Grundmann, *Religiöse Bewegungen*, p. 182.

15. For a good overview of the history of the name "beguine," see J. Van Mierlo, "Béguins, béguines, béguinages," *Dictionnaire de spiritualité,* 14 vols., editors vary (Paris: Beauchesne, 1937—), 1:1341–52.

16. The classic description of stages of beguine development comes from L.J.M. Philippen, *De Begijnhoven, Oorsprong, geschiedenis, inrichting* (Antwerp: n.p., 1918). This model continued to be cited by E.W. McDonnell, *Beguines and Beghards in Medieval Culture, with Special Emphasis on the Belgian Scene* (New Brunswick, N.J.: Rutgers University Press, 1954), pp. 5–6; by L.K. Little, *Religious Poverty and the Profit Economy in Medieval Europe* (Ithaca, N.Y.: Cornell University Press, 1983), p. 130; and by D. Devlin, "Feminine Lay Piety in the High Middle Ages," *Distant Echoes,* ed. John A. Nichols and Lillian Thomas Shank, Cistercian Studies Series 71 (Kalamazoo, Mich: Cistercian Publications, 1984), pp. 184–85.

17. Grundmann, *Religiöse Bewegungen,* chapter 5, "Die Eingliederung der religiösen Frauenbewegung in die Bettelorden," pp. 199–201.

18. What follows is based on Grundmann, *Religiöse Bewegungen,* chapter 6, "Die Beginen im 13. Jahrhundert," pp. 319–54.

19. Taken from "Casus et articuli, super quibus accusatus fuit a fratribus Predicatoribus, cum responsionibus ad singula," cited in Grundmann, *Religiöse Bewegungen,* pp. 323–24.

20. Janet Summers notes a similar two-tiered response to women among the Cistercian men. See "The First Century of Cistercian Nuns," especially chapter 5, "Development of Legal Relations Between Male and Female Cistercians."

21. Grundmann, *Religiöse Bewegungen,* pp. 332–33, n. 28.

22. *Corp. jur. can. VI, lib. 3, tit. 17, c. 1,* cited in Grundmann, *Religiöse Bewegungen,* p. 340.

23. Grundmann, *Religiöse Bewegungen,* p. 344.

24. Grundmann, *Religiöse Bewegungen,* p. 354.

25. See Lerner, *Heresy of the Free Spirit,* pp. 65–68, and McDonnell, *Beguines and Beghards,* pp. 516–520. McDonnell says this legislation was not directed against the "real" beguines, i.e., those beguines who were enclosed (p. 518). Lerner makes no such distinction.

26. McDonnell, *Beguines and Beghards,* p. 524. For the Latin, see P. Fredericq, *Corpus documentorum inquisitionis haereticae pravitatis neerlandicae,* 2 vols. (Ghent: n.p., 1889–1906) 1:167–68.

27. Fredericq, *Corpus documentorum*, 1:168.

28. McDonnell, *Beguines and Beghards*, pp. 524–28, seems to want to make this distinction, however.

29. Fredericq, *Corpus inquisitionis neerlandicae*, 1:168.

30. Richard Kieckhefer, *Repression of Heresy in Medieval Germany* (Philadelphia: University of Pennsylvania Press, 1979), pp. 19–21.

31. The shifts back and forth between persecution and protection are recounted in Kieckhefer, *Repression of Heresy*, pp. 19–51, and in Lerner, *Heresy of the Free Spirit*, pp. 85–163.

32. What follows is based on Lerner, *Heresy of the Free Spirit*, pp. 229–43.

33. Lerner, *Heresy of the Free Spirit*, p. 233.

34. Lerner, *Heresy of the Free Spirit*, p. 233.

35. Lerner, *Heresy of the Free Spirit*, pp. 239–40. Kieckhefer, *Repression of Heresy*, makes a similar point, p. 22.

36. See Lerner, *Heresy of the Free Spirit*, pp. 46–53. Lerner seems to imply this when he says that a particular beguine's greatest crime "consisted in being unlicensed and bereft of influential support" (p. 53).

37. Lerner, *Heresy of the Free Spirit*, p. 229.

38. Bernard Delmaire, "Les béguines dans le Nord de la France au premier siècle de leur histoire (vers 1230—vers 1350)," *Les religieuses en France au xiiie siècle*, ed. Michel Parisse, Table ronde organisée par l'Institut d'Etudes Mediévales de l'Université de Nancy II et le C.E.R.C.O.M. (Nancy: Presses Universitaires de Nancy, 1985), pp. 121–62. Delamire focuses his attention on those beguine houses which have not received earlier attention; therefore he does not discuss the role of the Capetian dynasty in the founding of beguine houses. His article is very valuable, however, for he lists the archives' locations which house the foundation documents.

39. Delmaire, "Les béguines dans le Nord," p. 136.

40. Léon Le Grand, "Les béguines de Paris," *Mémoires de la société de l'histoire de Paris et de l'Ile-de-France* 20 (1893):303. The statutes for the beguinage appear in an appendix at the end of the article, pp. 342–49.

41. Le Grand, "Béguines de Paris," pp. 304–6.

42. Arch. nat., JJ 64, n. 475, fol. 256 v, cited in Le Grand, "Béguines de Paris," pp. 317–18. The "reinstatement" probably refers to the escape clauses both in the Vienne decrees and those later

issued by John XXII (see Le Grand, p. 316). The phrase "in the said house" could refer to enclosed beguines in general and not necessarily to the particular beguinage in Paris. We will return to these concerns later in this section.

43. "Charles, etc. We make known to all present and those to come that since my lord Saint Louis, among the other works of mercy which he did during his lifetime, had acquired an enclosure of houses in Paris situated near the gate Barbeel, and there placed good and valiant women beguines for the purpose of chaste service to our Lord, and they possess and hold the said houses as their own, the property of the place protected and maintained by him, and since then our very dear lords father and brothers, the kings Philippe, Louis, and Philippe recently deceased, may God save him, for the purpose of good governance and estate of the said dwelling of the beguinage, had committed the care and the administration of this place to the prior of the order of the Friars Preachers of Paris, who by virtue and authority of his commissions made certain statutes and ordinances according to which the said beguines ought to live and conduct themselves. [The preamble continues with the statement noted above.]" Ibid., cited in Le Grand, "Béguines de Paris," p. 318, n. 1.

44. Le Grand, "Béguines de Paris," pp. 318–19. A few items were added in 1341, and Le Grand took care to indicate these additions.

45. Le Grand, "Béguines de Paris," pp. 321–22.

46. Le Grand, "Béguines de Paris," p. 323.

47. "And because the property of all the said houses had always been retained by our predecessors, we also retain it for ourselves and for our successors the kings of France. And the habitation of these [houses] along with improvements we have promised and do promise to women who live well and honestly in the said beguinage, as long as they desire to be obedient and keep our ordinances and persevere in good and holy works. And in the case where the contrary is found, we desire that the said houses, which are vacated through death, or through fault, or through voluntary departure, or through expulsion for misdemeanor, either be sold or freely managed by the counsel and consent of the said [Dominican] guardian and governor, and of the said mistress and of her council, as seems good to them." "Statuts du béguinage de Paris, 1341" (Arch. nat., JJ 73, fol. 52 v., n. 71), article 19, cited in Le Grand, "Béguines de Paris," p. 346.

48. See the discussion by Jane Tibbetts Schulenburg, "Strict Active Enclosure and Its Effect on the Female Monastic Experience (ca. 500–1100)," *Distant Echoes*, pp. 51–86; also Summers, "The First Century of Cistercian Nuns," pp. 112–24.

49. "Statuts," articles 1,3–5, cited in Le Grand, pp. 343–44.

50. "Statuts," article 2, cited in Le Grand, "Béguines de Paris," p. 343.

51. "Statuts," article 6, cited in Le Grand, "Béguines de Paris," p. 344.

52. "Statuts," article 10, in Le Grand, "Béguines de Paris," p. 344.

53. "Statuts," article 14, in Le Grand, "Béguines de Paris," p. 345.

54. "Statuts," article 23, cited in Le Grand, "Béguines de Paris," p. 347.

55. "Statuts," article 19, cited in Le Grand, "Béguines de Paris," p. 346.

56. "Statuts," article 19, cited in Le Grand, "Béguines de Paris," p. 346. "Our very dear lord and cousin the king Charles [IV], our abovesaid predecessor, in order to remove all doubts for the time to come, ordained, and we also ordain, that the beguines who have been given freely managed houses, they have neither made noticeable structures, whatever they have received for their ease, nor are they to be charged any rent, but are to be freely welcomed to the community."

57. "Statuts," article 19, cited in Le Grand, "Béguines de Paris," p. 346. "And those who have bought [houses] or built or noticeably repaired [them], can rent them reasonably according to the estimation and with the permission of the said governor, the mistress and her council. And anything which would be otherwise done without the permission of these is null and void. Instead, if any of these houses be sold or rented without the estimation and permission of the said governor, the mistress and her council, we desire and ordain that they [the houses] be taken over and applied freely for the common profit of the said beguinage."

58. "Statuts," article 20, cited in Le Grand, "Béguines de Paris," p. 347.

59. "Statuts," article 19, cited in Le Grand, "Béguines de Paris," p. 347.

60. Joseph R. Strayer, "France, the Holy Land, the Chosen Peo-

ple, and the Most Christian King," *Medieval Statecraft and the Perspectives of History: Essays by Joseph R. Strayer* (Princeton, N.J.: Princeton University Press, 1971), pp. 300–314.

61. See Joseph R. Strayer, *On the Medieval Origins of the Modern State* (Princeton: Princeton University Press, 1973), pp. 3–56.

62. Strayer, "France . . . Most Christian King," *Medieval Statecraft*, pp. 305–06, 309, 313.

63. Joseph R. Strayer, *The Reign of Philip the Fair* (Princeton, N.J.: Princeton University Press, 1980), chapter 4, "The King and the Church," p. 237.

64. Strayer, *Reign*, p. 240.

65. Strayer, *Reign*, pp. 237, 240–41.

66. Malcolm Barber, *The Trial of the Templars* (New York: Cambridge University Press, 1978, reprint 1987), Introduction, p. 1.

67. Barber, *Trial*, p. 2.

68. For instance, Peter Partner, *The Murdered Magicians: The Templars and Their Myth* (Rochester, Vt.: Thorsons Publishing Group, 1987), tells the story in terms of the way "uncontrolled private fears can turn into uncontrolled public disasters" (p. xx) and ultimately be part of the construct of a modern myth. Barber, *Trial*, and Strayer, *Reign*, are more concerned with assessing the available historical data in an effort to understand the reasons behind Philip's actions against the Templars. What follows is based on Strayer's analysis, with which Barber is in agreement for the most part (see his conclusion, pp. 246–47).

69. Strayer, *Reign*, pp. 287–88.

70. Strayer, *Reign*, pp. 288–89. Strayer also says that Pope Clement V went along with the royal accusations because the Templars had outlived their usefulness to the church (p. 292).

71. Strayer, *Reign*, p. 295.

72. The documents for Marguerite's trial have been published for a long time: Henry C. Lea, *A History of the Inquisition in the Middle Ages*, 3 vols. (New York: n.p., 1887), 2:575–78; Fredericq, *Corpus inquisitionis neerlandicae*, 1:155–60, 2:63–64. Eighty years later, Robert E. Lerner published the documents pertaining to the trial of Guiard in "An 'Angel of Philadelphia' in the Reign of Philip the Fair: The Case of Guiard of Cressonessart," *Order and Innovation in the Middle Ages: Essays in Honor of Joseph R. Strayer* (Princeton: Princeton University Press, 1976) pp. 343–64, and pp. 529–40. Paul Verdeyen published all the gathered documents in his article,

"Le Procès d'inquisition contre Marguerite Porete et Guiard de Cressonessart (1309–1310)," *Revue d'histoire ecclésiastique* 81 (1986):47–94.

73. Lerner, "An 'Angel of Philadelphia,' " pp. 356–58; Lerner, *Heresy of the Free Spirit,* p. 77; Verdeyen, "Le Procès," p. 49.

74. Lerner, "An 'Angel of Philadelphia,' " p. 346 and n. 13, p. 530.

75. Lerner, "An 'Angel of Philadelphia,' " p. 346.

76. See *Archives Nationales,* J.428, #16 & 17 in Lerner, "An 'Angel of Philadelphia,' " Appendix II, pp. 361, 362; and in Verdeyen, "Le procès," pp. 56–57, 62–63.

77. *Archives Nationales* J.428, #19, in Verdeyen, "Le procès," p. 61. The Latin gives a sense of her personal strength: "*Ipsam namque post multas contumacias in non comparendo commissas tandem coram se fecit personaliter presentari. Cui de dicenda veritate super sibi impositis et expositis ex officii sui debito detulit iuramentum, quod ipsa obstinata et pertinax subire seu prestare contumaciter recusavit, quamvis postea sufficienter informata ipsum fratrem Guillelmum inquisitorem plane recognosceret et etiam fateretur. Et propterea idem inquisitor ipsam, in sua contumacia persistentem, post multas exhortationes salubres sibi factas ab eo, maioris excommunicationis vinculo innodavit. Quam quidem excommunicationem fere per annum et dimidium in sue salutis dispendium animo sustinuit indurato, que prius et postea frequenter de iurando et respondendo per eundem inquisitorem legitime requisita, ipsi beneficium absolutionis in forma iuris impendendum sepius offerentem, jurare et respondere renuens contumaciter sicut prius, absolutionem sibi oblatam petere vel recipere, suam salutem refugiens, non curavit.*"

78. *Archives Nationales* J.428, #19, in Verdeyen, "Le procès," p. 61.

79. *Archives Nationales,* J.428, #16 and 17, in Lerner, "An 'Angel of Philadelphia,' " pp. 346, 361–62; and Verdeyen, "Le Procès," pp. 56–58, 61–63.

80. Revelation 3:7–13. *Archives Nationales,* J.428, #18, in Lerner, "An 'Angel of Philadelphia,' " pp. 346, 363–64; Verdeyen, "Le Procès," pp. 65–76.

81. Lerner, "An 'Angel of Philadelphia,' " p. 355; Verdeyen, "Le procès," p. 76.

82. Lerner, "An 'Angel of Philadelphia,' " pp. 357–58; Verdeyen, "Le procès," p. 77.

83. There has been some confusion about the date given in *Ar-*

chives Nationales, J.428, #15 (first section): "*Actum in loco predicto anno Domini MCCC nono, xia die Aprilis, indictione octava, pontificatus domini Clementis, divina providentia pape quinti, anno quinto.*" [Acted in the aforementioned place in the year of our Lord 1309, eleventh day of April, eighth indiction of the pontificate of lord Clement, by divine providence fifth pope, in the fifth year]; cited in Fredericq, *Corpus inquistionis neerlandicae,* 2:63–64. Also cited in Verdayen, "Le procès," p. 51, who reads "anno quarto" and thus changed the date noted in Fredericq from 11 April 1310 to 11 April 1309. Nevertheless, the weight of "*indictione octava*" and "*anno quinto*" indicates that the correct year is 1310. I am grateful to Robert Lerner who brought this alteration to my attention.

84. Lerner, *Heresy of the Free Spirit,* p. 71.

85. *The Mirror of Simple Souls,* chapter 140, p. 221. See also Lerner, *Heresy of the Free Spirit,* p. 72.

86. *The Mirror of Simple Souls,* chapter 140, p. 222.

87. Verdeyen, "Le procès," pp. 52–53.

88. *Archives Nationales,* J.428, #19bis, in Verdeyen, "Le Procès, pp. 78–79; also Fredericq, *Corpus inquisitionis neerlandicae,* 1:156–57. My translation.

89. Lerner, *Heresy of the Free Spirit,* p. 76; Verdeyen, "Le procès," p. 79.

90. Verdeyen, "Le Procès," p. 85.

91. Lerner, *Heresy of the Free Spirit,* pp. 207–8, mentions this possibility.

92. *The Mirror of Simple Souls,* chapter 122, p. 200.

93. Verdeyen, "Le Procès," p. 92. Also in Fredericq, *Corpus inquisitionis neerlandicae,* 2:64.

94. Verdeyen, "Le procès," p. 80.

95. Lerner, *Heresy of the Free Spirit,* pp. 73–75. See also Introduction, *CCCM* 69, which includes a full description of the Old French and Latin manuscripts. A Middle English translation with glosses by "M>N>," ed. Marilyn Doiron, is published in *Archivio Italiano per la Storia della Pietà* 5 (Rome: n.p., 1968):243–355.

96. E.g., Boethius, *The Consolation of Philosophy;* see also Jean de Meun, *Le Roman de la Rose.*

97. References to these courtly expressions are in the notes to the translation. For a good introduction to the courtly tradition see Robert W. Hanning, *The Individual in Twelfth-Century Romance* (New Haven, Conn.: Yale University Press, 1977). The literature is

vast. For a good selected bibliography, see *The Meaning of Courtly Love*, ed. F.X. Newman, Papers of the first annual conference of the Center for Medieval and Early Renaissance Studies, State University of New York at Binghamton, March 17–18, 1967 (Albany, N.Y.: State University of New York Press, 1968), pp. 97–102.

98. Marguerite Porete, *The Mirror of Simple Souls*, chapter 118, pp. 189–94. The stages are also treated in chapter 61, pp. 138–39.

99. Chapter 118, p. 189.

100. Chapter 118, p. 189.

101. Chapter 118, p. 190.

102. Chapter 118, pp. 190–91.

103. Chapter 118, p. 191. I follow the Latin, "*et ipsa non est, a qua nulla res est.*" The Old French reads: "*. . . et elle n'est mie, si n'est dont toute chose est.*" [. . . and she is not if she is not of the one from whom everything is.]

104. Chapter 118, p. 193.

105. Chapter 118, pp. 193–94.

106. Chapter 118, p. 194.

107. Chapter 59, p. 136.

108. Chapter 3, p. 81.

109. Chapter 62, p. 139.

110. Chapter 63, p. 140.

111. Chapter 118, p. 189; chapter 21, p. 103. When the word reason is capitalized, I am using the term as a personification as Marguerite does; used with lower case, the term refers to an aspect of Marguerite's faculty psychology.

112. Chapter 73, pp. 147–48. See Richard of St. Victor, *The Twelve Patriarchs*, 73.

113. Chapter 69, p. 144.

114. Richard of St. Victor in *The Mystical Ark* 5.12 expresses a similar emphasis in his assertion that the failure (*deficere*) of the spirit follows ardent longing.

115. Chapter 55, p. 132.

116. Chapter 77, pp. 151–52.

117. Chapter 57, p. 134.

118. Chapter 55, p. 132.

119. Chapter 1, p. 80, and chapter 2, p. 81.

120. Chapter 14, p. 96. For the traditional nature of these attributes see Peter Abelard, *Theologia Christiana* 4.100, *Theologia Scholastica* 2.16; Bernard of Clairvaux, *Epistola* 190.3 (*Contra quaedam*

capitula errorum Abaelardi); Richard of St. Victor, *De Trinitate* 1.16, 2.16–18, 6.15; and Aquinas, *I. I Sent.* d.31, q.1, a.2.

121. Chapter 67, pp. 142–43. See Pseudo-Dionysius, *Divine Names* 2.5, 2.7; Bonaventure, *I Sent.* d.2, a.u., q.2, *Brevil.* 1.3.

122. Chapter 113, p. 184. Augustine, *De Trinitate* 8.14.

123. Chapter 112, p. 184. The notion of goodness as self-diffusive comes from the Dionysian tradition. See Pseudo-Dionysius, *The Divine Names* 4.1, 4.4.

124. Chapter 108, p. 179.

125. Chapter 115, pp. 185–86.

126. Chapter 14, p. 96.

127. Chapter 43, pp. 122–23.

128. Chapter 110, p. 182.

129. Chapter 57, p. 134, for the understanding of the sad soul; chapter 55, p. 132, for the non-understanding of the lost soul.

130. Chapter 57, p. 133.

131. Chapter 111, pp. 183–84.

132. Chapter 80, p. 155.

133. Augustine, *The Spirit and the Letter* 53–55. Bernard of Clairvaux insists the will is free from necessity, *On Grace and Free Choice* 1.2.

134. Chapter 107, p. 179.

135. Chapter 103, p. 176. "Without a why," chapter 91, p. 167.

136. Chapter 104, p. 177.

137. Chapter 12, pp. 92–93. This notion is in opposition to a position like that found in William of St-Thierry's *The Golden Epistle* 257–258, where the soul indeed has a will, but a will which wills what God wills. Marguerite argues the contrary, that at the fifth stage the soul no longer has any will of her own, and only the divine will wills within her.

138. Chapter 89, p. 165.

139. Chapter 13, pp. 94–95.

140. Chapter 21, pp. 103–04.

141. Chapter 13, pp. 94–95.

142. Chapter 65, pp. 141–42.

143. Chapter 110, p. 182.

144. William of St-Thierry, *The Mirror of Faith* 15.27.

145. Richard of St. Victor, *Mystical Ark* 3.6.

146. Chapter 15, p. 98; chapter 57, p. 134; chapter 118, p. 190.

147. Chapter 60, p. 137.

148. Chapter 79, p. 153.

149. Chapter 118, p. 191.

150. Chapter 14, p. 96; chapter 130, pp. 210–11.

151. Chapter 81, p. 156.

152. Chapter 109, p. 181.

153. Chapter 45, pp. 124–25.

154. Chapter 130, pp. 210–11.

155. Chapter 118, p. 192: "The understanding of these two natures, of which we have spoken, the Divine Goodness and [the Soul's] wretchedness, is the ability which has endowed her with such goodness." See also chapter 130, pp. 210–11.

156. Chapter 117, p. 187.

157. Chapter 107, p. 179; chapter 109, pp. 180–81.

158. Chapter 131, pp. 211–13.

159. Chapter 131, pp. 213–14.

160. The term used is *sens*, or in the Latin, *sensus*, chapter 131, p. 214.

161. Chapter 43, pp. 122–23.

162. Chapter 40, p. 120.

163. Chapter 117, p. 187.

164. This necessity for the divine filling of the soul is very similar to Eckhart's views in his treatise *On Detachment*.

165. Chapter 118, p. 193.

166. Chapter 118, p. 192.

167. Chapter 88, p. 164.

168. Chapter 115, pp. 185–86. The role of the Holy Spirit is reminiscent of William of St-Thierry, *The Golden Epistle* 170, 257–266; *The Mirror of Faith* 99–101. See also Richard of St. Victor, *De trinitate* 6.14; *The Mystical Ark* 5. The generation of the Trinity for Marguerite bears some similarity to the birth of the Word in the soul for Eckhart, e.g., Sermon 2 and Sermon 6.

169. Chapter 42, p. 122.

170. Chapter 14, p. 96.

171. Chapter 110, p. 182.

172. Chapter 118, p. 193.

173. Chapter 61, p. 139.

174. Chapter 68, p. 143, and chapter 115, p. 185.

175. Chapter 91, p. 167.

176. Chapter 58, p. 135, and the sixth stage, chapter 118, pp. 193–94. Marguerite's notion of the aperture, or spark, may be related

to the "aperture" (*rima*) of contemplation in Gregory the Great, e.g., *Moralia* 5.29.52.

177. Chapter 61, p. 138.

178. Chapter 67, p. 143.

179. Chapter 51, pp. 128–29.

180. Chapter 7, p. 85, chapter 51, p. 129, and chapter 81, pp. 156–57.

181. Chapter 58, pp. 135–36.

182. Chapter 11, p. 90.

183. Chapter 9, pp. 86–87.

184. Chapter 11, p. 90.

185. Chapter 85, p. 160, and chapter 9, p. 87.

186. Chapter 90, p. 166.

187. Chapter 52, pp. 129–30.

188. Chapter 51, p. 129, and chapter 110, p. 182.

189. Chapter 115, p. 185.

190. Chapter 23, pp. 105–06.

191. Chapter 70, p. 145, and chapter 21, p. 104.

192. Chapter 52, p. 130.

193. Chapter 25, p. 107.

194. Chapter 82, p. 158. Eckhart uses a similar image of a drop of water in the sea to express a union of identity in *Sermon 80*. For an analysis of the uses of this image in the Middle Ages, see Robert E. Lerner, "The Image of Mixed Liquids in Late Medieval Thought," *Church History* 40 (1971):397–411.

195. Chapter 135, p. 218.

196. Chapter 61, p. 138.

197. Chapter 58, p. 135.

198. See above, p. 30; Augustine, *De trinitate* 8.14.

199. Chapter 14, p. 96. Emphasis is mine.

200. Chapter 115, p. 185.

THE MIRROR OF SIMPLE SOULS

THE MIRROR OF SIMPLE ANNIHILATED SOULS AND THOSE WHO ONLY REMAIN IN WILL AND DESIRE OF LOVE

Here commences the table in order to find the chapters of this book called "The Mirror of simple annihilated souls and those who only remain in will and desire of love."

THE MIRROR OF SIMPLE SOULS

THE MIRROR OF SIMPLE SOULS

THE MIRROR OF SIMPLE SOULS

THE MIRROR OF SIMPLE SOULS

THE MIRROR OF SIMPLE SOULS

THE MIRROR OF SIMPLE SOULS

HERE FOLLOW SOME CONSIDERATIONS FOR THOSE WHO ARE IN THE STAGE OF THE SAD ONES AND WHO ASK THE WAY TO THE LAND OF FREENESS

Explicit

Deo gratias

You who would read this book,
If you indeed wish to grasp it,
Think about what you say,
For it is very difficult to comprehend;
Humility, who is keeper of the treasury of
Knowledge
And the mother of the other Virtues,
Must overtake you.

Theologians and other clerks,
You will not have the intellect for it,
No matter how brilliant your abilities,
If you do not proceed humbly.
And may Love and Faith, together,
Cause you to rise above Reason,
[Since] they are the ladies of the house.

Even Reason witnesses
In the Thirteenth Chapter of this book,
And with no shame about it,
That Love and Faith make her live
And she does not free herself from them,
For they have lordship over her,
Which is why she must humble herself.

Humble, then, your wisdom
Which is based on Reason,
And place all your fidelity
In those things which are given
By Love, illuminated through Faith.
And thus you will understand this book
Which makes the Soul live by love.

EXPLICIT

THE MIRROR OF SIMPLE SOULS

Chapter 1: The Prologue

Soul, touched by God and removed from sin at the first stage of grace, is carried by divine graces to the seventh stage of grace, in which state the Soul possesses the fullness of her perfection through divine fruition in the land of life.

Here Love speaks: As for you actives and contemplatives, and perhaps those annihilated by true love, you will hear some powers of pure love, of noble love, of the high love of the Unencumbered Soul; how the Holy Spirit has placed his sail in her as if she were his ship. I pray you by love, says Love, that you hear through great effort of the subtle intellect within you and through great diligence, for otherwise all those who hear it will grasp it badly, if they are not of this kind.

Thus listen with humility to a little exemplum of love in the world and listen to it as a parallel to divine love.

Exemplum:[2] Once upon a time, there was a maiden, daughter of a king, of great heart and nobility and also of noble character; and she lived in a far off land. So it happened that this maiden heard tell of the great gentle courtesy and nobility of the king, Alexander, and very soon her will loved him because of the great renown of his gentility. But this maiden was so far from this great lord, in whom she had fixed her love from herself, that she was able neither to see him nor to have him. Thus she was inconsolable in herself, for no love except this one would be sufficient for her. When she saw that this faraway love, who was so close within her, was so far outside of her, she thought to herself that she would comfort her melancholy by imagining some figure of her love, by whom she was continually wounded in heart. And so she had an image painted which would represent the semblance of the king she loved, an image as close as possible to that which presented itself to her in her love for him and in the affection of the love which captured her. And by means of this image with her other habits she dreamed of the king.

Soul: In truly similar fashion, speaks the Soul who had this book written, I tell you of such a thing: I heard tell of a King of great power who was by gentle courtesy and by very great courtesy of nobility and largesse a noble Alexander. But He was so far from me, and I from Him, that I did not know how to take comfort for myself. And for the sake of my memory of Him, He gave me this book, which makes present in some fashion His love itself. But it is no hindrance that I have His image,[3] for it is not true that I am in a strange land and

80

far from the palace where the very noble friends of this Lord dwell, who are completely pure, perfect, and free through the gifts of this King with whom they remain.[4]

Author: Thus we shall tell you how our Lord is not at all freed from Love, but Love is from Him for us, so that the little ones might be able to hear it by means of you; for Love can do everything without any misdeed.

And thus Love speaks for your sake: There are seven stages of noble being, from which a creature receives being; so the Soul disposes herself to all the stages before she comes to perfect being. And we will tell you how before this book ends.

Chapter 2: Of the work of Love and why she has this book made.

Love: As for you little ones of Holy Church, says Love, I have made this book for you, so that you might hear in order to be more worthy of the perfection of life and the being of peace to which the creature is able to arrive through the virtue of perfect charity, the gift given by the whole Trinity, which gift you will hear explained in this book through the Intellect of Love and following the questions of Reason.

Chapter 3: Here Love speaks of the commandments of the Holy Church.

Love: Therefore we shall begin, says Love, with the commandments of the Holy Church, so that each might be able to take his nourishment in this book with the aid of God, who commands that we love Him with all our heart, all our soul, and all our strength; and ourselves as we ought, and our neighbors as ourselves.

First, that we love Him with all our heart: that means that our thoughts should be always truly in Him. And with all our soul: that means that until death we do not speak but the truth. And with all our strength: that is, that we accomplish all our works purely for Him. And ourselves as we ought: that means that in doing this we do not give attention to our gain but the perfect will of God. And our neighbors as ourselves: that is, that we neither do, nor think, nor speak toward our neighbors anything we would not wish they do toward us. These commands are of necessity for salvation for all: nobody can have grace with a lesser way.

Note here the example of the rich young man who said to Jesus Christ that he had kept these since infancy, and Jesus Christ said to him: "One thing is necessary for you to do, if you want to be perfect. It is: go and sell all the things which you possess and give them to the poor, and then follow me, and you will have treasure in the heavens."[5] This is the counsel of the complete perfection of the Virtues, and whoever keeps them will live in true Charity.

Chapter 4: The noble Virtue of Charity and how she obeys none other than Love.

Love: Charity obeys no created thing except Love.

Charity possesses nothing of her own, and should she possess something she does not say that it belongs to her.

Charity abandons her own need and attends to that of others.

Charity asks no payment from any creature for some good or pleasure that she has accomplished.

Charity has no shame, nor fear, nor anxiety. She is so upright that she cannot bow on account of anything that might happen to her.

Charity neither makes nor takes account of anything under the sun, for the whole world is only refuse and leftovers.

Charity gives to all what she possesses of worth, without retaining anything for herself, and with this she often promises what she does not possess through her great largesse, in the hope that the more she gives the more remains in her.

Charity is such a wise merchant that she earns profits everywhere where others lose, and she escapes the bonds that bind others and thus she has great multiplicity of what pleases Love.

And note that the one who would have perfect charity must be mortified in the affections of the life of the spirit through the work of charity.

Chapter 5: Of the life which is called the peace of charity in the annihilated life.

[*Love*]: Thus there is another life, which we call the peace of charity in the annihilated life. Of this life, says Love, we wish to speak, in asking what one could find:

1. A Soul
2. who is saved by faith without works

3. who is only in love
4. who does nothing for God
5. who leaves nothing to do for God
6. to whom nothing can be taught
7. from whom nothing can be taken
8. nor given
9. and who possesses no will

Love: Alas, says Love, who will give to this Soul what is lacking to her, for it was not ever given, is not now given, nor will be?

Love: This Soul, says Love, has six wings like the Seraphim. She no longer wants anything which comes by a mediary. This is the proper being of the Seraphim: there is no mediary between their love and the divine Love. They always possess newness without a mediary, and so also for this Soul: for she does not seek divine knowledge among the masters of this age, but in truly despising the world and herself. Great God, how great a difference there is between a gift from a lover to a beloved through a mediary and a gift that is between lovers without a mediary!

Love: This book speaks the truth about this Soul in saying that she has six wings like the Seraphim. With two wings she covers her face from Jesus Christ our Lord. That means that the more this Soul has understanding of the divine goodness, the more perfectly she understands that she understands nothing about it, compared to one spark of His goodness, for His goodness is not comprehended except by Himself.

With two other wings she covers her feet, which means that the more she has understanding of what Jesus Christ suffered for us, the more she understands perfectly that she understands nothing about it, compared to what He suffered for us, for this is not understood except by Himself.

With the two others the Soul flies, and dwells in being and rest. Thus all that she understands, and loves and praises of the divine goodness are the wings by which she flies. Dwelling in being she is always in the sight of God; and in rest she dwells forever in the divine will.

And what, nay, how would such a Soul have fear? Certainly she would neither be able nor need to fear anything or to doubt. For even if she should be in the world, and if it should be possible that the world, flesh, devil, the four elements and the birds of the air and the savage beasts torment and dismember or devour her, she cannot fear anything if God dwells in her. For He is everywhere present, omnipotent, omniscient, and total goodness. He is our Father, our Brother and our Loyal Lover. He is without beginning. He is incomprehensible except by Himself. He is without end, three persons and one God; and as such, says this Soul, He is the Lover of our souls.

Chapter 6: How the Soul, made loving by God, living in the peace of Charity, takes leave of the Virtues.

[*Love*]: This Soul by such love, says Love herself, can say to the Virtues that for a long time and for many days she has been in their service.

Soul: I confess it to you, Lady Love, says this Soul, there was a time when I belonged to them, but now it is another time. Your courtliness has placed me outside their service. And thus to them I can now say and sing:

> Virtues, I take my leave of you forever,
> I will possess a heart most free and gay;
> Your service is too constant, you know well.
> Once I placed my heart in you, retaining nothing;
> You know that I was to you totally abandoned;
> I was once a slave to you, but now am delivered from it.
> I had placed my heart completely in you, you know well.
> Thus I lived a while in great distress,
> I suffered in many grave torments, many pains endured.
> Miracle it is that I have somehow escaped alive.
> This being so, I no longer care: I am parted from you,
> For which I thank God on high; good for me this day.
> I am parted from your dominations, which so vexed me.
> I was never more free, except as departed from you.
> I am parted from your dominations, in peace I rest.

Chapter 7: How this Soul is noble, and how she takes no account of anything.

[*Love*]: This Soul, says Love, takes account of neither shame nor honor, of neither poverty nor wealth, of neither anxiety nor ease, of neither love nor hate, of neither hell nor of paradise.

Reason: Ah, for God's sake, Love, says Reason, what does this mean, what you have said?

Love: What does this mean? says Love. Certainly the one knows this, and no other, to whom God has given the intellect—for Scripture does not teach it, nor the human mind comprehend it, nor does creaturely work deserve to grasp it or comprehend it. Thus this gift is given from the most High, into whom this creature is carried by the fertility of understanding, and nothing remains in her own intellect. And this Soul, who has become nothing, thus possesses everything, and so possesses nothing; she wills everything and she wills nothing; she knows all and she knows nothing.

Reason: And how can it be, Lady Love, says Reason, that this Soul can will what this book says, when before it said that she had no more will?

Love: Reason, says Love, it is no longer her will which wills, but now the will of God wills in her; for this Soul dwells not in love which causes her to will this through desiring something. Instead, Love dwells in her who seized her will, and Love accomplishes Love's will in her. Thus Love works in her without her, which is why no anxiety can remain in her.

This Soul, says Love, no longer knows how to speak about God, for she is annihilated from all her external desires and interior sentiments, from all affection of spirit; so that what this Soul does she does by practice of good habit according to the commandment of the Holy Church, without any desire, for the will is dead which gave desire to her.

Chapter 8:   How Reason is surprised that this Soul has abandoned the Virtues and how Love praises them.

[*Reason*]: Ah, Love, says Reason, who can only understand the obvious and avoids subtleties, what a wonder! This Soul no longer has any sentiment of grace, nor desire of spirit, since she has taken leave of the Virtues who offer the manner of living well to every good soul, and without these Virtues none can be saved nor come to perfection of life; and whoever possesses them cannot be deceived. Nevertheless, this Soul takes leave of them. Is she not out of her mind, the Soul who speaks thus?

Love: Without a doubt, not at all, says Love, for such Souls possess better the Virtues than any other creatures, but they do not possess any longer the practice of them, for these Souls no longer belong to the Virtues as they used to; also they have been servants long enough to become free from now on.

Reason: Ah, Love, says Reason, when were they servants?

Love: When they lived in the love and the obedience of you, Lady Reason, and also of the other Virtues. And having lived there, they have become free.

Reason: And when are such Souls freed? says Reason.

Love: When Love dwells in them, and the Virtues serve them without any contradiction and without labor by such Souls.

Love: Without a doubt, Reason, says Love, such Souls who have become so free have known many days what Dominion knows how to do. And if someone were to ask them about the greatest torment a creature could suffer, they would say that it would be to live in Love and to be still in obedience to the Virtues. For it is necessary to give to the Virtues all that they demand at whatever cost to Nature. Thus it is that the Virtues demand honor and possessions, heart and body and life. This means that such Souls leave all things, and still the Virtues say to this Soul, who gave all this to them retaining nothing to comfort Nature, they say to her that the just are saved at great pain. And so this exhausted Soul who still serves the Virtues says that she would be assaulted by Fear and tormented in hell until Judgment Day, if afterward she would be saved for sure.

And this, says Love, is the truth about the sort of Dominion in which the Soul lived and over whom the Virtues possess power. But the Souls of which we speak have perfected the Virtues, for such Souls do nothing more for the Virtues. But instead the Virtues do everything which such Souls wish, without dominating and without contradiction, for such Souls are their mistresses.

Chapter 9: How such Souls no longer possess will.

[*Love*]: Whoever would ask such free Souls, sure and peaceful, if they would want to be in purgatory, they would say no; or if they would want to be certain of their salvation in this life, they would say no; or if they would want to be in paradise, they would say no. But then with what would they will it? They no longer possess any will, and if they would desire anything, they would separate themselves from

Love. For the One who possesses their will knows what is their good, and this is their sufficiency without them knowing it and without being assured of it. Such Souls, however, live by understanding, by Love, and by praise. This is the habitual practice of such Souls without moving themselves, for Understanding, Love and Praise dwell in them. Such Souls do not know how to consider themselves good or evil, no longer possessing understanding of themselves, nor knowing how to judge if they are converted or perverted.

Love: To speak more briefly, let us take one Soul as an example, says Love. Such a Soul neither desires nor despises poverty nor tribulation, neither mass nor sermon, neither fast nor prayer, and gives to Nature all that is necessary, without remorse of conscience. But such Nature is so well ordered through the transformation by unity of Love, to whom the will of this Soul is conjoined, that Nature demands nothing which is prohibited. Such a Soul has no anxiety about anything which she lacks, unless it is in the hour of her necessity. And no one can lose this anxiety if he is not innocent.

Reason: For the sake of God! says Reason. What are you saying?

Love: I answer you thus, Reason, says Love. As I said to you before, and again I say it to you, that none of the masters of the natural senses, nor any the masters of Scripture, nor those who remain in the love of the obedience to the Virtues, none perceive this, nor will they perceive what is intended. But of this be certain, Reason, says Love, for no one perceives it except those whom Fine Love[6] calls. But if by chance one finds such Souls, they will speak the truth about it, if they wish. And do not think that anyone can understand them, but only those whom Fine Love and Charity call.

This gift, says Love, is given any time in a moment of an hour, and whoever possesses it guards it, for it is the most perfect gift which God gives to a creature. This Soul is a student of Divinity, and she sits in the valley of Humility and on the plain of Truth, and rests on the mountain of Love.

Chapter 10: How Love names the Soul by twelve names for the Actives[7] at the request of Reason.

Reason: Ah, Love, says Reason, name this Soul by her right name, give to the Actives some understanding of it.

Love: She can be named, says Love, by twelve names; that is:

The very marvelous one.
The Not Understood.
Most Innocent of the Daughters of Jerusalem.[8]
She upon whom the Holy Church is founded.
Illuminated by Understanding.
Adorned by Love.
Living by Praise.
Annihilated in all things through Humility.
At peace in divine being through divine will.
She who wills nothing except the divine will.
Filled and satisfied without any lack by divine goodness
    through the work of the Trinity.
Her last name is: Oblivion, Forgotten.

These twelve names Love gives to her.
Pure Courtesy: And without fail, says Pure Courtesy, it is right that she be thus named, for these are her right names.
Reason: Ah, Love, you have named this Soul by many names, by which the Actives have some understanding of her, which would only be by hearing the very noble names by which you have named her.

Chapter 11:   How, at the request of Reason, Love gives understanding of this Soul to the Contemplatives, in declaring nine points, which were mentioned before.

Reason: Now, Love, says Reason, I pray you for the Contemplatives, who always desire to increase in divine understanding and who are and remain in desire of Love, that by your courtesy you explain the nine points of which you have spoken before, these nine points which this Soul possesses, whom Fine Love calls, in whom Charity is dwelling and rests through the annihilated life, by which the Soul is released through Pure Love.
Love: Reason, says Love, you name them.
Reason: The first point, says Reason, which you said is that one cannot find such a Soul.
Love: This is true, says Love. This means that this Soul knows in herself only one thing, that is, the root of all evil and the abundance of

all sins without number, without weight, and without measure. And sin is nothing. This Soul is completely submerged and tormented by these horrible faults of hers, which are less than nothing, and by means of this intellect this Soul is less than nothing, as long as she is with herself. Thus one can conclude that one cannot find this Soul, because such a Soul is so annihilated by humility that no creature who ever sinned merits so great a torment, so great a shame without end, as she according to her right judgment, so that God would wish to take vengeance for one thousandth of her faults. Such humility is true humility and it is perfected in the Annihilated Soul and none other.

Love: The second point is that this Soul is saved by faith without works.

Reason: For God's sake! says Reason, what can that mean?

Love: This means, says Love, that such an Annihilated Soul possesses so great understanding within her by the virtue of faith, that she is so occupied within herself with the sustenance which Faith administers to her of the power of the Father, of the wisdom of the Son, and of the goodness of the Holy Spirit, that a created thing, which passes briefly, cannot dwell in her memory, on account of this other occupation which surrounds the intellect of this Annihilated Soul. This Soul knows no longer how to work, and without fail she is thus excused and exonerated, without works, by believing that God is good and incomprehensible. This one is saved by faith without works, because faith surpasses all work, as Love herself witnesses.

Love: The third point is that she is alone in Love.

Reason: For God's sake, Lady Love, says Reason, what does this mean?

Love: This means, says Love, that this Soul possesses no comfort, nor affection, nor hope in a creature which God has created, nor in heaven, nor in earth, but only in the goodness of God. Such a Soul neither begs nor asks anything of any creature. She is the phoenix who is alone; for this Soul is alone in Love who alone is satisfied in her.

Love: The fourth point is that this Soul does nothing for God.

Reason: Ah, for God's sake, says Reason, what does this mean?

Love: This means, says Love, that God has nothing to do with her work, and this Soul does only what it is God's work to do. She does not care about herself. She cares about God, who loves her more than this Soul could love herself. This Soul has so great a faith in God that she has no fear of being poor, as long as her Lover is rich. For Faith teaches her that as much as she hopes in God, so she will find Him, and she hopes through faith that He is totally rich, which is why she cannot be poor.

Love: The fifth point is that this Soul omits nothing to do for God which she might be able to do.

Reason: Ah, for God's sake, says Reason, what does this mean?

Love: This means, says Love, that she cannot do anything if it is not the will of God, and also she cannot will some other thing; and so she omits nothing to do for God. She does not allow something to enter into her thought which might be contrary to God, and for this reason she omits nothing to be done for God.

Love: The sixth point is that one cannot teach her anything.

Reason: Ah, for God's sake, says Reason, what does this mean?

Love: This means that this Soul is so well established[9] that if she possessed all the understanding of all the creatures who ever were and who are and who are to come, so it would seem to her as nothing, compared to what she loves, which never was understood, is not now, and never will be. This Soul loves better what is in God, which never was given, is not now, nor ever will be given, than she [loves] what she possesses and what she will possess. Thus it is that she must possess all the understanding which all the creatures possess who are and who are to come.

[*Soul*]: And yet this is nothing, says this Soul, compared to what He is in Himself, but one cannot speak of it.

Love: The seventh point is that one cannot take anything from her.

Reason: Ah, for God's sake, Love, says Reason, say what this means.

Love: What does this mean? says Love. And what would one take from her? Certainly one could not take anything from her. For whoever would take from this Soul honor, wealth and friends, heart and body and life, still would take nothing from her, if God remains with her. Which is why it appears that one cannot take anything away from her, no matter how strong one is.

Love: The eighth point is that one cannot give anything to her.

Reason: Love, for God's sake, says Reason, what does this mean, that one cannot give anything to her?

Love: What does this mean? says Love. And what would one give to her? If one would give to her all that which ever was given and which will be given, this would be nothing compared to what she loves and will love.

90

If not God Himself, and the Soul says, Lady Love, [who] loves in me and will love [in me].[10]

[*Love*]: Guard your reverence, says Love, I am not [responding to] that. We will say, says Love for the sake of the hearers, that God loves better the greater part of this Soul in Him than the lesser part that is of herself.

But the Soul says: There is no lesser part, there is nothing except the All. This I can say well and truthfully.

[*Love*]: I say as well, says Love, that if this Soul would possess all the understanding and the love and the praise which ever was given and will be given by the divine Trinity, this would be nothing compared to what she loves and will love. And she will never attain this love through understanding.

Soul speaks to Love: Ah, certainly not, sweet Love, says the Soul. [She will attain] not even the least bit without more of my love. For God is none other than the One of whom one can understand nothing perfectly. For He alone is my God, about whom one does not know how to say a word. Not [even] all those in paradise know how to attain a single point, however much understanding they might possess of Him. And in this greater part, says this Soul, is enclosed the supreme mortification of the love of my spirit. It is the total glory of the love of my soul, and will be forever, and of all those who will ever grasp it.

This point is a small one to hear, says this Soul, compared to the greatest, of which no one speaks. But I want to speak about it and I don't know what to say about it. Nevertheless, Lady Love, she says, my love is so certain that I would prefer to hear something slanderous about you than that one should say nothing about you. And without fail I do this: I slander because everything I say is nothing but slander about your goodness. But whatever slander I commit must be pardoned me by you.

Because, my Lady, says the Soul, one slanders you who always speaks of you, even if nothing were said of your goodness. In similar fashion I speak of you myself. I have not finished speaking of you, whether by questions or through thoughts, or in hearing, if one tells me something of your goodness. But the more I hear tell of you the more I am amazed. For this would be for me a great villainy: that one should feign discernment to me, that one should pretend to tell me something. For they are deceived who believe it, because I certainly know that one cannot say anything. And, please God, I will never be

91

deceived and wish never to hear lying about your divine goodness, but that I might accomplish the enterprise of this book, of which Love is the mistress, who tells me that I complete all my enterprises in it. For insofar as I ask of Love something for myself on account of love,[11] I will be with myself in the life of the spirit, in the shadow of the sun where one cannot see the subtle images of the drawing power of divine Love and of the divine generation.

And what do I say? says this Soul. Certainly still this is nothing, because should I possess all that is said, compared to what I love of Him, which He will give to no one except to Himself; and it is necessary for Him to retain such for the sake of his divine righteousness. And thus I say, and it is true, that one cannot give to me anything which might be able to be. And this lament, about which you hear me complain, dear Reason, says this Soul, is my All and my Good, grasp it well. Ah, how it is [a] sweet goal. For God's sake, grasp the whole, for paradise is nothing other than this perception. *Love:* The ninth point, Lady Reason, says Love, is that this Soul possesses no will.

[*Reason*]: Ah, for the sake of God's love, what are you saying? You say that this Soul has no will?

Love: Ah, without fail, it is so. Because all that this Soul wills in consent is what God wills that she will, and this she wills in order to accomplish the will of God, no longer for the sake of her own will. And she cannot will this by herself, but it is the will of God which wills it in her. Which is why it appears that this Soul has no will without the will of God, who makes her will all that she ought to will.

Chapter 12: The true intellect by which this book says in different places, that the Annihilated Soul possesses no will.

[*Love*]: Now listen and grasp well, hearers of this book, the true intellect by which this book speaks in different places, that the Annihilated Soul neither possesses will, nor is able to possess it, nor is able to will to possess it, and in this the divine will is perfectly accomplished. The Soul does not possess sufficiency of divine Love, nor divine Love sufficiency of the Soul, until the Soul is in God and God in the Soul, of Him, through Him, in such a state of divine rest. Then the Soul possesses all her sufficiency.

Intellect of Reason: True, but it seems, says Intellect of Reason, that the ninth point says completely the contrary, for it states that the Annihilated Soul wills nothing compared to what she would will to will, which will she cannot possess, for God wills that she wills that her will be nothing compared to His sufficiency, which never will be given to her.

Reason: I perceive in this, says Reason, that the Soul wills to will, and that God wills that she will one will, which she cannot possess, and from this [she] has a lack and no sufficiency.

Intellect of Reason: It seems to me, Lady Love, says Intellect of Reason, that the ninth point makes me perceive this, contradicting this book, which point says indeed that the Unencumbered Soul neither possesses will, nor is able to possess it, nor is able to will to possess it, nor does the divine Unity will that she possess it, and so [she] possesses her full sufficiency in all things through divine Love, as this book says.

Soul: Ah, Intellect of Reason, says the Annihilated Soul, how you are so discerning! You take the shell and leave the kernel, for your intellect is too low, hence you cannot perceive so loftily as is necessary for the one who wishes to perceive the being of which we speak. But Intellect of Divine Love, who remains and is in the Annihilated Soul and who is unencumbered, grasps it well without hesitation, for she is this herself.

The Height of Intellect of Love: Now, Intellect of Reason, says the Height of Intellect of Love, understand now the coarse nature of your defective perception. If this Annihilated Soul wills the will of God—and the more she wills it, the more she would will to will it—she cannot possess this through the smallness of creaturehood, because God retains the grandeur of His divine righteousness. But God wills that she would will this, and that she would possess such a will. Such a will is the divine will, which gives being to a free creature. This divine will, which God makes her will, courses through her in the veins of divine Understanding and the marrow of divine Love and the union of divine Praise. But the [created] will of the Soul inhibits these.

[Love]: Therefore, says Love, how can the Soul possess will, since Clear Understanding understands that the will is one being among the beings, the most noble of all the beings, which a creature cannot possess if she possesses it by willing nothing?

Now Reason has heard, says Love, the answer to her questions, except that [question] where Reason says that the Unencumbered Soul possesses in her a lack of sufficiency. I will tell her in what she has a lack of sufficiency: it is from willing the divine will, which the more one wills it, one possesses less of such a willing of his sufficiency. But this same will is the will of God alone and the glory of the Soul.

Chapter 13: How Reason is content with the explanation of the things said above for the Contemplatives and the Actives, but she asks again for the sake of the common folk.

Reason: Now, Love, says Reason, you have condescended to our prayer, that is, to have declared the things said above for the Actives and Contemplatives. I pray again that you declare them for the sake of the common folk, of whom some will be able perchance to come to this stage, for there are several double words which are hard to grasp with their intellect. If you explain, this book will show to all the true light of Truth, and the perfection of Charity, and those who are preciously elected by God and called and supremely loved by Him.
Love: Reason, says Love, where are these double words, which you pray me to distinguish and clarify for the profit of those for whose sake you make to us so humble a request, and also for the hearers of this book, which we will name the "Mirror of Simple Souls Who Remain in Will and Desire"?
Reason: To this we respond to you, Lady Love, says Reason, that this book says greatly admiring things about this Soul—that is, in the seventh chapter—that this Soul takes no account of shame, nor of honor, nor of poverty, nor of wealth, not of ease nor of anxiety, not of love nor of hate, not of hell nor of paradise. And with this it says that this Soul possesses all and possesses nothing, she knows all and knows nothing, she wills all and wills nothing, as it says above in the ninth chapter. And so [the Soul], says Reason, neither desires nor despises poverty, neither martyrdom nor tribulations, neither masses nor sermons, not fasts nor prayers, and who gives to Nature all she asks of her without remorse of conscience.

And without fail, Love, says Reason, this no one can grasp with my intellect if he is not taught it by you through your teaching. For my intellect and my judgment and all my counsel is the best that I know how to counsel: that one desire contempt, poverty, and all manner of tribulations, and masses and sermons, and fasts and prayers, that one have fear of all kinds of love, whatever they might be, for the perils which can be there, and that one desire above all paradise, and that one have fear of hell; that one refuse all manner of honors and temporal things, and all comforts, in obstructing Nature [in] what she asks, except those things without which the Soul could not live, as in the exemplar of the suffering and passion of our Lord Jesus Christ. This is the best, says Reason, that I know how to say and counsel all those who live in my obedience. Thus I say to all, that none will grasp this book with my intellect unless they grasp it by the virtue of Faith, and by the power of Love, who are my mistresses because I obey them in all things. And moreover I wish to say, says Reason, that whoever has these two strings in his bow, that is, the light of Faith and the power of Love, has permission to do all that pleases him, by the witness of Love herself, who says to the Soul: My love, love and do what you will.[12]

Love: Reason, says Love, you are very wise and very certain about what is fitting for you, and you wish to have response to the words said above. And because you have prayed me that I state the meaning, I will respond to all your questions. I guarantee you, Reason, says Love, that such Souls, whom Fine Love governs, possess as equally dear, shame as honor, and honor as shame; poverty as wealth, and wealth as poverty; torment from God and his creatures, as comfort from God and His creatures; to be loved as hated, and hated as loved; to be in hell as in paradise, and in paradise as in hell; and in small estate as in great, and great estate as small: [this] for themselves and for their station in life. And Truth knows this well, that they neither will nor not-will anything of these prosperities nor of these adversities. For such Souls no longer possess any will, except what God wills in them, and the divine will does not occupy these lofty creatures with such encumbrances as we have described.

Love: I have already said above, says Love, that such Souls possess as equally dear all adversities of heart—for the body and for the soul—as prosperity, and prosperity as adversity. And it is true, says Love, if the adversities and prosperities come to them, their will would not be the cause of it. And also these Souls know not what is best for them, nor in what manner God wishes to find their salvation or the salvation of their neighbors, nor by what means God wishes to dispense justice or mercy, nor through what means God wishes to give to the Soul the supreme gift of the goodness of His divine nobility. And for this the Unencumbered Soul possesses no longer any will to will or not-will, except only to will the will of God, and to accept in peace the divine ordinance.

Reason: Still, Lady Love, I add one thing to my question; that is, that this book says that this Soul possesses all things and so possesses nothing.

Love: This is true, says Love, for this Soul possesses God by divine grace, and whoever possesses God, possesses all things. And so [the book] says she possesses nothing, for all that this Soul possesses from God within her by the gift of divine grace, seems to be nothing to her. And thus it is [nothing] compared to what she loves, which is in Him, which He will not give to anyone except Himself. And according to this intellect this Soul possesses all and so possesses nothing, she knows all and so knows nothing.

Chapter 14: How this Soul by faith has understanding of God.

[*Love*]: She knows, says Love, by the virtue of Faith, that God is all Power, and all Wisdom, and perfect Goodness, and that God the Father has accomplished the work of the Incarnation, and the Son also and the Holy Spirit also. Thus God the Father has joined human nature to the person of God the Son, and the person of God the Son has joined [human nature] to the person of Himself, and God the Holy Spirit has joined [human nature] to the person of God the Son. So then God possesses in Him one sole nature, that is divine nature; and the person of the Son possesses in Him three natures, that is, this same nature which the Father possesses, and the nature of the soul and the nature of the body, and is a person of the Trinity; and the Holy Spirit possesses in Him this same divine nature which the Father and the Son possess. To believe this, to say this, to think this is true contemplation. This is one Power, one Wisdom, and one Will. One God alone in three persons, three persons and one God alone. This God is everywhere in His divine nature, but humanity is glorified in paradise, joined to the person of the Son as well as to the Sacrament of the Altar.

Chapter 15: Here is spoken of the Sacrament of the Altar.[13]

[*Love*]: True Christians receive this divinity and this humanity when they take the Holy Sacrament of the Altar. How this humanity remains with them is taught by Faith, and the clergy know this.

Light of Faith: And for this purpose we will tell you, says Light of Faith, how we will make a comparison of this Sacrament in order to grasp it better.

Take this Sacrament, place it in a mortar with other things, and grind this Sacrament until you can no longer see nor feel the Person which you have placed there.

Faith: I tell you truly, says Faith, that He is not there. Now you can ask therefore, "Has he thus gone away from it?"

Truth: Not at all, says Truth. He was there, but now He is there no longer (understand in a holy way, not humanly). Now you can ask if the humanity has gone away, as it thus came into it. I say to you, says Truth, that the humanity of Jesus Christ neither comes nor goes.

Temptation: What can this be, then? says Temptation.

Truth: It was there, says Truth, when one could see and feel it, and now it is no longer there, since one cannot see or feel it. Thus had divine power ordained it. This same humanity, which belongs to the Sacrament of the Altar, is not seen in another semblance, [and] neither the angels nor the saints nor the Virgin Mary see it other than as we see it ourselves. And if they see it in the semblance that we see it, it is by the intellect of the spirit. For to see the glorified humanity of Jesus Christ in the Sacrament of the Altar pertains no longer to the glory of those who are in glory and therefore they no longer see Him glorified except by [this] intellect.

[*The Soul by Faith*]: And we see [the glorified humanity] by the virtue of Faith, in contradicting the reason of our mind which sees nothing there but bread, nor anything else not felt or tasted or smelled. But our faith contradicts all these for it believes firmly, without doubt, that there is neither whiteness, nor odor, nor taste, but it is the precious body of Jesus Christ who is true God and true man. Thus we see it by faith. And those in glory do not do this, for a thing glorified no longer uses faith, and thus they do not see it as we do. The divine Trinity has ordained the Holy Sacrament of the Altar in such being for the purpose of feeding and nourishing and sustaining the Holy Church. Such is the ordinance of the Sacrament of the Altar, says the Soul by Faith Illumined by the Divine Trinity, in the knowledge of God and in belief in me through divine Power.

Courtesy of the Goodness of Love: Do not be surprised, says the Courtesy of the Goodness of Love, if we tell you these things by love, for I can tell you surely, without being blamed, that no one can arrive at a profound depth nor to a high edification if he does not arrive there through subtlety of a great natural sense and through the sharpness of the Light of Intellect of the Spirit. And with this one cannot know very much in petitioning the divine will. For Intellect, which gives light, shows to the soul what she loves by her nature. And the Soul receives the approach and the juncture through Light of Intellect, and, through Concord of Union in Fertile Love, she receives the being toward which she tends in order to have her rest and repose. She hears willingly Understanding and Light, who carry to her news of her Love. For she comes from Love and there she wishes to be dissolved, so that she possesses only one will in Love: that is, the sole will of the one whom she loves.

Chapter 16: Here Love responds to Reason concerning what she said, that the Soul knows all and knows nothing.

[*Love*]: Reason, says Love, to what I said, that the Unencumbered Soul knows all and so knows nothing, I answer you that she knows by the virtue of Faith what is necessary for her to know for her salvation. And so she knows nothing about what God possesses in her by Himself for her sake, [He] who will not give to anyone except to her. Thus through this intellect this Soul knows all and so knows nothing. She wills all things, says Love, and so wills nothing; for this Soul, says Love, wills so perfectly the will of God that she neither knows, nor is able, nor wills in her own will except the will of God, because Love holds her in strong captivity. And so she wills nothing, for it is so small a thing that she wills what God wills in her, compared to what she would will to will, that she can only have what God wills she might will. For her will is nothing, compared with her sufficiency which will never be given to her and thus the will is from the will of God, as was said above. Therefore by this intellect this Soul wills all things and so wills nothing.

Love: This daughter of Zion desires neither masses nor sermons, neither fasts nor prayers.

Reason: And why, Lady Love? says Reason. This is the food of holy souls.

Love: This is true, says Love, for those who beg; but this Soul begs for nothing, for she has no need to desire something which would be outside of her. Now listen, Reason, says Love. Why would this Soul desire these things named above since God is surely everywhere, without this as with this? This Soul has no thought nor word nor work except the practice of the grace of the divine Trinity. This Soul has no anxiety about sin which she might have ever committed, nor about suffering which God might have suffered for her, nor about the sins or anxiety in which her neighbors remain.

Reason: God! and what does this mean, Love? says Reason. Teach my intellect, since you have appeased my other questions.

Love: This means, says Love, that this Soul does not belong to herself, which is why she cannot have anxiety. For her thought is at rest in a peaceful place, that is, in the Trinity, and thus she cannot move herself from it, nor have anxiety, as long as her Lover is content. From this [place] no one falls into sin, and any sin which was ever done, responds Love to Reason, is as displeasing to her will as it is to God's. It is His displeasure itself which gives to this Soul such displeasure.

But nevertheless, says Love, the Trinity has no anxiety in her on account of such displeasure, and so also this Soul who is at rest in [the Trinity] has no anxiety. But if this Soul, who is at rest so high, could help her neighbors, she would aid them with all her power in their need. But the thoughts of such Souls are so divine because they are not impeded with things passing or created, which might conceive anxiety within them, since God is good without containment.

Chapter 17: Here Love responds to Reason about what she said, that these Souls give to Nature what she asks.

[*Love*]: This Soul gives to Nature whatever she asks. And it is true, says Love, that this Soul has neither care nor love for temporal things which she would know how to gain in refusing Nature her demand; but a guilty conscience would cause to be taken from her what is her own. But such creatures are so excellent that one would not dare to speak overtly about them, especially about their practice by which these Souls possess being from good intellect. But there are few who taste such intellect.

Love: I have said before, says Love, that one dare not speak overtly about it. And no doubt on account of the simple intellects of other creatures, lest they misapprehend to their damage.

Such Souls of whom this book speaks, which touches on some things about their practice, possess, by righteousness of their being which is pure and divine being, such a condition within them that they possess nothing. And they are confident that even if they live until the Judgment Day, they would not be able to have anxiety of the heart one hour about anything that they might need for all the gold of the world, with the exception, and not more, of the portion where Nature needs what is necessary in order to give them what is theirs. If such Souls possess something—and few people know where these Souls are, but it is necessary that they be of the righteous goodness of Love in order to sustain the faith of the Holy Church—thus, if they possess something, and should they know that others might have greater need than they, such Souls would never withhold anything, even if they were certain that nothing would be growing on earth any more, neither bread nor grain nor other sustenance.

This is true, says Love, do not doubt any of it. Such is their nature, through pure righteousness; and such righteousness is Divine Righteousness, who has given his measure to the Soul.

Divine Righteousness: This is correct, says Divine Righteousness. It is necessary that complete justice be fulfilled in her. If the Soul keeps what is necessary from her neighbor, she only keeps what she does not possess according to the perfection of the peace of charity in which she lives completely, for this is her just food. Also why would such Souls feel guilty about taking what is necessary if necessity asks it? For these Souls this would be to fault the innocence and to encumber the peace in which such a Soul rests from all such things. Who would make his conscience guilty about taking the necessities from the four elements, as light from heaven, warmth from fire, dew from the water, and from the earth what sustains us? We receive the service of the four elements in all the ways that Nature has need of them without reproach to Reason. These elements were graciously made by God as other things. As such Souls make use of all things made and created of which Nature has need, in complete peace of heart, so they make of the earth upon which they walk.

[*Love*]: They possess the good foundation, says Love, and the high place which holds them in repose from all things.

Chapter 18:   How such creatures know no longer how to speak of God.

[*Soul*]: Such creatures know no longer how to speak of God, for they know not how to say where God is any more than how to say who God is. For whoever speaks of God when he wishes and to whom he wishes and where he wishes to speak, must not doubt, but know without doubt, says this Soul; such a one never once felt the true seed of divine Love, which makes the Soul completely surprised without being aware of it. For the true pure seed of divine Love, without creaturely matter, which is given by the Creator to the creature, [*takes away such practice entirely, that is, of speaking*].[14] And the custom of such Souls is to understand much and to forget quickly through the subtlety of the Lover.

Chapter 19:   How Faith, Hope, and Charity ask knowledge about these Souls from Love.

[*Faith, Hope, and Charity*]: O Holy Trinity, say Faith, Hope, and Charity, where are such supreme Souls who are such as this book describes? Who are they? Where are they? What do they do? Teach us about them through Love who knows all, so those who are astounded at hearing this book will be appeased. For the whole Holy Church, if she hears it read, will be amazed by it, say these three divine Virtues.

[*Faith*]: It is true, says Faith herself.

[*Love*]: In truth, Holy Church the Little, says Love; this is the Church who is governed by Reason, and not Holy Church the Great, says Divine Love, who is governed by us.

Love: Now tell me, says Love to the three divine Virtues, why you ask of us who these Souls are and where they are, and what they do? And without fail, as you know, says Love, a thing which God has created knows not how to find these Souls. As for where they are, all three of you know it, for you are with them in all moments of the hours, for you make them noble. What they do, this you know also. But who they are—for the purpose of speaking of their worth and their dignity—this is known neither to you nor to them, which is why the Holy Church cannot know it.

Reason: And who knows this, for God's sake! says Reason.

Love: God alone, says Love, who has created them and redeemed them, and perhaps re-created them[15] many times for the sake of Love by whom alone they are exiled, annihilated and forgotten. How is it, says Love, that the Holy Church is astounded if the Virtues serve these lofty celestial Souls? And why wouldn't they do it? Are not all the Virtues praised, written and commanded for the sake of these Souls, and not the Souls for the sake of the Virtues? As such Virtues are made to serve such Souls, such Souls are made to obey God, in order to receive the singular gifts of the pure courtesy of His divine nobility, which gifts God gives to no creature who remains in desire and in will. But whoever wishes to have these gifts [must] accompany[16] neither desire nor will, for otherwise he will not have [the gifts].

Love: And why would the Holy Church understand these queens, these daughters of the King, sisters of the King and spouses of the King? Holy Church could understand them perfectly if Holy Church were within their souls. But no created thing enters within their souls except God alone who created the Souls, so that none would understand such Souls except God who is within them.

Chapter 20: Love responds to Reason about what she said, that no one understands such Souls except God.

Reason: Ah, Love, says Reason, do not be displeased, for another question occurs to me, and if you do not tell it to me I will be distressed. *You say that no one understands these souls except God who created them.*[17]

Love: Now, says Love to Reason, say what your question is.

Reason: I will say it to you, says Reason. This book says that no one understands these Souls except God who is within such Souls. And so as was said above, no one can find them nor understand them, except the one whom Fine Love calls. But whoever finds such Souls would tell the truth about it. So this book has said above. Thus it seems that those-who-are-such understand those-who-are-this, if they were, or if they are.

Love: This is true, says Love, for those-who-are-such, if they were, or if they are, would understand their companions by their practice, but even more by the virtue of the gift which is given to them, which is singular.

Reason: Singular, says Reason, and without fail it is singular, for in hearing it I am singularly amazed.

Love: Reason, says Love, the same word has two meanings, for if those-who-are-such have understanding of the practice of such Souls, and even if this were the most perfect being which God gives to a creature, even so such souls would not understand the dignity of these Souls, for God alone understands them, God who created them. .

Chapter 21: Love answers the argument of Reason for the sake of this book which says that such Souls take leave of the Virtues.

[*Reason*]: Now, Love, says Reason, I still have a question, for this book says that this Soul has taken leave of the Virtues in all respects, and you say that the Virtues are still with these Souls more perfectly than with any other. These are two contradictory statements, it seems to me, says Reason, and I do not know how to grasp them.

Love: Let me calm you, says Love. It is true that this Soul takes leave of the Virtues, insofar as the practicing of them is concerned, and insofar as the desire for what they demand is concerned. But the Virtues have not taken leave of her, for they are always with her, but this is from perfect obedience to them. By means of this intellect, the Soul takes leave of the Virtues and they are always with her. For if a man serves a master, it is he whom the man serves, and the master does not belong to him. Yet the time comes when the servant has gained all the wisdom of the master and perceives that he is richer and wiser than the master, and the servant leaves the master for a better master. And when the one who had been the master sees that his former servant is more worthy and knows more than he, he arranges to remain with the one who had been his servant in order to obey him in everything. So you can and must grasp everything about the Virtues and such Souls. For at first this Soul did whatever Reason taught her, whatever the cost to heart and body, since Reason was the mistress of this Soul. And Reason constantly told her to do all that the Virtues wished, without resistance, until death. Thus Reason and the Virtues were the mistresses of this Soul and this Soul was truly obedient to all that was commanded, for she wanted to live the Spiritual Life.

So this Soul has gained and learned so much with the Virtues that she is now superior to the Virtues, for she has within her all that the Virtues know how to teach and more, without comparison. This Soul has within her the mistress of the Virtues, whom one calls Divine Love, who has transformed her completely into herself, is united to her, and which is why this Soul belongs neither to herself nor to the Virtues.

Reason: To whom does she belong then? says Reason.

Love: To my will, says Love, which transformed her into me.

Reason: But who are you, Love? says Reason. Are not you one of the Virtues with us even though you be above us?

Love: I am God, says Love, for Love is God and God is Love,[18] and this Soul is God by the condition of Love. I am God by divine nature and this Soul is God by righteousness of Love.[19] Thus this precious beloved of mine is taught and guided by me, without herself, for she is transformed into me, and such a perfect one, says Love, takes my nourishment.

Chapter 22: How this Soul is compared to an eagle, and how she takes leave of Nature.

[*Love*]: And so this Soul is like the eagle, because this Soul flies high, indeed, very high, higher than any other bird because she is feathered by Fine Love. She sees more clearly the beauty of the sun, the rays of the sun, and the splendor of the sun, and the rays which feed her with the marrow of the high cedars.[20]

Soul: Thus this Soul says to the unhappy Nature who through many days has made her remain in servitude: "Lady Nature, I take leave of you; Love is near me and I free myself by her without fear, and contrary to all else."

Love: This Soul is not fearful of tribulation; she is not detained for consolation, nor is she lowered on account of temptation, nor is she diminished by any subtraction. She is common[21] to all things through the largesse of Pure Charity and so she asks nothing of anyone on account of the nobility of the courtesy of Pure Goodness with which God has filled her. She is at all times sober without sadness, joyous without dissolution, for God has sanctified His name within her and there the Trinity is at home.

To you little ones who in desire and will take prey for your nourishment, desire that you be such as she is. For whoever desires the lesser part and desires not the greater part, such a one is not worthy of the least of God's blessings because of the cowardice of a poor heart. Thus he allows himself to fall, and so it appears that he is always hungry.

Chapter 23: How this Soul is balanced between two equal weights, and how she is drunk from what she never drinks.

[*Love*]: This Unencumbered Soul, says Love, is balanced by means of a yoke with two equal weights, that is, one on the right and other on the left. With these two weights the Soul is strong against her enemies, like a castle on a hill in the midst of the sea, which one cannot penetrate. One of these weights, which maintains the Soul strongly against her enemies and which guards the gifts of her richness, is her true understanding of her poverty. The left weight, on which she leans at all times, is strength. The one on the right is the high understanding which the Soul receives from the pure Deity.

With these two weights the Soul is balanced, which is why she pays no attention to her enemies on the right or left. She is so deeply awed, says Love, by the understanding of her poverty that she seems to the world and to herself completely beside herself. And she is so inebriated by the understanding from Love and from the grace of the pure Deity that she is forever inebriated by Understanding and filled with Praise by Divine Love. And she is inebriated not only from what she has drunk, but very intoxicated and more than intoxicated from what she never drinks nor will ever drink.

Reason: For God's sake, Love! says Reason, what does this mean, that this Soul is inebriated from what she never drinks, nor ever will drink? It seems, says Reason, as far as I can grasp these words, that it is a greater thing for this Soul that she becomes inebriated from what her Lover Himself drinks and has drunk and will drink from the divine beverage of His goodness, than from what she herself has drunk and will drink of the divine beverage from this barrel.

Love: That is right, says Love: the greater part makes her intoxicated, but not because she has drunk the greater part, as was said. But [she is so inebriated] because her Lover has drunk from it, for between Him and her, through transformation by Love, there is no difference, whatever there might be of natures. Love accomplishes this transformation in her through righteousness, [Love] who makes her inebriated from the greater part of her beverage. Never will it be otherwise. It happens that there are several taps in the one barrel. But the clearest wine, the newest, the most profitable, the most delicious and the most intoxicating is the wine from the tap at the top. This is the supreme beverage which none drinks except the Trinity. And from this beverage, without her drinking of it, the Annihilated Soul is inebriated, the intoxicated Unencumbered Soul, the drunken Forgotten Soul, very inebriated, more than inebriated from what she never drinks nor ever will drink.

Now hear and pay attention for the purpose of a greater clarification. In this barrel of divine beverage are, without fail, several taps. This is known to the humanity which is joined to the person of the Son of God, the humanity who drinks at the most noble tap after the Trinity. And the Virgin Mary drinks at the one after and this noble lady is intoxicated by the most High. And after her, the ardent Seraphim drink, on the wings of whom these Free Souls fly.

Holy Church: Ah, dear God, says Holy Church, how it is appropriate to love purely and guard closely such a Soul who flies so high!

Love: Such a Soul, says Love, possesses memory, intellect, and will, in an abyss through humility and is highly penetrated with understanding through subtlety, and very free in all places by the love from the Deity.

Chapter 24: At what point such Souls are in the righteous freeness of Pure Love.

[*Reason*]: Ah, Love, says Reason, when are such Souls in the righteous freeness of Pure Love?

Love: When they possess neither desire, nor feeling, nor at any time affection of spirit. For these things would enslave them because it is too far from the peace of freeness where few folk allow themselves to remain. Also these Souls, says Love, do nothing which would be contrary to the peace of the being of their interior, and so they carry in peace the ordinance of Love. Such persons are so filled that they possess the divine sun within themselves, without begging for anything beyond themselves, by which they can guard a purity of heart. And no others than they, says Love, have understanding of the greater part. And if they did not have understanding of it, they could beg for the lesser part, and still they would not have their sufficiency.

Such Souls are alone in all things, and common in all things, for they do not encumber their being on account of something which might happen to them. For as completely as the sun has light from God and shines on all things without taking any impurity into it, so also such Souls have their being from God and in God, without taking impurity into themselves on account of things which they might see or hear outside themselves.

Chapter 25: Reason asks Love if such Souls feel any joys within themselves.

[*Reason*]: Now tell me, Love, says Reason, do such Souls feel any joys within them or outside them?

Love: Not at all as regards your question, says Love, because their nature is mortified and their spirit is dead. For all will has departed from them, and on account of this [such a Soul] lives and remains, and is, because of such mortification, in divine will.

Now listen, Reason, says Love, in order to grasp better your question. That which burns has no cold, and the one who swims has no thirst. Thus such a Soul, says Love, is so enflamed in the furnace of the fire of Love that she has become properly fire, which is why she feels no fire. For she is fire in herself through the power of Love who transforms her into the fire of Love. This fire burns of itself in all places and in all moments of an hour without consuming any matter, nor is it able to will to consume beyond itself. For whoever feels something of God through matter which he sees or hears outside himself, because of work which he does by himself, this is not the total fire. Instead, there is matter along with such fire. For human labor, and the desire to have matter beyond the self in order to increase the love of God within, is only blindness about the understanding of the goodness of God. But the one who burns with this fire, without seeking matter and without having it and without willing to possess it, sees clearly in all things that he consumes things according to the way one ought to consume them. For such a Soul has no matter within her which impedes her from seeing clearly since she is alone in Him by the virtue of true humility. And she is common to all things through the largesse of perfect charity, and alone in God through the divine enterprise of Fine Love.

Chapter 26: How this Soul loves nothing except for the sake of the love of God.

[*Love*]: Such a Soul no longer loves anything in God, nor will she love anything, however noble it may be, if it is not solely for the sake of God and for the sake of what He wills, and for the sake of God in all things and all things for the sake of the love from Him. And through such love is this Soul alone in the Pure Love of the love of God. Such a Soul is so transparent in understanding that she sees herself to be nothing in God and God nothing in her.

Now give attention, noble lovers, to the one dwelling through meditation on Love, without creaturely hearing. For such meditation —which the Soul takes in Love, without willing any of Love's gifts, called consolations, which comfort the Soul by the feeling of the sweetness of prayer—such meditation teaches the Soul, and no other practice teaches her except Pure Love. For whoever would wish the comforts of God through the feeling of consolation, the consolations will impede the enterprise of Fine Love.

Chapter 27: How Meditation on Pure Love has only one intent alone.

Love: Meditation on Pure Love has only one intent alone, which is that the Soul love always loyally without wishing to have anything in return. And the Soul can do this only if she is without herself, for Loyal Love would not deign to have any consolations which might come from her own seeking. Without fail not. Meditation on Love knows well according to the better part that she must not excuse herself from her work, which is to will perfectly the will of God. She allows God to work and to do what is according to His will. For the one who wills that God cause him to experience God's will in comforts does not trust perfectly in God's goodness alone, but in the gifts of His riches which He has to give.

Soul: And without fail, says this Soul, whoever would love well would not remember to take nor to ask, but instead always would wish to give without retaining anything in order to love loyally. For whoever would have two goals in one same work will enfeeble the one for the other. And so Loyal Love has only one sole intent, that she might always be able to love loyally. For she has no doubt about the love of her Lover, that He always does what is best, but she doubts that she would always do what she must do. And she wills accordingly only that the will of God be done in her.

Love: She has righteousness, says Love, for that is everything. And also of her [own] power she cannot will anything, for her will is no longer her own nor in her, but instead is in the One who loves her. And this is not her work but instead is the work of the whole Trinity, who works His will in such a Soul.

Chapter 28:   How this Soul swims in the sea of joy.

[*Love*]: Such a Soul, says Love, swims in the sea of joy, that is in the sea of delights, flowing and running out of the Divinity. And so she feels no joy, for she is joy itself. She swims and flows in joy, without feeling any joy, for she dwells in Joy and Joy dwells in her. She is Joy itself by the virtue of Joy which transforms her into Joy itself.

That is, she says that she rejoices more in that which can be communicated to no one than what can be communicated, because the latter is mediocre and only of the moment, and the former is infinite and eternal.[22]

Now there is one common will, as fire and flame, as the will of the Lover and the one who is loved, for Love has transformed this Soul into Love herself.

Soul: Ah! very sweet Pure Divine Love, says this Soul, how it is a sweet transformation by which I am transformed into the thing which I love better than myself! And I am so transformed that I have lost my name in it for the sake of Love, I who am able to love so little. However little I can love, it is in love, for I do not love except by Love.

Chapter 29:   Reason asks Love when it is that this Soul is in the pure freeness of Love.

[*Reason*]: Now, Lady Love, says Reason, I pray you that you say what you meant when you said that this Soul is in the righteous freeness of Pure Love, when she does nothing which might be contrary to the demand of the peace of her being within.

Love: I will tell you what it means, says Love. It means that she would do nothing, regardless of what happens, which might be contrary to the perfect peace of her spirit. Instead the truly innocent one does it, and the being of which we speak is true innocence.

Reason, says Love, I give you an example. Look at the infant who is purely innocent: does he allow a thing to be done, great or small, if he is not pleased by it?

Reason: Without fail, Love, no, and well I can perceive it, and by this I am wise from my question.

Chapter 30: How Reason speaks to Love that she might satisfy this Soul by saying everything that she can about God.

[*Reason*]: Ah, Lady Love, says Reason, I ask mercy of you, in praying that you satisfy this Soul by saying at least all that one can say about Him who is all in all things.

Love: She knows this, says Love, for she always finds Him there, that is, in all things. Appropriately, one finds something in the place where it is, and because He is everywhere, this Soul finds Him everywhere. All things are fitting for her, for she does not find anything anywhere but that she finds God there. Now, Reason, says Love, why do you wish that I satisfy this Soul by saying about God all that one can say?

Reason: So that, says Reason, she can repose peacefully in her being of innocence without having to move or remove herself in order to hear you speak.

Love: I will say it to you willingly, says Love. I certify to you, says Love to Reason, and I swear on myself, that everything which this Soul has heard about God, and all one can say about Him, is at best nothing (to speak properly) compared to what He is of Himself, which never was said, is not now said, nor will be; compared to all that one ever says, all that ever was said, and all that one could allow to be said about Him.

Love speaks to the Soul: But yet again, Love says more to the Soul in order to increase her joy and her sadness, and in order to complete all her enterprises: Lady Soul, says Love, I say to you once and for all, without your desiring anymore to inquire of me, for you would lose your pain, that all creatures, without exception, who remain and will remain in the vision of the sweet face of your spouse, have comprehended and will comprehend less about Him, compared to what He is worthy of or what He makes understood and loved and praised, and what He Himself understands of Himself, [compared to] what one might be able to say with truth, [or compared to] what one might understand or love or praise about anything.

Soul: Alas! Love, says this Soul, what will I do now? Certainly I never believed anything better than what you tell me now. But one thing, Lady Love, I would willingly say to you if I may.

Love: Now, sweet Soul, says Love, say what would please you, for I wish to hear it.

The Amazed Soul: Now very sweet Love, says the amazed Soul, for the sake of God, tell me why He would be so gracious to create me and ransom me and recreate me in order to give me so little, He who has so much to give? But what is more difficult, one dare not speak of a thing which He might will to do. Truly, says this Soul, I know not, but if it might be that I had something to give, I would not make for Him so small a portion, I who am nothing, and He is all. Certainly I would not be able to hold back anything from Him, because I would give Him everything if I had something to give. And however little I have [that is] worthy, I have held nothing from Him, neither body nor heart nor soul, and He knows it well. Now I have given Him everything,[23] I who have nothing to give, which is why it seems that willingly I would give to Him if I had something to give. Now He has taken whatever I might possess of value, and He has given nothing to me, but keeps everything. Ah, Love, for God's sake, is this the portion of the lover?

Love: Ah, sweet Soul, says Love, you know more than you are saying. And if you have given Him everything, the best part has come to you. And, what is more, you have not given Him anything which was not His own before you gave it to Him. Now look at what you do for His sake.

Soul: You speak truly, sweet Love, says the Soul; I could not deny it even if I wanted to.

Chapter 31: How Love calms the Soul because she has given her Spouse all she has.

[*Love*]: Ah, very sweet Soul, says Love, what do you want Him to give you? Are you not a creature? Do you want to have from your Lover something which is not entrusted to Him to give you, nor to you to take? Calm yourself, sweet Soul, if you believe me. He does not give to a creature something other than what you have, and such a gift He promised you.

Soul: Ah, Lady Love, says this Soul, but you did not tell me this when I met you for the first time. For you told me that between a lover and a beloved there is no lordship. But indeed there is, as it seems to me, since the One has everything and the other has nothing compared to His All. But if I could improve it, I would improve it, because thus I would be able to the same degree as you are able—I would love you in the same degree as you are worthy.

Love: Oh my very sweet Soul, you cannot say any more. Calm yourself. Your will suffices for your Lover. And He declares this to you through me that you might have faith in Him, and I say to you that He will love nothing without you, thus you are not without Him. It is one very great favor, and this is sufficient for you, sweet Soul, if you believe me.

Soul: Ah, Lady Love, for the sake of God be quiet about this, says this Soul, for certainly I cannot be silent in order to save the whole world, if by silence it must be saved. For I do not have anything which I love more strongly than the one who suffices me. For if what I love is not sufficient for me, I would disintegrate or diminish from so little of love as I have. But even so, Lady Love, says the Soul, one thing is sufficient for me which I will tell you. That is, the One whom I love better than myself, and no other thing do I love if not for His sake, has within Him what no one understands except for Himself, as you have told me. And therefore since I love Him better than myself, and since He is the sum of all goodness and my Lord and my God and my All, He is totally my comfort, says the Soul. And therefore if I am discomfited by what is lacking to me, nevertheless I am recomforted by the [fact] that nothing is lacking to Him. For He has in Him the abundance of all goodness without any lack. And this is the sum of my peace and the true repose of my thought, for I do not love except for His sake. Thus, since I do not love except for His sake, nothing is lacking to me, something I have said above. It is without fail not [the case]—not according good perception. But I would wish to speak about Him because no one would tell me about Him where I would have willingly heard about Him, and Lady Love has told me the truth by which I calm myself. For the best thing which one could say about Him to me is nothing compared to what He is in Himself. And it is no longer necessary for me to hear someone speak about Him, except as one might tell me that my Lover is incomprehensible. And it is true, because no one would be able to comprehend the smallest thing to which one might compare Him. This is why my love finds no limit in Love in order to have eternally new love from Him who is total Love, as great as He is. This is the end of what one might say about Him to me, says this Soul. Nothing would have calmed me except that Love spoke of Him, which is why I say to all that I have the sum of my questions in what cannot be said to me about Him. And such is the Lover of my soul, says the Soul herself.

Chapter 32: How Love makes such Souls remain in their minds.

[*Discretion*]: For God's sake! says Discretion, think how such Souls remain in their minds!

[*Soul*]: I know it well, says the Soul. Love makes them remain, Love who is the mistress of the doing of this book. I said above, says the Soul, that nothing is lacking to me since my Lover possesses in Himself sufficiency of His righteous nobility without beginning, and will have it without end. And what therefore could be lacking to me? I do not love myself nor Him nor His works except for the sake of Himself. And so what He possesses is more mine than what I possess or ever will possess, than what I have and will have in possession of Him.

Reason: Prove it, says Reason.

Soul: It is easy to prove, says the Soul. Look here at the proof. I love the best by far, one hundred thousand times to one, the abundant goodness which remains in Him than I do the gifts from Him which I have and will have in possession. Thus I love better what is in Him beyond my intellect than I do what is in Him and in my intellect. For this reason what He understands and what I do not understand is more mine than what I understand about Him and which is mine. Where the greater part of my love is, there is the greater part of my treasure.[24] And because I love better the greater part of Him, which I will never understand, than I do the least part, which I will understand, thus He is more mine on account of the greater part of my love, as Love herself witnesses. This is the goal of the love of my spirit.

And still, Lady Love, says the Soul, I really want to say that if one of His creatures might have so much power and will, giving me joy and glory like all those in His court receive, if He himself would not give it to me properly from Himself, I would lack it for all time forever, because I could neither take it nor wish to take it from any other than from Him. No, rather to die for eternity! For indeed I could not, for He has so enflamed me of Himself that I cannot will anything without Him.

Sweet Love, says the Soul, for God's sake, suffer me, for I am completely distressed on account of Him, and what is more, I do not know what to ask. And what would I ask from Him? I know truly that no more than one could count the waves of the sea when the wind is strong could anyone describe or comprehend the Spirit, so little does one comprehend God. And this is not surprising because the body is too heavy to speak of the enterprises of the Spirit. But, speaking in worldly terms, what is more worthy is better than nothing. Likewise I say to you, says this Soul, that to hear one describing it and talking about it is better than hearing nothing said!

Chapter 33: The Soul is amazed when she ponders the gifts from the goodness of God.

[*Soul*]: Ah, Lord, says the Soul, how am I still remaining in my mind when I ponder the gifts of your goodness, you who have given my soul the vision of the Father and the Son and the Holy Spirit whom my soul will see for eternity? Since I will see so great a thing as the Trinity, the understanding of angels, souls, and saints will not be taken from me, nor even the vision of little things, which is to say, all things which are less than God!

Ah, Lord, says the Soul, what have you done for me? Truly, Lord, I am completely amazed over what I understand about it, so that I do not know what amazes me, nor do I have any other practice, nor can I have, for the continuation of this understanding. Lord, as I have no other cause to be amazed than that you have given to my soul the vision of the whole Trinity, of angels and souls, such as you have not given to your precious body which is joined to the nature of the Father in the person of the Son, so it is a marvel that I am able to live! But still, Lord, it is so great a thing to see the angels and the souls to whom you have given the vision of your sweet face. Corporality is not worthy to see such angels and souls, and, by greater reason, corporality cannot see the Trinity since it cannot see the angels nor the souls. Nevertheless, you have given this gift to my spirit for eternity, as long as you are God.

Chapter 34:   How the Soul says that she can do nothing.

[*Soul*]: For God's sake, Love, says this Soul, I pray that you say what I will do, for you know this and you know the gifts from the goodness of my Lover.

Love: I will tell it to you, says Love, and after this do not ask me any more about it. The best that I can tell you is that if you understand perfectly your nothingness you will do nothing, and this nothingness will give you everything. If you cannot come perfectly to understand your nothingness which is of the truth as much as of you, it is necessary for you to do something, truly, the best that you can do, or you will diminish, says Love, from what you have conceived in your spirit. As God has transformed you into Himself, so also you must not forget your nothingness. That is, you must not forget who you were when He first created you,[25] and what you might become if He keeps your works, and who you are and will be, if not by the One within you.

Soul: Ah, Lord, says this Soul, I am certain that I am worthy of nothing other than my horrible faults for which you have suffered death in order to give me life. But Lord, even so, my goal and my hope is, and this is true, that, if none had sinned except me alone, so you would have ransomed my soul by your overflowing love, in dying completely naked on the cross for me, in using power ordained for the destruction of sin. Therefore, Lord, all that you have suffered in your sweet humanity, you suffered for me, even if no one had sinned except me alone. This is why, Lord, I alone am indebted to you. And more than this I owe you: that is, more than my own worth, I owe you to the degree that you are more worthy than I for whom you have given yourself. And all the same you know, Lord, that I can do nothing, and so you have indebted me to you instead. But I pray you, Lover sweet and courteous, that you free me of this debt, you who have the power to do all things. And without fail, Lord, this you will do, says the Soul, so that from now on I might will in all things your perfect will.

Chapter 35:   How this Soul argues against Reason and says that without beginning she has been loved by God.

[*Soul*]: Now, very sweet Love, says the Soul, I pray you show me how I have functioned by [the power of] the Trinity.

Love: Say what your thought is, says Love, for you must not hide it from me.

Soul: Lady Love, says the Soul, I will tell it to you. You have said that He who is in Himself and of Himself without beginning will never love anything without me, nor I without Him.

Love: It is true, says Love, I assure you.

Soul: Well, since He will never love, that is, eternally, anything without me, I say therefore that it follows that He never loved anything without me. In addition, since He will be in me through love forever, therefore I have been loved by Him without beginning.

Reason: Watch what you say, Lady Soul! says Reason. Have you forgotten that you have just barely been created, and that once you were not? For God's sake, sweet Soul, watch that you do not fall into error!

Soul: If I err in holding this opinion, Lady Reason, says the Soul, Love errs with me who makes me believe and think and speak.

Reason: Now prove what you say, Lady Soul, says Reason.

Soul: Ah, Reason, says the Soul, how tedious you are, and those have pain and suffering who live in your counsel! Reason, says the Soul, if I am loved without end by the three Persons of the Trinity, I have also been loved by them without beginning. For as He will love me without end through His goodness, thus have I been in the knowledge of His wisdom so that I must be created by the work of His divine power. Thus, as long as God is, who is without beginning, I have been in the divine knowing, that I might be without end, since He loved from that time, says the Soul, in His goodness the work which He would do in me by His divine power.

Love: This is true, says Love, for since that time He did not will to keep Himself from loving you any more than He would do so now.

Soul: Now, Reason, says the Soul, you have heard the testimony of Love. Now be silent before you tangle with me further.

Reason: Now, Lady Soul, says Reason, since Love leads you and you do not lead Love, that is, since Love dwells in you, Love who accomplishes her will in you without you, I would not dare to combat you nor to contradict you. Instead, Lady Soul, now before all, I promise you obedience and peace with all my ability. To do this is most necessary for me, in spite of myself, because Love wills it I cannot do the contrary. Thus I give my all to you.

Chapter 36: How the Soul is freed and beyond the subjection of Reason.

[*Soul*]: Now the debts are turned, says the Soul to Reason, and with good cause, for the nobility of the courtesy of my Spouse would not deign any longer to leave me in your service, nor in that of any other. For it is necessary that the Bridegroom should free the bride whom He has taken by His will.

Love: This is the truth, most sweet Soul, says Love, I swear it and confess it to you.

Reason: Ah, for God's sake! Lady Soul, says Reason, you think and say and do whatever you wish, since Love wills it and confirms it.

Soul: Ah, Reason, says this Soul, how rude you are! Love wills and confirms me that I might say, think, and do all that I would will. And why would she not do it? says the Soul. What is done is proper to herself, for by myself I cannot do anything if my Lover Himself does not do it in me. You are amazed, says the Soul to Reason, that He wills what I will? Willing is always necessary for Him, for I do not will except that He wills in me, and He wills that I might will. In this He gives me rest by His courtesy, that He wills what I will, and He does not will what I do not will. And therefore, Reason, I have peace, says the Soul, because He and I have between us this concord.

Ah, most sweet Master of this work, how can I have such peace, I who know such loss from my work? And without fail, Lord, so I can have such peace, for your courtesy and your nobility will that, since you have peace, I should have it also. So, Lord, I understand well that by this debt, that is, by giving peace to me, you have made yourself the master. For whatever portion of my sins I find, whether to come or already there, always your peace dwells in me.

Chapter 37: Here the Soul says that in paradise her sins will be understood to her great glory.

[*Soul*]: Lord, says the Soul, no one in this world can understand my sins in so ugly and hideous a figure as they are—only you can. But, Lord, in paradise all those who will be there will understand them, not to my distress but to my very great glory. For in seeing that by my sins I have angered you, your mercy, Lord, and your largesse full of courtesy will be understood.

[*Love*]: Such courtesy, says Love, gives peace of conscience to this Soul, whatever she might do or leave undone in order to will your will, *Lord*,[26] for to will perfectly your will is perfect charity. And whoever always would have perfect charity in his will, he will never have remorse nor a blameworthy conscience. For remorse or a blameworthy conscience in the Soul is nothing other than a lack of charity. For the Soul was created for nothing other than to have within her without end the being of pure charity.

Soul: Ah, Lord, says this Soul, what have I said about you?

Love: Think about it, says Love, and then you will know how to understand your words.

Soul: Ah, Lady Love, says this Soul, you have given to me the understanding, and now behold. Nothing comes from a work when it is necessary that the work is nothing. Thus it is fitting, says this Soul, that I be certain that what I have said is less than nothing. But whatever is in me or through me of divine understanding, you yourself, Lady Love, have said it in me and through me by your goodness for my profit and that of others. Therefore yours is the glory of it, and ours the profit, and so it is also for the hearers who will read this book.

Chapter 38: How the Soul recognizes the courtesy of Love in perfectly recognizing her poverty.

[*Soul*]: O overflowing and abundant Lover, and courtesy without measure for my sake—for thus it seems to me, says this Soul—when you will to suffer [me]! To suffer, Lord? Indeed, you will to suffer [me], more willingly than anyone could say, lest I remain in what I deserve, that is, in this wretched body without limiting the time. And at the same time, because of whatever mercy might be in you, I cannot recover the loss of past time, for it is necessary, sweet Lover, to guard your righteousness. Nevertheless, it cannot be that the lost time might never be returned to me, and that I would be so far from loving and understanding and praising you.

How many moments of an hour have I been idle, and in how many deficiencies have I fallen, I who am in the abyss of total poverty? And nevertheless, so it seems to me, you have willed to place the gift of such grace, which you have described above, in this abyss of poverty. Described? says the Soul. Truly, Lady Love, everything you have said about this grace through the mouth of a creature would only be muttering compared to your work.

Reason: Ah, for God's sake! Lady Love, says Reason, I indeed have heard what is said, willingly I would hear no more, except that I might grasp this perfectly, says Reason. But, Love, this can be only for you alone, to whom this gift is given.

Love: Truly, says Love, and it is given by the Holy Spirit Himself.

Reason: Therefore I say, says Reason, that I cannot grasp it, except that it seems to me that everything which this Soul has done, which is by you, is very well done.

Chapter 39: How Reason wishes to serve and to belong to this Soul.

[*Reason*]: Now, Lady Love, says Reason, I pray you, guide me so that I might serve her completely as her simple handmaid. For I understand that I cannot have greater joy nor greater honor than to be the servant of such a lady.

Love: I confess it to you, says Love, that you cannot do better than to confess and say it.

Reason: Ah, most sweet Love, says Reason, what would I do with the people whom I have to govern who will never see any ordering in this Soul, that is, in her practices and activities?

Love: Why do you say that? says Love. Is there a better ordering than that of this Soul?

Reason: Not at all, says Reason, not to those who see a little or to those who are chosen in this manner, but of such types there are few on the earth. I dare to say it.

Love: Now Reason, says Love, what do you call an ordering?

Reason: I call an ordering, says Reason, the life of the works of the Virtues in perpetuity, through my counsel and the counsel of Discretion, as in the exemplar of the works of our Lord Jesus Christ.

Love: Reason, says Love, what the humanity of Jesus Christ suffered, the divinity did not feel. I speak in a similar way to you, says Love, concerning the Soul. For what you say about the Virtues and of yourself, Reason, says Love, this Soul takes no account. She is able to do better, for Love, who has transformed her into Love, dwells in her. This Soul herself is Love, and Love has no difference from her. In everything it is appropriate to have discretion,[27] except in Love. I

119

give you another example. Even if a lord wishes to have allegiance in his land because one owes his right to him, nevertheless he never owes allegiance to his servants, but the servants owe it to their lord. Similarly I say to you, Reason, says Love, all things owe me allegiance, including the works of the Virtues counseled by Reason, refined by Discretion, except the one alone who is grasped by Love and transformed into Love. This one owes me only love, and for this is he free, for Love has freed him.

Chapter 40: How Love calls this Soul supremely wise and why.

[*Love*]: Among my chosen ones, I call this Soul supremely wise, but a small mind does not know how to estimate or understand a thing of great value.
Reason: Ah, Lady Love, says Reason, what do you call wise?
Love: The one in the abyss of humility, says Love.
Reason: Ah Love, says Reason, who is the one in the abyss of humility?
Love: The one, says Love, who has no injustice in anything and knows he has no righteousness in anything. One who is in this understanding of his injustice sees so clearly that he sees himself beneath all creatures, in the sea of sin. And because the demons are slaves of sin, and this Soul has seen for a long time that she is beneath them, a slave to sin (without any comparison by her regarding them, insofar as the comparison is of her or of her works), and in this regard this Soul has become nothing and less than nothing in all her aspects. She has heard for a long time through the Holy Spirit that God will put the least in the highest solely by His loyal goodness.

Chapter 41: How the Soul has no anxiety of sin, nor hope in any good which she might have ever done.

[*Love*]: Thus such a Soul has no anxiety from sin which she might have ever committed, nor hope in something which she might be able to do, but only in the goodness of God. And the secret treasure of this goodness alone so annihilates her within herself that she is dead to all feeling from within and without, to the extent that such a Soul no longer does any works, neither for God's sake nor for her own. And so she has thus lost all her senses in this practice to the point that she knows not how to seek nor how to find God, nor even how to conduct herself.

Love: This Soul, says Love, is no longer with herself, which is why she must be excused from everything. And the One in whom she is does His work through her, for the sake of which she is entirely freed by the witness of God Himself, says Love, who is the worker of this work to the profit of this Soul who no longer has within her any work.

Fear: Ah Love, says Fear, where then is such a Soul since she is no longer with herself?

Love: She is where she loves, says Love, without her feeling it. Thus such a Soul lives without reproach of conscience, because she does nothing from within herself. For whoever does anything by the movement of himself, says Love, is no longer without himself; instead he has Nature and Reason with him. But the one, says Love, who has died from love neither feels nor understands either Reason or Nature. Such a Soul wills none of the joys of paradise, however many one might place before her to choose, nor does she refuse any torments of hell, even if it would be completely within her will.

Holy Church: Ah, what then, for God's sake? says Holy Church.

Love: It is because she is in her understanding, says Love.

Holy Church: And what is such a Soul? says Holy Church. Most sweet Holy Spirit, teach it to us, for this word surpasses our Scripture, and so we cannot grasp by Reason what Love says. And we are so amazed, says Holy Church, that we dare not oppose her.

Chapter 42: How the Holy Spirit teaches what the Soul knows, and what she wills and what she possesses.

[Holy Spirit]: O Holy Church, says the Holy Spirit, do you wish to know what this Soul knows and what she wills? I will tell you, says the Holy Spirit, what she wills. This Soul knows only one thing, that is, she knows nothing. And so she wills only one thing, that is, she wills nothing. This knowing-nothing and this willing-nothing give her everything, says the Holy Spirit, and allow her to find the secret and hidden treasure which is enclosed in the Trinity forever; not, says the Holy Spirit, through divine nature, for that cannot be, but through the power of Love, as it is necessary to be.

Love: Now, Holy Church, says Love, you have heard why this Soul possesses all things.

121

Holy Spirit: True, says the Holy Spirit; yet all that I possess is of the Father and of the Son. And since she possesses all that I have, and the Father and the Son have nothing which I do not have in myself, says Love, thus this Soul possesses in her, says the Holy Spirit, the treasure of the Trinity, hidden and enclosed within her.

Holy Church: Thus, since it is so, says Holy Church to the Holy Spirit, it is necessary that the Trinity dwells and lives in her.

Holy Spirit: That is right, says the Holy Spirit, because she is dead to the world and the world is dead in her, the Trinity will dwell in her forever.

Chapter 43: How these Souls are called Holy Church, and what the Holy Church can say about them.

[*Holy Church*]: O true God, Holy Spirit! says Holy Church.

Love: It is true, Holy-Church-Below-This-Church, says Love. For these Souls, says Love, are properly called Holy Church, for they sustain and teach and feed the whole Holy Church. And not merely they, says Love, but the whole Trinity within them. It is true, says Love, without any doubt.

O-Holy-Church-Below-This-Church, now speak, says Love. What do you wish to say about these Souls who are commanded and praised above you, you who do everything according to the counsel of Reason?

Holy Church: We wish to say, says Holy Church, that these Souls are of the life above us, for Love dwells in them and Reason dwells in us. But this is not against us, says Holy Church the Little, for we teach her and advise her about it according to the glosses on our Scriptures.

Reason: But, Lady Love, says Reason, we would wish to grasp better, if it please you, more openly, this gift which the Holy Spirit gives to such Souls by His simple goodness, provided that no one be harmed on account of rudeness in hearing this divine lesson.

Love: Ah, Reason, says Love, you will always be one-eyed, you and all those who are fed by your doctrine.[28] For, to be sure, one has faulty vision who sees things before his eyes and does not understand them at all. And so it is with you.

Holy Spirit: I have said, says the Holy Spirit, that I will give to this Soul all that I have—I will so give, says the Holy Spirit. For so it was promised to her before by the whole Trinity, and given by His goodness in the knowledge of His wisdom without beginning, all that we have. And so it is right, says the Holy Spirit, that we not hold back from these Souls anything we possess. For this Soul, says the Holy Spirit, has given everything to us, whatever she held dear. And so what we have, we have given to her, in a manner of speaking. For one says, and it is true, that a good will is known by works. This Soul, says the Holy Spirit, is of such a condition that if she has in her what we have, she renders it back to us, completely as we have done, without wishing anything in return in heaven or on earth, but for the sake of our will alone. Thus we possess all things, says the Holy Spirit, by our divine righteous condition, and this Soul gives everything to us mediated through will, which is enclosed in Love without mediation. Because such a Soul has given to us everything she possesses and everything that she is (which she no longer possesses mediated through will), it is necessary, says the Holy Spirit, that we give to her what we possess, by right of Love. Thus what we possess in us, says the Holy Spirit, is by divine nature, and this Soul possesses it from us in herself by right of Love.

Holy Church: Ah, Lord, says Holy Church, we grasp and believe in truth that your worthy nobility gave such a gift to her in return for love, for love cannot be returned in any manner sufficiently except in Love.

Love: This Soul, says Love, for a long time has seen and known that there is not any greater discernment than temperance, nor a greater richness than sufficiency, nor a greater power than love. This Soul, says Love, possesses memory, understanding and will in the abyss completely in One Being, that is, in God. And such Being gives being to her, without knowing, feeling, or willing any being, except the ordination of God alone. This Soul, says Love, has for many a day languished in love.

Chapter 44: What the Soul does who languishes in love, and at what point the Soul has died from love.

[*Reason*]: Ah, Lady Love, says Reason, what does a Soul do who languishes in love?

Love: She wars against vices, says Love, in acquiring virtues.

Soul: Ah, very sweet Love, says this Soul, how great and perilous a war it is! And without a doubt, says this Soul, one must certainly call such a strenuous life sickness and a life of war.

Love: She has so languished in love, says Love, that she has died from love.

Reason: Ah, Love, says Reason, for the sake of God, tell us at what point the Soul is who has died from love.

Love: She has finished with the world, says Love, and the world has taken leave of her and has finished with her. Because she lives in God, neither sin nor vice can find her. She is so hidden and placed in God, that neither the world nor the flesh nor demons are able to hurt her, for they cannot find her in their works. Thus such a Soul lives in the repose of peace, for she takes no account for her own sake of anything which is created. And because such a Soul has such peace there, she lives in the world without any reproach.

Reason: Such a Soul, says Reason, has no more will; and our being must become such being.[29] For we have no merit before God except as we leave our will for the sake of His will and insofar as we give our will completely, without willing anything except only according to the measure of His work in the ordination of His goodness.

Soul: I believe this, says this Soul, and so nothing is lacking to me, since I will nothing. For no Souls have perfect peace unless they have no more will.

Love: What do you know, Lady Soul? says Love.

Soul: Without a doubt so it is, Lady Love, says this Soul, for I have proven it by certain tests, and I almost died from it. And there I might have been,[30] if willing nothing had not thrust me outside, through the school of the divine goodness. One has no more will who wills nothing. This one, not any other, has given his will, and so has nothing with which to will except the will of Him to whom his will has been given.

Chapter 45: How those who have no more will live in freeness of charity.

[*Love*]: Such ones live in freeness of charity who have no more will. And whoever would ask such persons what they want, in truth they would say that they want nothing. Such persons have arrived at the understanding of their nothingness, that is, were something created in them, they could understand nothing about their nothingness, for their understanding would be too small to understand such a loss. But they have arrived at belief in the greater part, and the understanding of such belief is that one can understand nothing about it.

Reason: Nothing? says Reason.

Love: No, says Love. For if one could understand something as totally as one would understand in paradise, or again if one could compare [something] totally with something which one could comprehend by parts or otherwise, still all that one would comprehend would be nothing. Again, concerning this comprehension, this nothingness would not be something which one could compare, even if one did not place in this comparison His power, His judgment, His knowledge, His goodness. It might be only a spark of His pure goodness, and still it would be nothing. Whoever thus would comprehend Him, beyond what one will comprehend about Him, as has been said in this comparison, [it] would still be nothing compared to the smallest part which remains in Him, which is not comprehended except by Him. This is to say, to say it better,[31] that whoever would understand everything which has been said about Him, this would still be nothing compared to the great understanding which remains in Him, beyond our understanding. Truly, the smallest part of His goodness which one could compare in a manner of speaking still would be nothing compared to the grandeur of the smallest part of His goodness. And it would be less than a spark, compared to the whole of Him.

Soul: O Lord God, says this Soul, what will the Soul do who believes this about you?

God: She will do nothing, says God; but I will do my work in her without her. For the understanding of her nothingness and belief in me have placed her in such nothingness that she cannot do anything. So that the understanding of this nothingness, compared to the grandeur of this All, releases her completely and frees her, for nothing is lacking to her since she wills nothing.

Chapter 46: How the Soul has understanding of the greater part; according to her she understands nothing of God compared to the greater part of Him.

[*Love*]: Now this Soul has fallen and arrived at understanding of the greater part. Truly, but only in the sense that she understands nothing of God, compared to the whole of Him.

Reason: Ah, dear! says Reason. Does one dare call nothing a thing which is of God?

Soul: What? says this Soul. Truly, whatever might be given us or will be from Him is indeed nothing. Truly, suppose that He gives us what is mentioned above in this writing. By comparison, if this were true, still it would be nothing compared to one sole spark of His goodness, which remains in His understanding, beyond our understanding.

Soul: Oh, says this Soul, and what might be thus from the whole of Him, since one can speak so much of the goodness of the least part of Him? Ah, most sweet Love, says this Soul, this you alone know, and it is sufficient for me.

Chapter 47: How the Soul has arrived at understanding of her nothingness.

[*Love*]: Now you have heard how this Soul has arrived at belief in the greater part. Now I will tell you, says Love, how she has arrived at understanding of her nothingness. Thus she understands that neither she nor any other understands the nothingness of her horrible sins and faults, compared to what is in the knowledge of God about them. Such a Soul, says Love, has retained no will, but instead has arrived at and fallen into willing nothing and the certain knowledge of knowing nothing. And this knowing-nothing and willing-nothing have released and freed her. Such a Soul, says Love, maintains the counsel of the Gospel which says: "Have a simple eye and then you will not sin."[32]

So this Soul is at peace in all that God suffers from her, for she has true intention in all her undertakings and peaceful repose in the actions of her neighbors. For in everything about which she has intention, she makes no judgment except that it is always in goodness.

This Soul has her peace in all places, for she carries peace with her always, so that, because of such peace, all places are comfortable for her, and all things also. Thus such a Soul seats herself without moving herself on the throne of peace in the book of life, in the witness of a good conscience and in freeness of perfect charity.

Chapter 48: How the Soul is not free who desires that the will of God be done in her to her honor.

[*Love*]: Thus the Soul wills nothing, says Love, since she is free; for one is not free who wills something by the will within him, whatever he might will. For when one is a servant of oneself, one wills that God accomplish His will to one's own honor. The one who wills this only wills that the will of God be accomplished in him and in another. To such a one, says Love, God refuses His kingdom.

Reason: Without doubt, says Reason, thus they would do.

Soul: Indeed, so they would do this. Truly, says this Soul, they must do this, or they would lose what little they possess.

Reason: It is true, Lady Soul, says Reason, I confess it to you.

Love: Such folk, says Love, are not calm no matter how much they think they are, and because of such opinion, their state is sufficient for them.

Soul: They do not have as much worthiness, says this Soul, as to think there is no one greater than they, and this keeps them from arriving at what is better, and so they remain in their good wills.

Love: They will never be satisfied, such folk, says Love.

Soul: Certainly not, says this Soul. Since will remains in them they are servants of their will. A Soul enters such servitude, says this Soul, who believes completely these two Virtues, that is, Reason and Fear, and this insatiable Will. But the one alone is free, says this Unencumbered Soul, whom Faith and Love govern, for they remove such a one from all servitude, without fear of frightening things, without desire of delectable things.

Chapter 49: How such a Soul, who no longer has will, is noble.

[*Love*]: Such a Soul no longer has will, and thus it does not matter to her what God might do, only that He might always do His will. For this Soul, says Love, is unencumbered and content. She does not need hell, or paradise, or any created thing. She neither wills nor not-wills anything which might be named here.

Holy Church the Little: But what [does she will], for God's sake? says Holy Church the Little.

Love: Nothing, says Love, she wills nothing. But to say this seems indeed strange to those who desire great burdens from multiplicities of love. And this is not surprising. But, without fail, no one of this sort could think or believe what seems so strange to them, which is a great pity for them.

Soul: Such folk, says this Soul, are so blind that a great thing seems little to them.

Love: This is true, sweet Soul, says Love, what you say. For as the work of God is more worthy than the work of a creature, so this willing nothing in God is more worthy than willing good for God's sake. Indeed truly, says Love, suppose that willing this good they could do miracles and receive martyrdom each day for the sake of their love of God, and still, says Love, there would be no comparison since will remains. No indeed, says Love, and they could even be raptured into heaven each day to see the Trinity, on account of such a will, as was Saint Paul the Apostle![33]

Chapter 50: How this Soul is engraved in God like wax from a seal.

Love: This Soul is engraved in God, and has her true imprint maintained through the union of Love. And in the manner that wax takes the form of the seal, so has this Soul taken the imprint of this true exemplar.

Soul: For even if God loves us, says this Soul, as He has shown us through divine works and through human sufferings, He did not love us, says this Soul, in contradiction to Himself. If He died for us and took human flesh, this was in accordance with Himself, by the witness of His goodness which owes it to me since the divine will willed it. However, says this Soul, He did not love us in contradiction to Himself. All that the Trinity had created in His wisdom would have to have been condemned eternally if Jesus Christ the Son of God had not been taken away from Truth in order to save us all.

Alas for me! says this Soul, where does what I have said come from? Does not everyone know that this cannot be?

Love: Yes, sweet beloved, says Love, my friends know it well that this cannot be.

[*The Person of God the Father*]: But I have said it to you, you who are my dear love, says the Person of God the Father, because such must be my first-born daughter who is heir-apparent to my realm, who knows the secrets of the Son through the Love from the Holy Spirit, who has given this from Himself to this Soul.

Chapter 51: How this Soul is similar to the Godhead.

[*Love*]: It is fitting, says Love, that this Soul be similar to the Godhead, for she is transformed into God, says Love, which is why she has retained her true form, which is granted and given to her without beginning from One alone who has always loved her by His goodness.

Soul: Ah, Love, says this Soul, the meaning of what is said makes me nothing, and the nothingness of this alone has placed me in an abyss below less than nothingness without measure. And the understanding of my nothingness, says this Soul, has given me the All, and the nothingness of this All, says the Soul, has taken from me prayer, and I pray nothing.

Holy Church the Little: And what do you do then, our very sweet Lady and Mistress, says Holy Church the Little.

Soul: I repose completely in peace, says this Soul, alone and nothing and all in the courtesy of the goodness of God alone, without moving myself away from the one will for the sake of whatever richness He has in Himself. It is the goal of my work, says this Soul, always to will nothing. For as long as I will nothing, says this Soul, I am alone in Him without myself, completely unencumbered. And if I should will something, she says, I am with myself, and therefore I have lost freeness. But when I will nothing I have lost everything beyond my will, therefore nothing is lacking to me. To be unencumbered is my conduct. I would will nothing at all.

Love: O very precious Esther, says Love,[34] you who have lost all your practices, and through this loss have the practice of doing nothing, truly you are very precious. For in truth this practice and this loss is accomplished in the nothingness of your Lover, and in this nothingness, says Love, you are unconscious and remain dead. But you live, beloved, says Love, in His will completely which is His chamber, and there He is pleased to remain.

Chapter 52: How Love praises this Soul, and how she remains in the abundances and flowings of divine love.

Love: O very high-born one, says Love to this precious pearl [Marguerite],[35] it is well that you have entered the only noble manor, where no one enters if he is not of your lineage and without bastardy.

This Soul, says Love, has entered into the abundances and flowings of divine Love, not, says Love, by the attainment of divine Understanding; for it could not be that any intellect, however enlightened, could attain any of the flowings of divine Love. But the love of such a Soul is so conjoined to the flowings of the greater part of this absolute divine Love (not by attainment of the Intellect of Love, but by attainment absolute of her love), that the Soul is adorned with the adornments of this absolute peace in which she lives, and endures, and is and was and will be without being. All this, says Love, is like iron invested with fire which has lost its own semblance because the fire is stronger and thus transforms the iron into itself. So also this Soul is completely invested with this greater part, and nourished and transformed into this greater part, because of the love of this greater part, taking no account of the lesser. So she remains and is transformed into the greater part of the absolute eternal peace without anyone finding her. This Soul loves in the sweet country of absolute peace and there is nothing which might aid or torment those who love there, not created creature, nor a thing given, nor anything which God commands.

Reason: But what? says Reason.

Love: What never was given, nor is, nor will be, makes her naked and places her in nothingness without her caring about whatever might be, and she desires neither assistance nor to be spared, neither from His power, nor from His wisdom, nor from His goodness.

The Soul speaks of her Lover and thus says: He is, says this Soul, and nothing is lacking to Him. I am not, and so nothing is lacking to me. And so He has given me peace and I live only from Peace, which is born from His gifts in my soul without thought. I can do nothing if it is not given to me to do. He is my All and my Best Good. Such being makes me have one love and one will and one work in two natures. Annihilation by the unity of divine righteousness has such power.

[*Love*]: This Soul leaves the dead to bury the dead,[36] and the sad ones to work the Virtues, and so she rests from the least part of her in the greater part, but she uses all things. This greater part shows her her nothingness, naked without covering; such nakedness shows her the All Powerful through the goodness of divine righteousness. These showings make her deep, large, supreme, and sure. For they make her always naked, All and Nothing, as long as they hold her in their embrace.

Chapter 53: How Reason asks for clarification of what was said above.

[*Reason*]: O most sweet abyssed one, says Reason, at the bottom without bottom of total humility, and very noble rock on the broad plain of truth, alone on the mountaintop except for those in your domain: I pray that you say what is meant by these hidden meanings which Fine Love mentions.

Soul: Reason, says this Soul, if anyone would tell these to you and should you hear, still you will never grasp them. Instead, your questions have dishonored and ruined this book, for there are many who have understood it with few words. But your questions have made it long because of the answers you need, both for yourself and for those whom you nourish who move along at a snail's pace. You have revealed this book to those in your domain who move along at a snail's pace.

Love: Revealed? says Love. Truly, in this matter Reason and all her students can only be against what does not seem to them to be well said, whatever is grasped about it.

Soul: This is true, says the Soul, for that one alone understands it whom Fine Love rules. And so it is necessary that whoever grasps clearly be dead by all mortifying deaths, for no one tastes this life if he is not dead by all deaths.

Chapter 54: How Reason asks how many deaths it is necessary that the Soul should die before one understands this book.

[*Reason*]: Ah, treasure house of Love, says Reason, tell us about how many kinds of death it was necessary for you to die before you understood this book perfectly.

Soul: Ask Love, says this Soul, for she knows the truth about it.

Reason: Ah, Lady Love, for the sake of God's mercy, says Reason, tell it to us, not only for me and for those whom I have nourished, but also for those who have taken leave of me, to whom this book will bring light, if it please God.

Love: Reason, says [Love], those who have taken leave of you will still have something of your nourishment after two kinds of death by which this Soul has died. But the third death, by which this Soul died, no one living grasps except the one on the mountain.

Reason: Ah, for God's sake, says Reason, say what kind of folk are on the mountain.

Love: They have neither earthly shame nor honor, nor fear of anything which might come.

Reason: Ah, God, Lady Love, says Reason, for God's sake, answer our questions before you say any more, for I have horror and fear to hear of the life of this Soul.

Chapter 55: How Love responds to the questions from Reason.

[*Love*]: Reason, says Love, those who live as described in this book (these are the ones who have attained the being of such a life) understand quickly without it being necessary to explain the glosses. But I will clarify your questions for you. Now listen closely.

There are two types of folk who live the life of perfection by the works of Virtues in affections of the spirit.

There are those who completely mortify the body in doing works of charity; and they possess such great pleasure in their works that they have no understanding that there might be any better being than the being of the works of the virtues and death by martyrdom, in desiring to persevere in this with the aid of an orison filled with prayers, in multiplying good will, always for the purpose of retaining what these folk possess, as if this might be the best of all that could be.

Such folk are happy, says Love, but they are lost in their works, on account of the sufficiency which they have in their being.

Such folk, says Love, are called kings, but they are in a country where everyone is one-eyed.[37] But without fail, those who have two eyes consider them to be servants.

Soul: Servants they are truly, says this Soul, but they don't understand it. They are like the owl who thinks there is no more beautiful bird in the wood than young owls. So it is, says this Soul, with those who live in perpetual desire. For they think and believe that there is no better state than the state of desire where they dwell and wish to dwell. Thus they perish on the way because they are satisfied by what desire and will give to them.

Chapter 56: How the Virtues complain about Love, who offers so little honor to them.

Virtues: Ah, God, alas! say the Virtues. Lady Love, who will offer honor to us since you say that those perish who live totally by our counsel? And truly if anyone should say such a thing to us, say the

Virtues, we would consider him a heretic and a bad Christian. For we cannot perceive that one can perish who does everything according to our teaching, through the ardor of desire which gives true sentiment of Jesus Christ. Yet we believe perfectly and without any doubt all that you say, Lady Love.

Love: To be sure, says Love. There is mastery in the intellect, for there is the kernel of divine food.

Virtues: We believe it, Love, say the Virtues, but it is not our office to grasp it. We are indeed acquited, if we believe you, on account of the intellect we possess, for we are made by you for the purpose of serving such Souls.

Soul: Ah, without doubt, says this Soul to the Virtues, that is well said! One would do well to believe you. And for this purpose I say to all those who hear this book: whoever serves a poor Lord a long time becomes poor in waiting for a small wage. Thus it is that the Virtues have understood and perceived well (heard by all who have wished to hear) that they do not grasp anything about the being of Noble Love. And so I say, says this Soul, how will the Virtues teach their pupils what they do not possess and never will possess? But whoever wishes to perceive and learn how those perish who live in the Virtues should ask Love.

Indeed, they should inquire of this Love who is the mistress of Understanding, not of that Love who is the daughter of Understanding, for she knows nothing about this. But again for the better, let that person ask this Love who is the mother of Understanding and of Divine Light, for she knows the whole of it on account of the greater part of the All in which this Soul stops and remains, and so she cannot do other than remain in the All.

Chapter 57: Concerning those who are in the stage of the sad ones and how they are servants and merchants.

[*Love*]: You have heard about those who are lost, and in what, and by what and why. Now we will tell you also about those who are sad who are servants and merchants, but they act more wisely than the lost do.

Soul: Ah, by love, Lady Love, says this Soul, you who make all things easy, tell us why the sad souls remain in the Virtues as well as the lost, why they serve the Virtues, and why they feel and desire through ardor the sharpening from the work of the spirit. Even the lost do this, as well as the sad. Where, therefore, is the better thing by which you praise them more than the lost?

Love: Where is it? says Love. Certainly it is in this stage, for it is the one good necessary to arrive at the stage, from which the lost cannot have any aid.

Soul: Ah, love Divine Love, says this Unencumbered Soul, I pray that you tell us why these sad ones are wise compared to the lost, since they both have the same practice, except in this one regard, for which you esteem the former more than the latter.

Love: Because, says Love, the sad ones maintain that there is a being better than theirs, and so they understand well that they do not have understanding of this better thing which they believe. Moreover, this belief gives them so little understanding and sufficiency in their being, that they maintain instead that they are miserable and sad. And so they are, without doubt, compared to the being of freeness of those who are in it, who never move themselves. Because they maintain and know for truth that they are sad, they often ask the way, through ardent desire, of the one who knows it—that is, Lady Understanding, who is illumined by divine grace. This lady has pity on their calls, and those who are sad know this. Thus she teaches them the right royal road, which runs through the land of willing nothing. This is the true direction: the one who is directed there knows if I speak the truth. And so such folk who are sad know this, these folk who regard themselves as miserable. And so, if they are sad, they can come to the being of the unencumbered ones, of whom we speak, according to the teaching of this Divine Light, to whom this little sad soul calls to find the way and to direct her path.

Reason: Little? says Reason. Truly! Ever little.

Holy Spirit: Again the Holy Spirit speaks: Truly, so long as a soul makes any calls to Understanding or to Love, so that she will take account only of something which could be, either in love, or in understanding, or in praise. For no wise man asks without cause, nor concerns himself with what cannot be. Thus one can indeed say that the one who asks often is little or poor, and [this is true] of whoever asks for something. For every being, whatever it might be, is but a game of catch or child's play compared to the supreme being of willing nothing, the being in which the unencumbered ones remain without moving. For the unencumbered one in his righteous being could neither refuse, nor desire, nor promise anything in exchange for something which someone could give him; but instead, [the unencumbered one] would want to give everything for the sake of maintaining loyalty.

Chapter 58: How the Annihilated Souls are at the fifth stage with their Lover.

[*Reason*]: Ah, for God's sake, says Reason, what do these Souls have to give who are so annihilated?

Love: To give? says Love. Truly, says Love, whatever God has of value. The Soul who is such is neither lost nor sad. Instead, she is in the depths of the fifth stage with her Lover. There nothing is lacking to her, and so she is often carried up to the sixth, but this is of little duration. For it is an aperture, like a spark, which quickly closes, in which one cannot long remain;[38] nor would that soul ever have authority who knew how to speak of this.[39]

The overflowing from the ravishing aperture makes the Soul, after the closing, free and noble and unencumbered from all things. This happens from the peace of the work of the overflowing and the peace lasts as long as the opening of the aperture. After such an encounter, the Soul keeps herself freely at the fifth stage, without falling to the fourth, because at the fourth she has will, and at the fifth she has none.[40] And because at the fifth stage, of which this book speaks, she has no more will—where the Soul remains after the work of the Ravishing Farnearness, which we call a spark in the manner of an aperture and quick closure—no one would be able to believe, says Love, the peace upon peace of peace which the Soul receives, if he were not this himself.

Understand these divine words in a divine manner through Love, hearers of this book! This Farnearness, which we call a spark in the manner of an aperture and quick closure, receives the Soul at the fifth stage and places her at the sixth as long as His work remains and endures. And therefore she is other. But she remains in the being of the sixth stage for a short time, for she is put back at the fifth stage.

And this is not surprising, says Love, for the work of the Spark, as long as it lasts, is nothing other than the showing of the glory of the Soul. This does not remain in any creature very long, except only in the moment of His movement. Thus such a gift is noble, says Love, for He does His work before the Soul has any perception or awareness of His work. But the peace, says Love, from the operation of my work, which remains in the Soul when I work, is so delicious that Truth calls it glorious food. None who remain in desire are able to be fed by it. Such Souls would govern a country if it had the need, and all without themselves.

Chapter 59: By what means this Soul has conquered, and how and when she is without herself.

[*Love*]: At the beginning this Soul conquered by means of the life of grace, grace which is born in the death of sin. Afterward, says Love, she conquered by means of the life of the spirit, which is born in the death of nature. And now, she lives the divine life, which is born in the death of the spirit.

Love: This Soul, says Love, who lives the divine life, is always without herself.

Reason: And when, for God's sake, says Reason, is she without herself?

Love: When she belongs to herself.

Reason: And when does she belong to herself?

Love: When she is no part of herself, neither in God nor in herself, nor in her neighbors; but in the annihilation by which this Spark opens her by the approach of His work. This work is so preciously noble that nothing can be said about the aperture of one movement of glory which the gentle Spark gives, nor does any Soul know how to speak about this precious closing by which she is forgotten through the annihilation of the understanding which this annihilation gives to her.[41]

Soul: By God's name, says this Soul, how one would be a grand lord who could comprehend the profit of one movement of such annihilation.

Love: That is true, says Love, he would be so.

Soul: If you have heard in these words a high matter, says this Soul to the hearers of this book, do not be displeased if I speak afterward about little things, for it is necessary for me to do so if I want to accomplish the enterprise of my goal—not, she says, for the sake of those who are this, but for those who are not who yet will be, and will beg continuously as long as they are with themselves.

Chapter 60: **How it is necessary to die three deaths before one arrives at the free, annihilated life.**

[*Love*]: Reason, says Love, you have asked us about how many deaths it is necessary to die before one arrives at such a life. And I answer you that before the Soul could be born into this life, it was necessary that she die three entire deaths. The first is the death of sin, as you have heard, by which the Soul must die completely so that there no longer remains in her color, or taste, or odor of anything which God prohibits in the Law. Those who die thus are folk who live by the life of grace, and this is sufficient for them, that they keep themselves from doing what God prohibits, and that they be able to do what God commands.

Ah, to you most noble ones, annihilated and uplifted by great admiration and stupefied by conjunction of union of Divine Love, do not be displeased if I touch on something for the little ones, for I will speak soon enough about your being. For one sees white and black better when they are next to each other, than when each is viewed by itself.

Now you who are elected and called to this supreme being, pay attention and hasten yourselves, for it is a very great way and a very long road from the first stage of grace to the last stage of glory which the gentle Farnearness gives. I have said, says Love, to pay attention and to hasten because this intellect is strong and subtle and very noble, for which the full-blooded have the help of nature. And without the haste of the will piercing the ardor of desire of the spirit, the hot-tempered have some help from nature. And when these two natures are together, that is, nature and the ardor of the desire of the spirit, it is a very great advantage. For such persons apply themselves and attach themselves so strongly to what they undertake that they are completely given over to it through the strength of spirit and of nature. When these two natures are in accord with each other and with the third nature, which must join these two natures eternally through righteousness (this is the dream[42] of glory which draws one by means of nature in his nature through righteousness), this concord is finely noble. And in order to understand it better, I pose a question: which is more noble—the dream of glory which draws the Soul and adorns the Soul with the beauty of its nature, or the Soul who is joined to such glory?

137

Soul: I do not know, says this Soul, if it annoys you, but I cannot do any better. Please excuse me, for jealousy of Love and the work of charity, by which I am burdened, cause this book to be made, so that you little ones might be of this sort without interruption, at least in will, if you still have it. And if you are already unencumbered from all things, if you are those without will in the life which is above your intellect, then at least you could explain the glosses of this book!

Chapter 61: Here Love speaks about the seven stages of the Soul.

[*Love*]: I have said, says Love, that there are seven stages, each one of higher intellect than the former and without comparison to each other. As one might compare a drop of water to the total ocean, which is very great, so one might speak of the difference between the first stage of grace and the second, and so on with the rest: there is no comparison. Even so, of the first four stages none is so high that the Soul does not still live in some great servitude. But the fifth stage is in the freeness of charity, for this stage is unencumbered from all things. And the sixth stage is glorious, for the aperture of the sweet movement of glory, which the gentle Farnearness gives, is nothing other than a glimpse which God wills the Soul to have of her glory itself, which will be hers forever. Thus, by His goodness, He makes for her this showing of the seventh stage in the sixth. The showing is born from the seventh stage, which gives the being of the sixth. The showing is so quickly given that [this Soul] to whom it is given has no perception of the gift which is given.

Soul: What is this wonder? says the Soul herself. If I myself perceived when such a gift were given, I would become myself what is given by the divine goodness. The gift will be given to me eternally when my body has left my soul.

The Spouse of the Soul: This is not something she can make happen, says the Spouse of this Soul. I have sent you betrothal gifts[43] by my Farnearness, but no one asks me who this Farnearness is, neither the works He does nor that work when He showed the glory of the Soul, for one cannot say anything about it save this: the Farnearness is the Trinity Himself, and [He] manifests His showing to her, which we name "movement," not because the Soul moves herself in the Trinity, but because the Trinity works the showing of her glory in this Soul. Of this none know how to speak, save the Deity alone. Then the Soul, to whom the Farnearness gives Himself, has so great an understanding of God and of herself and of all things that she even sees within God through divine understanding. And the light of this understanding takes from her all understanding of herself and of God and of all things.

Soul: This is true, says this Soul, there is nothing else. And so if God wills that I possess this great understanding, He takes from me and keeps what I understand, for otherwise, says this Soul, I would not possess any understanding. And if God wills that I understand myself, this understanding also He takes from me, for otherwise I would not be able to possess anything of it.

Love: This is true, says Love, Lady Soul, what you say. There is no surer thing to understand, there is no more profitable possession than this work.

Chapter 62: Concerning those who are dead to mortal sin and born into the life of grace.

[*Love*]: Now, Reason, says Love, listen. I return to our topic for the little ones. Such folk, of whom we have spoken, who are dead to mortal sin and born into the life of grace, have no reproach or remorse of conscience, but instead they are acquitted before God by what He commands alone. They desire honors, indeed, and are bewildered if someone despises them, but they keep themselves from vain glory and from impatience, which guides them toward death to sin. They love riches, so they are saddened that they are poor. And if they are rich, they are saddened when they lose something. But always they are preserved by death to sin insofar as they no longer love their riches contrary to the will of God, whether in loss or gain. And so they love ease and repose for their pleasure, but they keep themselves from inordinate excess. Such folk are dead to mortal sin and born into the life of grace.

Soul: Ah, without doubt, says the Unencumbered Soul, such folk are little on earth and very little in heaven, and are saved in an uncourtly way.

Reason: Ah, Lady Soul! says Reason, watch what you say! We would not dare to say that any are little who will see God eternally.

Love: Truly, says Love, but their littleness could not be described compared to the greatness of those who die the death to nature and who live by the life of the spirit!

139

Reason: Indeed, I believe it, says Reason, and so they are, for if they would say otherwise, they would be lying. But they do not wish to do anything else. They indeed say to me, Reason, that they are not restricted by anything if they do not wish to be, for God has not commanded them to do more. Instead, indeed, He has counseled nothing more for them.

Soul: They speak the truth, says this Soul, but they are completely uncourtly.

Desire: Ah, without fail, says Desire, uncourtly they are. They have forgotten that it would have not been sufficient for Jesus Christ to act on their behalf if He had not done all that humanity could accomplish unto death.

Chapter 63: How Love calls those peasants for whom it is sufficient only to be saved.

[*Soul*]: Ah, most sweet Jesus Christ, says this Soul, do not trouble yourself about such folk. They are so exceedingly selfish that they forget you, on account of their rudeness in which they have sufficiency.

Love: Ah, without fail, says Love, this is great crudity.

Soul: This is the manner, says this Soul, of the merchant folk, who in the world are called crude, for indeed crude they are. For the gentleman does not know how to mingle in the marketplace or how to be selfish. But I will tell you, says this Soul, in what I appease myself concerning such folk. In this, Lady Love, that they are kept outside the court of your secrets, much like a peasant would be kept from the court of a gentleman in the judgment of his peers, where no one can be a part of the court if he is not of correct lineage—and certainly not in the court of a king. And in this I take my repose, says this Soul, for so also are they kept outside of the court of your secrets, where the others are called who will never forget the works of your sweet courtesy, that is, the rejection and the poverty and the insufferable torments which you have suffered for us. These will never forget the gifts of your suffering, which are always a mirror and exemplar for them.

[*Love*]: For such folk, says Love, are all necessary things prepared, for Jesus Christ has promised it in the Gospel. Those here [in the court], says Love, are saved much more courteously than are the others. And nevertheless, says Love, these, too, are small, indeed so small that one could not compare them to the greatness of those who are dead to the life of the spirit *and live the divine life.*[44]

Chapter 64: Here one speaks concerning the Souls who are dead to the life of the spirit.

[*Love*]: No one tastes of this life if he has not died by this death.
Truth: This [life] carries there, says Truth, the flower of the love from the Deity. There is no mediary between these Souls and the Deity, and they desire no mediary. Such Souls cannot suffer the memory of any human love, nor the will of divine sentiment, for the sake of the pure divine Love which this Soul has by Love.
Love: This domination by Love alone, says Love, gives her the flower from the boiling of love, by the witness of Love herself.

This is true, says Love. This love of which we speak is the union of lovers, the inflaming fire which burns without consuming.

Chapter 65: Here one speaks about those who are seated in the high mountain, above the winds.

[*Love*]: Now, Reason, says Love, you have heard something about these three deaths by which one comes to these three lives. Now I will tell you who it is who is seated on the mountain above the winds and the rain. They are those who, on earth, have neither shame nor honor, nor fear on account of something which might happen. Such folk, says Love, are secure, and so their doors are open, and yet nothing can disturb them, and no work of charity dares to penetrate. Such folk are seated on the mountain, and none other than these are seated there.
Reason: Ah, for the sake of God, Lady Love, says Reason, tell us what will become of Modesty, who is the most beautiful daughter which Humility has; and Fear also, who has done for this Soul so many benefits and so many lovely services, and even myself, says Reason, who has never slept while these Virtues had need of me. Alas! says Reason, are we to be set outside of her resting place[45] now, because she is thus arrived into lordship?
Love: Not at all, says Love, since you three will remain in her entourage, and you three will be the guardians of her gate in case someone who would be against Love, to whom each of you is pledged, might want to attack her lodging. You will show loyalty only in this, that

you be as gates, for otherwise havoc would be created by you. Thus you will be heard only in this, for otherwise she would sink low in need or necessity. Such a creature, says Love, is better vested by the divine life, of which we have spoken, than she is in her own spirit, which was placed in her body in its creation. And her body is better vested by her spirit than the spirit is by her body, for the grossness of the body is taken away and diminished by divine works. Thus it is better that the Soul be in the sweet country of understanding-nothing, where she loves, than she is in her own body to which she gives life. And the freeness of Love has such power.

Chapter 66:   How the Soul is joyous since she has taken leave of Reason and of the other Virtues.

[*Holy Church the Little*]: Ah, most sweet Divine Love, says Holy Church the Little.
Soul: And truly she is little, for she will not remain very long until she arrives at her end, says this Soul, from which she will have great joy.
Reason: All the same, says Reason, tell me what has given you more joy?
Soul: Lady Love, says this Soul, will say it for me.
Love: It is from this, says Love, that she has taken leave of you and of the works of the Virtues. For as long as this Soul was cloaked in love, she took lessons in your school through desire of the works of the Virtues. Now she has entered upon and is so surpassing in divine learning that she begins to read where you take your end. But this lesson is not placed in writing by human hand, but by the Holy Spirit, who writes this lesson in a marvelous way, and the Soul is the precious parchment. The divine school is held with the mouth closed, which the human mind cannot express in words.

Chapter 67:   Here is described the country where this Soul dwells, and the Trinity.

Reason: Ah, Love, says Reason, I pray that you say something to me about the country where this Soul dwells.
Love: I say to you, says Love, that the One who is, where this Soul is, is of Himself, in Himself, through Himself, without receiving anything from another except from Himself alone. Therefore this Soul, says Love, is in Him, of Him, and according to Him without receiving anything from another except from Him alone.

Truth: Thus is she in God the Father, says Truth. For we believe that there is no person in the Trinity who has not received from His person, save only the person of the Father.

Love: This is the truth, says Love, for God the Father possesses the divine power of Himself without receiving it from any other. He possesses the outpouring of His divine power and gives to His Son the same which He possesses of Himself, and the Son receives it from the Father. So that the Son is born of the Father and so is equal to Him. And from the Father and from the Son is the Holy Spirit, one person in the Trinity. He is not born, but He is. The Son is born of the Father and the Holy Spirit is from the Father and from the Son.

Chapter 68: How by the divine work the Soul is joined to the Trinity, and how she calls those who live according to the counsels of Reason, donkeys.[46]

[*Love*]: This Soul, says Love, is totally dissolved, melted and drawn, joined and united to the most high Trinity. And she cannot will except the divine will through the divine work of the whole Trinity. And a ravishing Spark and Light joins her and holds her very close. And on account of this the Soul speaks thus:

Soul: O very small person, rude and poorly behaved, she says.

Reason: Who are you talking to? says Reason.

Soul: To all those, she says, who live by your counsel, who are such beasts and donkeys that on account of their rudeness I must hide from them and not speak my language to those who prefer death to the being of life where I am in peace without moving myself. I say, says the Soul, that on account of their rudeness I must be silent and hide my language, which I learned in the secrets at the secret court of the sweet country, in which country courtesy is law, and Love moderates, and Goodness is the nourishment. The sweetness draws me, the beauty pleases me, the goodness fills me. What therefore can I do, since I live in peace?

Chapter 69: The Soul says that the practice of the Virtues is only care and labor.

[*Reason*]: For God's sake, says Reason, dear sweet Flower without blemish, how does our practice seem to you?

Soul: It seems to me, says this Soul, to be labor full of care. At the same time, nevertheless, one earns one's bread and sustenance by means of one's labor in this care. Jesus Christ exalted it by His own body, He who saw the bestiality of those in this labor who would be saved, and for them He certainly came. And Jesus Christ, who would not ever will to lose them, has bound them to Himself through His death, and through His Gospels, and through His Scriptures where laboring folk are guided to the right way.

Reason: And from whence does your guidance come, our sweet Lady? says Reason, you who do nothing nor take care for any labor in this regard beyond faith—whence do you possess this gift?

Soul: Truly, says this Soul, I am freed from this, for my better thing is elsewhere, which is so far from this that one would not be able to compare it: the end of my better thing is in God who is beyond time. But I possess time in order to attain what is mine from Him.[47] And what is mine is that I might be established[48] in my nothingness.

And so, Reason, says this Soul, you ask us whence are we guided? I say to you, from Him alone, says this Soul, who is so strong that He can never die, about whom the teaching is not written, neither by the works of exemplars or by teachings of men, for His gift cannot be given form. He knows, completely without beginning, that I would believe Him well without a witness. Is there, says this Soul, a greater villainy than to wish a witness in love? Certainly not, it seems to me, since Love is the witness to love: it is enough for me. If I should wish more, then I do not really believe Him at all.

Reason: Ah, Lady Soul, says Reason, you have two laws, one for yourself and one for us. Ours is in order to believe, and yours is in order to love. Tell us your will about it, and why you have called our children cattle and donkeys.

Soul: Such folk, says this Soul, whom I call donkeys, seek God in creatures, in monasteries for prayer, in a created paradise, in words of men and in the Scriptures. Without a doubt, says this Soul, in such folk Benjamin has not been born because Rachel is still living. It is necessary that Rachel die in the birth of Benjamin, for until Rachel dies, Benjamin cannot be born.[49] It seems to the novices that such folk, who seek Him on the mountains and in the valleys, insist that God be subject to their sacraments and their works.[50]

Alas! They are miserable and it is a pity. And they will remain that way, says this Soul, as long as they have such custom and practice! But those are in good and profitable times who adore God not only in temples and monasteries, but adore Him in all places through union with the divine will.

Reason: Very well, then, O high-born one, says Reason, tell us for God's sake: where do you seek and where do you find Him?

Soul: I find Him everywhere, says this Soul, and He is there. He is One Deity, One sole God in Three Persons, and this God is everywhere. There, I find Him.

Chapter 70: How such a Soul is what she is by the grace of God.

[*Reason*]: Now, our sweet Lady, says Reason, tell us who you are that you speak thus to us.

Soul: I am what I am, says this Soul, by the grace of God. Therefore I am only that which God is in me, and not some other thing. And God is the same thing that He is in me, for nothing is nothing. Thus He is Who is. Therefore I am not, if I am, except what God is, and nothing is beyond God.[51] I do not find anything but God, in whatever part I might find myself, for He is nothing except Himself, to speak the truth.

This Soul loves in Truth, that is, in the Deity, but Truth loves in the One by whom this Soul has being, and thus is all work of charity complete in her.

Love: This is true, says Love, for all others, except this Soul, are hidden through the lack of innocence, on account of the sin of Adam.

Chapter 71: How this Soul does not do any work for God, nor for herself, nor for her neighbors.

[*Love*]: This Soul, says Love, does not do any work for God's sake, nor for her own, nor for her neighbors' either, as was said above. But God does it, if He wills, [He] who is able to do it. And if He does not will, it does not matter to her one way or the other; she is always in one state. Therefore there is in this soul the ray of divine understanding which draws her from herself without herself into an inexpressible divine peace, carried by one elevation of flowing love from the most high Jealous One,[52] who gives sovereign freeness to her in all places.

Soul: Jealous? says this Soul. Jealous He is truly! He shows it by His works, which have stripped me of myself completely and have placed me in divine pleasure without myself. And such a union of full peace joins me and conjoins me through the supreme height of the creation with the splendor of divine being, by which I have being which is Being.

Love: When this Soul, says Love, is thus drawn by Him without herself, by God for her sake, this is divine work. A work of charity was never accomplished by a human body. The ones who accomplish such a work could not accomplish it [by themselves].

Soul: Grasp carefully, says this Soul, the two meanings of Love, for they are difficult to grasp [for] whoever has the intention of glossing this.

Love: This is true, says Love, for the work of a creature (that is, the work done by human effort) cannot be compared to the divine work done by God in the creature by His goodness for the sake of the creature.

Chapter 72: Here one speaks about the distance from the land of the lost and sad ones to the land of freeness, and why the Soul possesses will.

Soul: Grasp carefully, says this Soul, the two meanings of Love, for they are beyond the land of the sad ones in the land of freeness filled with peace, where the established ones remain.

Love: This is true, says Love, I will tell them one meaning.

Soul: Truly, says this Soul, in spite of will in which the lost and sad ones remain, who lead a life of perfection such as it is.

Love: When the divine Trinity created the angels by the courtesy of His divine goodness, those who were evil through their perverse choice gave themselves over to the evil will of Lucifer, who willed to have by his nature what he could not have except by divine grace. As soon as they willed this with their forfeited will they lost being from goodness. Therefore they are in hell without being, and without ever recovering the mercy of seeing God. Their will made them lose this high vision, which they would have had in return for giving over their will which they have held onto. Now see what they have come to!

Truth: Alas, alas! says Truth. Why, Souls, do you love will so much, since such a loss is accomplished by will?

Love: I will tell you, says Love, why the Soul has will: because she still lives in spirit, and the life of spirit is still the will.

Reason: Ah, for God's sake, Lady Love, says Reason, tell me why you have named this chosen Soul, so beloved by you, "soul" from the beginning of this book, since you say that because sad persons have will they still live in the life of spirit. And you have named her so many times by as short a name as "soul," which is a shorter name than the name "spirit."

Love: You know, says Love, this is a good question. For to be sure, all those who live in the life of grace through the accomplishment of the commandments, and allow themselves to be satisfied in this, have the name of "soul" truly, but not all have the name of "spirit." But all have the name of "soul" through the life of grace. For all the hierarchies of paradise do not have the same name which is the longest name. For instance, all angels are called "angels," but the first angel did not have the name of Seraphim, but instead only the name of angel; but the Seraphim have both the name "angel" and the other name "Seraphim."

Grasp it without my saying what this means, says Love. For likewise I say to you that those who keep the commandments, and for whom this suffices, have the name "soul" and not the name "spirit." Their right name is "soul" and not "spirit," for such folk are far from the life of the spirit.

Reason: And when is the soul completely spirit? says Reason.

Love: When the body is completely mortified and the will delights in dishonor, in poverty, and in tribulations, then it[53] is completely spirit, and not otherwise. Therefore such spiritual creatures have purity in conscience, peace in affection, and intellect in reason.

Chapter 73: How the spirit must die before one loses the will.

[*Reason*]: Ah, for the sake of God, says Reason, Lady Love, I pray that you tell me why the spirit must die before one loses the will.

Love: Because, says Love, the spirit is completely filled with spiritual will, and no one can live the divine life as long as he has will, neither can he have sufficiency unless he has lost the will. When the spirit is perfectly dead, then he has lost the sense of his love and killed the will which gives life to [this sense], and in this loss the will is perfectly filled by the sufficiency of divine pleasure. And in such a death grows the supreme life, which is always unencumbered and glorious.

Truth: Ah, for God's sake, Lady Divine Love, I pray that you show me, says Truth, a soul perfected in this being.

Love: Willingly, says Love, and if she is not as I have told you, I command you to take her back, and to tell her that she is badly prepared and apparelled for speaking to me in my secret chamber, where no one enters if he is not prepared properly, as you have heard me say.[54] No one is my beloved, says Divine Love, who fears to lose or to gain, but only the one who loves for the sake of my pleasure; for otherwise she would be for her own sake, and not for my sake and with me. So this spouse of mine cannot be for her own sake. And if she had committed as many sins as the whole world ever did, and as many good deeds as all those who are in paradise, and if all her good deeds and all her evil deeds were apparent before the people, such a Soul, says Love, would have neither dishonor nor honor for her own sake, nor the will to hide or conceal her evils. For if she did otherwise, says Love, she would be for her own sake and with herself, and not for my sake and with me.

What dishonor, says Love, would those have in my paradise, however, if someone sees their sin and my gifts of glory which they receive from me? Certainly they have no will to hide their sins, nor any dishonor if one should recognize them; nor do they desire to show my glory.

Truth: Ah, without fail, says Truth, they leave it to the concern of their Master, who hides or shows their sins according to His will. And in this way these Souls of whom we speak behave, [those] who are vessels by such election: the Farnearness makes present to them this noble gift.

Chapter 74: Why Love calls this Soul by so short a name as "soul."

[*Love*]: Now Reason, you ask us why I have named this Soul by so small a name as "soul."

Reason, says Love, on account of your rudeness I have named her many times by her surname. And because one understands the gloss by means of a category,[55] we will be helped by it, and so let us proceed—but her right name is perfectly noble. She has the name "pure," "celestial," and "spouse of peace." For she is seated in the bottom of the valley, from which she sees the height of the mountain, and from which she sees the mountain from the height as well. No

148

intermediary can penetrate her. And for security the wise man places his treasure there, that is, the gift of unity of divine love. And this unity gives her peace and essential and marvelous nourishment from the glorious land where her beloved dwells. Her dominions extend only in the glorious life. This is the nourishment of my chosen bride; this is "Mary of peace," and so she is "married by peace," because Fine Love makes her peaceful in this land.[56] Martha, you know, is too impeded and she does not know it. Her impediments trouble her, which is why she is far from such a life.

Chapter 75: How the Illuminated Soul gives the meaning of the things said above through the exemplar of the transfiguration of Jesus Christ.

[*Intellect of Divine Light*]: Ah, through Love, says Intellect of Divine Light, now tell me, you who have something to hide, what you mean in this.

Soul: I will tell you, says the Soul by Light, what I mean by this.

[*Those who have something to hide*]: We perceive, they say, that Jesus Christ was transfigured on Mount Tabor, where there were only three of his disciples. He told them that they must neither speak about it nor say anything about it until His resurrection.[57]

Unencumbered Soul: Well said, says this Unencumbered Soul to the servants of Nature who hide themselves for this reason, you have given me the stick with which to beat you.

Soul: Now I ask you: why did God do this?

[*Those who hide*]: He did it for our sakes, say those who hide. And since He teaches us this, why would not we do it?

Soul: Ah, sheep! says this Soul, how your intellect is bestial! You leave the kernel and take the chaff. Now I tell you that, when Jesus Christ was transfigured before three of His disciples, He did it so that you might know that few folk will see the brightness of His transfiguration, and that He shows this only to His special friends, and for this reason there were only three. And still this happens in this world when God gives Himself through the ardor of light into the heart of a creature. Now you know why there were three.

Now I will tell you why this was on the mountain. This was in demonstrating and in signifying that no one can see the divine things as long as he mixes himself or mingles with temporal things, that is, with anything less than God. Now I will tell you why God told them that they were to say nothing until His resurrection. This was to demonstrate that you cannot say a word about the divine secrets lest you take vainglory from them. As far as this is concerned one must not speak of it to anyone. For thus I swear to you, says this Soul, that whoever has something to conceal or hide, he has something to show; but whoever has nothing to show, he has nothing to hide.

Chapter 76: Here one shows by the example of the Magdalene and the saints that the Soul has no shame about her sins.

[*Soul*]: Ah, for the sake of God, behold the repentant sinner. She had no dishonor because of what Jesus Christ said to her, that she had chosen the better part and the most sure, and, what is greater, that it would never be taken from her.[58] And also she had no dishonor from the fact that her sins might be made known before all people, through the witness of the Gospel itself, which says, in the hearing of all, that God delivered seven enemies from her.[59] She had dishonor from no one, except those by whom she had been condemned. For she was overtaken, captured, and filled, and so she concerned herself with no one except Him.

What dishonor would Saint Peter have, since God resuscitated the dead in his shadow even after he denied God three times?[60] Certainly he had no dishonor since he received great honor.

What shame and what glory did Saint John the Evangelist have, since God wrote through him the true apocalypse even after he had fled from the capture by which Jesus Christ was taken?[61]

Soul: I maintain, says this Soul, that he and the others had neither dishonor from this nor honor, nor the wish to hide or conceal themselves, and that it is of no concern to them that God might accomplish something through them, and for their sake and for the people, since it would be a divine work. These examples are sufficient for those who have intellect to grasp what remains to be said. This book is not written for the others.

Chapter 77: Here the Soul asks if God has set an end and limit to the gifts of His goodness.

Soul: I have said, says this Soul, that from what God accomplished in them they would have neither dishonor nor honor, nor the wish to

hide themselves on account of anyone, as you can see by what is said.
Truth: Ah, without fail, says Truth, they would not have known why,
for they were freed from themselves and were completely in God.
Soul: Ah, for the sake of God! says this Soul. Since God has accomplished this grace for them, is [grace] still as large for giving as it was?
Has He now set end and limit to the gifts of His goodness?
Courtesy: And without fail, not at all, says Courtesy, His divine goodness could not suffer it. He retains what He also gives, that is, the
great gifts which He has to give are the same things which were
never given, nor spoken by a mouth, nor pondered by a heart,[62] if one
might desire or know how to dispose oneself. Grasp through love,
Love prays you, that Love has so much to give, and so she sets no
limit to it; in one moment she makes of two things one.
Soul: But one thing pleases me to say, says this Soul, not for those
who are in being, for they have nothing to do, but for those who are
not in being, who will yet be (and these do have something to do).
That is, that they might be on guard, so that if Love asks of them
something of what she has furnished them, that they not refuse her
because of anything which might happen, at whatever hour it be, nor
because of any Virtue which Love sends to be the messenger. For the
Virtues carry as messengers the will of Love through letters sealed by
their mistress, as the angels do from the third hierarchy.

And also all those to whom Love sends her messengers know
that if they refuse at that point what the Virtues ask through the
interior, which must have lordship over the body, they know that
they will never make their peace with the sovereign who sends the
messenger. They know that they will be accused and troubled in
understanding and encumbered with themselves through a lack of
faith. For Love says that someone in great need sees one's friend.
Reason: Now answer me this, says Reason,[63] if one does not aid her in
her need, when will one aid her? Tell me.
Love: If I remember it, says Love, is that surprising? It is necessary
that I guard the peace of my divine right and render to each one what
is his; not, says Love, what is not his, but what is his.

Now give attention, says Love, to the gloss on this book. One
values something according to its worth and as one has need of it, and
not more. When I desired, says Love, and when it pleased me, and
when I had need of you (I mean *need*, because I *command* it to you),[64]
you refused me through many of my messengers. No one knows it,
says Love, except me, I alone. I sent you Thrones to purify[65] you and

151

adorn you, the Cherubim to illumine you, the Seraphim to enflame you. Through all these messengers I called you, says Love, and they would have you know my will and the stages of being to which I call you, and you never took account of it. And I swear, says Love, I leave you in your own blind protection[66] in saving yourselves. For if you had obeyed me, you would have been otherwise, by your own testimony. But you will be saved well enough by yourselves, which is why you are in a life encumbered by your own spirit, which will never be without some burden. Because you did not obey my messengers and the Virtues, when I wanted by means of such messengers to chain your body and free your spirit. Because also, says Love, you did not obey when I called you by the subtle Virtues which I sent to you, and by my angels by whom I disputed with you, I cannot give you by means of righteousness the freeness which I have, for righteousness cannot do it. And if you had obeyed, says Love, when I called you to the will of the Virtues which I sent, and by my messengers by whom I disputed with you, you would have had by righteousness the freeness which I have.

Love: Ah Soul, says Love, how you are encumbered with yourself!

Soul: Truly, says this Soul, my body is feeble and my soul is fearful. For often I am burdened, whether I want to be or not, with these two natures, which the unencumbered neither have, nor are able to have.

Chapter 78: How those who do not obey the teachings of perfection live encumbered with themselves until death.

[*Love*]: Ah, Soul enchained, says Love, how you have such pain and so little gain! And all because you have not obeyed the teachings of perfection, about which I disputed with you in order to unencumber you in the flower of your youth. Nevertheless, you have never willed to change, and you have not willed to do anything. Instead you always refused my calls about what I would have you know through such noble messengers, as you have heard before. Such folk, says Love, live encumbered with themselves until they die.

Ah, without fail, says Love, if they would will it, they could be delivered from that to which they are and will be in great servitude for so little profit, from which, if they had willed it, they might have been delivered in return for so small a thing. Truly, for so small a thing, says Love, as giving themselves over to the place where I would want them to be, which I showed them by the Virtues, whose function this is.

I say, says Love, they could be completely free both in soul and in body if they had followed my counsel by the Virtues, who tell them my will and, says Love, what is necessary for them to do so that I might fill them with my freeness. And because they would not do it, they are all living, as you heard, with themselves. The annihilated free ones, adorned by delights, know this, for they see through themselves the servitude of the others. Because the true Sun shines in their illumination, they see the little specks in the rays of the Sun by means of the splendor of the Sun and of the rays.[67] Thus when such a Sun is in the Soul, and such rays and such dazzling brightness, the body is then no longer feeble and the Soul is no longer fearful. For the true Sun of Justice never healed any soul without healing the body when He did His miracles on earth. And often still it is so, but He does not do this for anyone who has no faith in Him.

Now you can see and hear that such a one is great and strong and very free and unencumbered from all things. The one who trusts in God, God sanctifies.

I have said, says Love, that those with whom I disputed through their interior life concerning obedience to the Virtues and who did nothing, I have said that they will live encumbered with themselves until they die. And again I say that even if they drive themselves each day with themselves to enlarge upon the perfection of the apostles by the effort of the will, they will not be unencumbered from themselves (no one pays attention), that is, neither from the body nor from the soul. Truly not, says Love, since rudeness and the disputes about the interior life do not give deliverance, one cannot return there no matter what is done with oneself, it will still only be self-encumbrance. Those know this who undertake works with themselves without the whirling fiery ardor of the interior life.

Chapter 79: How the Unencumbered Soul advises that one not refuse the calls of a good spirit.

[*Unencumbered Soul*]: Therefore I say, says this Unencumbered Soul, to all those who live in the effort of the life of perfection, that they take care that they do not refuse the calls of the ardor of the desire of the will of the spirit, that they hold dearly to the attaining of the better thing after this life which one calls the sad life and the life of the spirit.

153

Love: I have said, says Love, that they should take care, for it is necessary for them if they wish to arrive at and attain the better thing. This life is the handmaid and servant who prepares the place for the arrival and lodging of the great being of the Freeness of Willing Nothing, by which the Soul is in all points satisfied. That is, [the Soul is satisfied] by this nothingness which gives all things. For the one who gives all, possesses all, and not otherwise.

Soul: Ah, again, says this Soul, I would say to those who are sad that the one who guards the peace and satisfies perfectly the will of the ardor of desire piercing the work of his spirit, as I have said, in regulating his judgments so strictly that they possess no work through deliberation outside of the will of the spirit, such a one will attain, as the rightful heir, worthy proximity to this being of which we speak.

Such is the first-born daughter of the most high King, who does not have within her any lack of gentility. And such a lady, says Love, has attained this being of which we speak, where it is the most noble. And I will tell you how, says Love. She has no emptiness in her which would not be completely filled by me, which is why she cannot host either care or memory, and so she possesses no semblance of them. And yet, says Love, piety and courtesy are not departed from such a Soul, as long as there is time and place.

Indeed this is right, says this Soul, that piety and courtesy not be departed from me, for neither were they departed from Jesus Christ, through whom I have derived life. And however much His sweet soul might be glorified as soon as it was joined to a mortal body and to the divine nature in the person of the Son, nevertheless there remained in it piety and courtesy. And whoever would be courteous would never love except what he ought. One never loves the Humanity who loves temporality. One never loves divinely who loves something corporally. And those who love the Divinity feel little of the Humanity. One would never be joined nor united nor divinely filled who feels corporally. And with what would one feel? As God is not changed, so a thing is not changed. *Now grasp the gloss through nobility of intellect.*[68]

Reason: Ah, says Reason, how strong such souls are shows in the Baptizer!

Love: Would one ever be weak, says Love, who was not encumbered with himself?

Soul: Certainly not, says this Soul. Love does not destroy but instead instructs and nourishes and sustains those who pledge faithful loyalty to her, for she is satisfying and deep and a richly flowing sea.

Chapter 80: How the Soul sings and chants.

[*Soul*]: I sing, says this Soul, one hour singing, another chanting, and all for those who are not yet unencumbered, so that they might hear something about freeness, and whatever else is necessary until they arrive at this stage.

[*Love*]: This Soul has perceived by divine light the being of the land of which she must be. And [she] has crossed the sea in order to suck the marrow of the high cedar.[69] For no one receives or attains this marrow if he does not cross this high sea, if he does not plunge his will into its waves. Give attention, lovers, to what this means.

I have said above that such a Soul has fallen from me into noth-ingness, moreover, into less than nothingness without limit. For as God is incomprehensible with regard to His power, so also is this Soul indebted by her incomprehensible nothingness by even one hour of time that she had possessed a will contrary to Him. To Him she owes without subtraction the debt which her will owes, as often as she had willed to steal her will from God.

Soul: O true God, You who see and suffer this, says this Soul, who will pay such a debt?

The Soul herself responds: Ah, dear Lord, You Yourself will pay it. For Your full goodness overflowing with courtesy could not allow that I not be freed of it by the gift of Love by whom You caused to pay in one moment all my debts. This sweetest Farnearness has carried away the last denarius of my debt,[70] and tells me that as much as You have to render to me, so much have I to render to You. For if I owe You as much as You are worth, You owe me as much as You have, for such is the largesse of Your divine nature. And thus, says this gentle Farnearness of whom I have spoken, these two debts continue, one contrary to the other, and are made completely one from now on. And I completely consent to it, for it is the counsel of my nearest one.

Reason: Ah, for God's sake, Lady Soul, says Reason, who is your nearest one?

Soul: The Ravishing Most High who overtakes me and joins me to the center of the marrow of divine Love in whom I am melted, says

155

this Soul. Thus it is right that He come to my aid of Himself, for I am dissolved in Him. It is necessary to be silent about this being, says this Soul, for one cannot say anything about it.

Love: No, truly, says Love, no more than one could enclose the sun in a dwelling could this Soul say anything about this life, compared to what is there, to speak the truth.

Astonishment: Ah, Lady Soul, says Astonishment, you are a well-spring of divine Love, from which well-spring of divine Love is born the fount of divine Understanding; from which well-spring of divine Love and from which fount of divine Understanding is born the flow of divine Praise.

Soul: I relinquish everything, says this one confirmed in nothingness, perfectly in the divine will.

Chapter 81:   How this Soul has no concern about herself, nor about her neighbor, nor even about God.

[*Love*]: Now this Soul, says Love, has her right name from the nothingness in which she rests. And since she is nothing, she is concerned about nothing, neither about herself, nor about her neighbors, nor even about God Himself. For she is so small that she cannot be found, and every created thing is so far from her that she cannot feel it. And God is so great that she can comprehend nothing of Him. On account of such nothingness she has fallen into certainty of knowing nothing and into certainty of willing nothing.

And this nothingness, of which we speak, says Love, gives her the All, and no one can possess it in any other way.

This Soul, says Love, is imprisoned and held in the country of complete peace, for she is always in full sufficiency, in which she swims and bobs and floats, and she is surrounded by divine peace, without any movement in her interior, and without any exterior work on her part. These two things would remove this peace from her if they could penetrate to her, but they cannot, for she is in the sovereign state where they cannot pierce or disturb her about anything. If she does any exterior thing, it is always without herself. If God does His work in her, it is by Him in her, without herself, for her sake. Such a Soul is no more encumbered by this than is her angel by guarding her. No more is an angel encumbered by guarding us than if he never guarded us at all. So also neither is such a Soul [encumbered] by what she does without herself than if she had never done it at all. For she has nothing of herself. She has given all freely without a why, for she is the lady of the Bridegroom of her youth. He is the Sun who shines and warms and nourishes the life of being separate from His Being. This Soul has retained neither doubt nor anxiety any longer.

Reason: Why therefore? says Reason.

Love: A sure alliance and a true concordance by willing only the divine ordinance.

Chapter 82: How this Soul is unencumbered in her four aspects.

[*Love*]: This Soul, who is what she is perfectly, is unencumbered in her four aspects. For four aspects are required in a noble person before he might be called a gentleman and thus of a spiritual intellect.

The first aspect in which this Soul is unencumbered is that she has no reproach in her at all, even though she does not do the work of the Virtues. Ah, for the sake of God! give attention, you who hear if you can! How could it be that Love could be able to have her practice along with the works of the Virtues, when it is necessary that works cease when Love has her practice?

The second aspect is that she has no longer any will, no more than the dead in the sepulchers have, but only the divine will. Such a Soul is not concerned about either justice or mercy. She places and plants everything in the will alone of the One who loves her. This is the second aspect by which this Soul is unencumbered.

The third aspect is that she believes and maintains that there never was, nor is there, nor will there ever be anything worse than she, nor any better loved by the One who loves her according to what she is. Note this and do not grasp it poorly.

The fourth aspect is that she believes and maintains that it is no more possible for God to be able to will something other than goodness than it is for her to will something other than His divine will. Love has so adorned the Soul with Herself that She makes her maintain this about Him, who by His goodness has transformed her into such goodness through His goodness; who, by His love, has transformed her into such love through love; and [who], by His will, has

157

purely transformed her into such will through divine will. He is of Himself in her for her sake this same One. And this she believes and maintains. She would not be unencumbered in all her aspects by any other means.

Grasp the gloss, hearers of this book, for the kernel is there which nourishes the bride. This is so as long as she is in the Being by which God makes her to be, there where she has given her will, and thus cannot will except the will of the One who has transformed her of Himself for her sake into His goodness. And if she is thus unencumbered in all aspects, she loses her name, for she rises in sovereignty. And therefore she loses her name in the One in whom she is melted and dissolved through Himself and in Himself. Thus she would be like a body of water which flows from the sea, which has some name, as one would be able to say Aisne or Seine or another river. And when this water or river returns into the sea, it loses its course and its name with which it flowed in many countries in accomplishing its task. Now it is in the sea where it rests, and thus has lost all labor.[71] Likewise it is with this Soul. You have from this enough of an example to gloss the intention of how this Soul came from the sea and had a name, and how she returns into the sea and so loses her name and has a name no longer, except for the name of Him into whom she is perfectly transformed, that is, into the love of the Bridegroom of her youth, who has transformed the bride completely into Himself. He is, therefore this Soul is. And this satisfies her marvelously, thus she is marvelous; and this is pleasing to Love, and so this Soul is love. And this delights her.

Chapter 83: How this Soul has the name of the transformation by which Love has transformed her.

[Love]: Now such a Soul is without a name, and because of this she has the name of the transformation by which Love has transformed her. So it is with the waters of which we have spoken, which have the name of *sea* because they are wholly sea as soon as they have entered into the sea.

So also no nature of fire adds any matter into itself, but instead it makes of itself and the matter one thing, no longer two but one. So it is with those of whom we speak, for Love draws completely their matter into herself. Love and such Souls are one thing, no longer two things, for this would be discord; but instead they are one thing alone, and thus there is accord.

Chapter 84: How the Unencumbered Soul in her four aspects ascends into sovereignty and lives unencumbered by divine life.

[*Love*]: I say, says Love, that such a Soul, who is thus unencumbered in these four aspects, rises after this in sovereignty.

Reason: Ah, Love! says Reason. Is there no higher gift?

Love: Yes, says Love, there is, which is her nearest one. For when she is thus unencumbered in her four aspects and gentle in all her offspring, which are descended from her (no one vile is taken in marriage there, and thus she is very noble), then she falls from this, says Love, into an astonishment, which one calls "pondering nothing about the nearness of the Farnearness," who is her nearest one. Then such a Soul, says Love, lives not by the life of grace, or by the life of spirit only, but by the divine life, unencumbered—but not gloriously, for she is not glorified—but she lives divinely, for God has sanctified her of Himself in this point, and nothing which might be contrary to goodness can reach there.

Grasp this in a divine manner, this is for as long as she is in this being: God gives you being there forever without departure from it. I say this to the persons for whose sake Love has had this book made and to those for whose sake I have written it. To you who are not this, who were not, nor will be, you make yourselves suffer in vain if you wish to grasp it. He tastes nothing of it who is not this: either in God without being, or God in him in being. Grasp the gloss, for whatever nourishes is savory, and, as one says often, what nourishes badly is unsavory.

Encumbered Reason: Ah, without fail, well said! says Encumbered Reason.

Astonished Soul in Pondering Nothing: Truly, says this Soul astonished in pondering nothing about the nearness through this Farnearness who delights her in peace, rudeness could neither speak nor ponder nor encumber her with Reason. It is clear enough to [Reason's] disciples, a donkey would not do the work which they would want to hear about. But God has guarded me well, says this Soul, from such disciples. They no longer hold me in their counsel, nor do I wish to hear their doctrine any more, for I have been held there too long, even though it might have been good for me. But now it is not my better thing, even though they do not know it. For a petty mind cannot appreciate something of great value, nor grasp something of which Reason is not the mistress. And if they should grasp it, it is not very often.

Thus I say, says this Soul, that I will not hear their rudeness anymore; they will say it no more to me, I cannot suffer it further, for I indeed have neither what nor why. This work now belongs to God, who accomplishes His works in me. I do not owe Him any work since He Himself works in me. If I should place my own [work] there, I destroy His work. And so the disciples of Reason wish to place me back in the poverty of their counsel, if I would believe them. They thus lose their worthiness, for such a thing is impossible; but I forgive them their intentions.

Chapter 85: How this Soul is free, more free and very free.

[*Love*]: This Soul, says Love, is free, yet more free, yet very free, yet finally supremely free, in the root, in the stock, in all her branches and all the fruits of her branches. This Soul has her portion of purified freeness, each aspect has its full measure of it. She responds to no one if she does not wish to, if he is not of her lineage. For a gentleman would not deign to respond to a peasant, even if such a one would call him or attack him in a battlefield. And for this anyone who calls her will not find such a Soul. Her enemies have no longer any response from her.

Soul: That is right, says this Soul, since I believe that God is in me, it is necessary that He be my help, and His goodness cannot lose me.

Love: This Soul, says Love, is scorched through mortification and burned through the ardor of the fire of charity, and her ashes are thrown into the open sea through the nothingness of will. This Soul is gently noble in prosperity, and supremely noble in adversity, and excellently noble in all places whatever they might be. This Soul who is such no longer seeks God through penitence, nor through any sacrament of Holy Church; not through thoughts, nor through words, nor through works; not through creature here below, nor through creature above; not through justice, nor through mercy, nor through glory of glory; not through divine understanding, nor through divine love, nor through divine praise.

160

Chapter 86: How Reason is astounded by what is said about this Soul.

[*Reason*]: O God! O God! O God! says Reason. What is this creature saying? She is now completely beside herself! But what will my children say? I do not know what to say to them, nor how to respond to excuse this.

Soul: I am not surprised, says this Soul, for these are folk with feet but no path, hands but no work, mouth but no words, eyes but no vision, ears but no hearing, reason but no reasoning, body but no life, and with a heart but no intellect, as long as they are at this stage. For this reason do your children marvel upon marvel of marvel.

Love: True, these are astounded, says Love, well astounded, for they are so far from the country where one has such practice in order to possess the heights. But those who are from the country in which God lives, these are not astounded at all by it.

Soul: Not at all! If it please God, says the Unencumbered Soul, this would be a mark of crudity, and I will say to you and show you how by an example. If a king should give one of his servants, who loyally served him, a great gift, by which gift the servant would be eternally rich, without ever doing any service again, why would a wise man be astounded by this? Without fail, he must not be astounded by it at all, for in doing so he would blame the king and his gift and the liberality of the gift.[72]

Courtesy: And I will tell you, says Courtesy, in what and by what. Because a wise man is never astounded when another does what is fitting for him to do. Instead he praises and values and loves this. And if he would be astounded by it, he would show in this that this would not be proper to do. But the heart that is villainous and of little wisdom, which does not know on account of a lack of judgment what is honor or courtesy, or about a gift of a noble lord, has great astonishment over this.

Truth: This is not astounding, says Truth; one has the why within him, as you have heard.

Nobility of the Unity of the Soul: Ah, for God's sake, says the Nobility of the Unity of the Unencumbered Soul, why is anyone astounded who has judgment within him, if I say great things and new things, and if I have through All, by All, in All my full sufficiency? My lover is great who gives me a great gift, and so He is all new and gives me a new gift. And so of Himself He is fertile and full of abundance of all goodness. And I am pregnant and full and abundantly full of the abundances of delights from the flowing goodness of His divine goodness, without seeking it through pain or through the peddling of pain's remedies, which this book describes.

Soul: He is, says this Soul, and this satisfies me.

Pure Courtesy: Without fail this is right, says Pure Courtesy. It is appropriate for the Lover, since He is of valor, that He satisfy His beloved with His goodness.

> Troubled is Martha, peace has Mary.
> Praised is Martha, but more so Mary.
> Loved is Martha, much more Mary.

Mary has only one sole spirit in her, that is, one sole intent, which makes her have peace. And Martha has some of it sometimes, which is why sometimes she has an uneasy peace. And for this reason the Unencumbered Soul cannot have but one sole intent.

> Such a Soul often hears what she hears not,
> and often sees what she sees not,
> and so often she is there where she is not,
> and so often she feels what she feels not.

And so she holds her Lover and she says:

Soul: I hold Him, says she, for He is mine. I will never let Him go.[73] He is in my will. Let come whatever might be, He is with me. It would be a lack in me if I should be astounded.

Chapter 87: How this Soul is the lady of the Virtues and daughter of Deity.

[*Love*]: This Soul, says Love, is the lady of the Virtues, daughter of Deity, sister of Wisdom, and bride of Love.

Soul: Truly, says this Soul, but this seems to Reason to be strange language. But it is not strange, and in a little while [Reason] will be no more. But I was, says this Soul, and I am, and I will be always without lack, for Love has no beginning, no end, and no limit, and I am nothing except Love. How would I have anything else? This could not be.

Reason: Ah God! says Reason. How dare one say this? I dare not listen to it. I am fainting truly, Lady Soul, in hearing you; my heart is failing. I have no more life.[74]

Soul: Alas! Why did it take so long, this death! says this Soul. For as long as I had you, Lady Reason, I could not freely receive my inheritance, what was and is mine. But now I can receive it freely, since I have wounded you to death by Love.

Soul: Now is Reason dead, says this Soul.

Love: Therefore I will say, says Love, what Reason would say, if she were alive in you. She would ask [something] of you, Beloved of us, says Love to this Soul who is Love herself and nothing other than Love, ever since Love, by her divine goodness, had put Reason and the works of the Virtues under her feet and led them to their death, without return.

Chapter 88: How Love asks what Reason would ask if she were still alive, that is, who is the mother of Reason and the other Virtues.

[*Love*]: I will say, says Love, what Reason would ask if she were still alive. She would ask, says Love, who is the mother of her and of the other Virtues who are of Reason's generation, and if they are mothers of anyone.

Love: Yes, says Love herself who answers. All the Virtues are mothers.

Soul: Of whom? says this Soul. Of Peace?

Love: Of Holiness, says Love.

Soul: Then all the Virtues, who are of the generation of Reason, are mothers of Holiness.

Love: True, says Love, of that Holiness which Reason grasps, but no other kind.

Soul: Then who is mother of the Virtues?

Love: Humility, says Love. Not that Humility who is Humility through the work of the Virtues, for she is a sister of the same generation of Reason. Thus I say sister, for it is a greater thing to be a mother than a child, even a much greater thing, if you can see this.

Soul speaks in the persona of Reason: From whom, then, says this Soul who speaks in the persona of Reason, is this Humility who is the mother of these Virtues? To whom is she daughter, from whom does she come, who is the mother of so great a lineage as the Virtues, and aunt of the Holiness of whom these Virtues are the mothers? Who is grandmother to this Holiness? Does no one know how to say whence comes such a lineage?

Love: Not at all, says Love. The one who knows it, does not know how to put it into words.

Soul: This is true, says this Soul, but I would lie as soon as I said something.

This Humility, who is aunt and mother,
is daughter of Divine majesty and so is born from Divinity.
Deity is her mother and grandmother of her branches,
by whom the buds make such great fruitfulness.
We are silent about it, for speaking ruins them.
This one, that is, Humility,
has given the stem and the fruit from these buds,
because she is there, close
to the peace of this Farnearness
who unencumbers her from works,
and turns away the speaking,
makes dark there the pondering.
This Farnearness unencumbers,
no one encumbers her with anything.
This one is freed from all service,
for she lives by freeness.
Whoever serves, he is not free,
whoever senses, he has not died,
whoever desires, he wills,
whoever wills, he begs,
whoever begs, he has a lack of divine sufficiency.

But those who are always loyal to her are always overtaken by Love and annihilated through Love, and completely stripped by Love, and so have no care except for Love, in order to suffer and endure torments forever, because [these loyal ones] would be as great as God is great in goodness. The Soul never loved perfectly who doubted that this would be true.

Chapter 89: How this Soul has given everything through the freeness of nobility.

[Love]: This Soul has given everything through the freeness of the nobility by the work of the Trinity, in which Trinity this Soul plants her will so nakedly that she cannot sin if she does not uproot herself. She has nothing to sin with, for without a will no one can sin. Now she is kept from sin if she leaves her will there where it is planted, that is, in the One who has given it to her freely from His goodness. And thus, by His beneficence, He wills the return of His beloved nakedly and freely, without a why for her sake, on account of two things: because He wills it, and because He is worthy of it. And before this she had no fertile and restful peace until she was purely stripped of her will.

This one, who is such, always resembles one who is inebriated. It does not matter to someone inebriated what happens to him, whether his fortune comes or not. And if it did matter to him, he would not be inebriated very well. So also, if this Soul has something to will with, this means that she is poorly planted and that she can still indeed fall if she is assailed by adversity or by prosperity. And this is not all; for she is not nothing if she has something to will with, for her poverty or her wealth are in her willing to give or to retain.

And again, indeed, so I would like to say, says Love, to all those who are asked and called by the desire of their interior life in the works of perfection through the effort of Reason, whether they want to or not, that if they would want to be what they could be, they would come to the stage of which we speak, and they would indeed be lords over themselves, and over heaven and earth.

Reason: How lords? says Reason.

Soul: This none know how to say, says the Unencumbered Soul, who holds all things without heart, and who possesses all things without heart, and if her heart senses it, she is not this.

Chapter 90: How one can come to perfection by doing the contrary of one's will.

[*Love*]: I have said, says Love, that whoever fulfills the demand of the interior life of the spirit—if he is called to arrive at a good will,

165

otherwise I do not speak—and if he leaves his will completely out-side in order to live in the life of spirit, he would come indeed into complete lordship.

Spirit: Ah, for the sake of God, says the Spirit who seeks this very thing in the sad life, tell us how!

Soul: This no one knows how to say, says the Unencumbered Soul, except the One who is such in the creature, by His goodness for the sake of the creature. But I can tell you, says this Freed Soul, what is necessary before one arrives at it, that one do perfectly the contrary of his own will in feeding the Virtues until they are fat,[75] and restrain-ing oneself without weakening, so that the spirit always has lordship without contradiction.

Truth: Ah, my God, says Truth, how ill in the heart would the body become where there was such a spirit?

Soul: I dare say, says this Unencumbered Soul, that the kind of will that it is necessary to have in the sad life, that is in the life of the spirit, would destroy in one brief moment the fluids of all illnesses. The ardor of the spirit has such healing powers.

Love: This is true, says Love, whoever doubts it, if they try it they will know the truth about it. Now I will tell you, says Love. (It is the contrary in the case of the Unencumbered Soul.) The life of which we have spoken, which we call the life of spirit, cannot have peace unless the body always does the contrary of its own will, that is, that such folk do the contrary of sensuality, or else they would fall into perdition from such a life, if they do not live contrary to their pleasure.

Those who are unencumbered do the opposite. For insofar as it is necessary that in the life of the spirit they do the contrary of their own will if they wish not to lose peace, so likewise in an opposite way, the unencumbered ones do everything that pleases them if they wish not to lose peace, since they have arrived in the stage of free-ness, that is, since they have fallen from the Virtues into Love, and from Love into Nothingness.

Chapter 91:   How the will of these Souls is the will of Love, and why.

[*Love*]: They do nothing unless it pleases them and if they do [what does not please them] they take away peace, freeness, and nobility from themselves. For the Soul is not refined until she does what is pleasing to her, and until she experiences no reproach for doing her pleasure.

This is right, says Love, for her will is ours. She has crossed the Red Sea, her enemies have been drowned in it. Her pleasure is our will, through the purity of the unity of the will of the Deity where we have enclosed her. Her will is ours, for she has fallen from grace into the perfection of the work of the Virtues, and from the Virtues into Love and from Love into Nothingness, and from Nothingness into clarification by God,[76] who sees Himself with the eyes of His majesty, who in this point has clarified her with Himself. And she is so dissolved in Him that she sees neither herself nor Him, and thus He sees completely Himself alone, by His divine goodness.[77] He will be of Himself in such goodness which He knew of Himself before she ever was, when He gave her His goodness by which He made her a lady. [This goodness] was Free Will, which He cannot take from her without the pleasure of the Soul. Now He possesses [the will] without a why in the same way that He possessed it before she was made a lady by it. There is no one except Him; no one loves except Him, for no one is except Him, and thus He alone loves completely, and sees Himself completely alone, and praises completely alone by His Being itself. And the limit is at this point, for it is the most noble stage which the Soul might be able to have here below.

And so there are five [stages] below this one where it is necessary to unite to the perfection of the demand of each, before the Soul might be able to have this one, which is the sixth, which is the most profitable, the most noble, the most noble of them all. And in paradise is the seventh, and this one is perfect and without any lack. Thus God accomplishes by His goodness His divine works in His creatures. The Holy Spirit breathes there wherever He is, and so He is in His creatures marvelously.[78]

Chapter 92:   How the Soul is unencumbered from God, and from herself and from her neighbor.

[*Soul*]: Ah, Lord, says this Soul, you have suffered so much from us, and you have worked so much in us, through yourself, of yourself, that these two works, Lord, have found their end in us. But it is too late.

Now work in us of yourself for our sakes without ourselves, as it pleases you, Lord. As for me, from now on I am not afraid. I unencumber myself from you, and from myself, and from my neighbors, and I will tell you how. I release you, and myself, and all my neighbors, in the knowledge of your divine wisdom, in the outflowing of your divine power, in the governance of your divine goodness, for the sake of your divine will alone.

[*Satisfied Soul*]: And these divine things alone, annihilated, clear, and clarified by the divine majesty, says the Satisfied Soul, have given me freeness from all things without expecting anything in return, for otherwise there would not be this gift if there were a lack.

Soul: Now pay attention, if you will, if you have such a gift, says this Soul to the servants of Reason and Nature in order to make them envious. I owe nothing, *otherwise Love would be a slave and otherwise nothingness exists, which cannot be.*[79] And when such nothingness is, then God sees Himself in such a creature, without any hindrance from His creature.

Chapter 93: Here one speaks of the peace of the divine life.

[*Soul*]: The peace of such a life by divine life cannot be thought or spoken or written, as long as the Soul is in such love without the work of the body, without the work of the heart, without the works of the spirit: through divine work the law is fulfilled. Reason esteems the Magdalene well in that she sought Jesus Christ, but Love is silent about her. Note this well and do not forget it, for when [the Magdalene] sought Him, she lacked the divine life which Truth names the glorious life. But when she was in the desert, Love overtook her, which annihilated her, and thus because of this Love worked in her for her sake, without her, and so she lived by divine life which made her have glorious life.[80] Thus she found God in herself, without seeking Him, and she had no why since Love had overtaken her. But when she possessed love, she sought Him by desire of will in the feeling of the spirit, and so she was human and small, for she was sad, but not Maria.[81] She did not know when she sought Him that God was completely everywhere, so that she might not seek Him.[82] I have found no one who always knew this, except for the Virgin Mary. She never willed through sensuality, nor worked in the spirit outside the will of the Deity by the divine work. This was and is and will be [the Virgin's] divine aspect, her divine feast, her divine love, her divine peace, her divine praise, her full labor and her full rest—to will only the divine will. And because of this, she had, without any intermediary in her soul, the glorious life of the Trinity in her mortal body.

Chapter 94: Concerning the language of divine life.

[*Soul*]: The language of such a life of divine life is a hidden silence of divine love. She has had this for a long time, and so she has willed this for a long time. There is no greater life than always to will the divine will.

You have nothing to delay in giving up yourselves, for no one can rest in the highest restful repose if he is not fatigued first—of this I am certain. Let the Virtues have what is theirs in you by sharpening the will in the core of the affection of your spirit until they have acquitted you of what you owe Jesus Christ. And it is necessary to do this before one comes to [this] life.

For the sake of God, understand what Jesus Christ Himself says. Did He not say in the Gospel that "whoever will believe in me will do works as I do, and even greater ones will he do"?[83]

Where is written the gloss on this meaning, I ask you! Until one has paid to Jesus Christ all that one owes Him, one cannot have the peace of the country of divine being where life remains. God gives you briefly the accomplishment of your natural perfection, concord of the powers of the soul, and sufficiency in all things. It is necessary that you have this, for it is the way of divine life, which we call the glorious life. And this being, of which we speak, the form of which Love gives us of Her goodness restores today the first day in the soul.[84] That one restores today the first day who attains on earth the innocence through divine obedience which Adam lost in terrestrial paradise through disobedience. Pain remained in [humanity], for Jesus Christ took it [upon Himself], and so it is just that it remain with us. The truly innocent never possess a regulation, [and] no one ever makes them unjust. They are completely naked; they have nothing to hide. All still hide by the sin of Adam, except those who are annihilated: those have nothing to hide.[85]

Chapter 95: How the land of the sad is far from the land of those who are annihilated.

[*Love*]: It is a very long road from the land of the Virtues, who hold the sad, to the land of the forgotten ones, the naked annihilated ones, the clarified ones, who are in the highest stage, where God is relinquished by them in themselves. Thus He is neither known, nor loved, nor praised by such creatures, except only in this, that one cannot know Him, nor love, nor praise Him. This is the summation of all their love, the last course of their way: the last accords with the first, for the middle is not discordant. It is right, since [the Soul] has finished the course, that she repose in Him who is able [to do] whatever He wills by the proper goodness of His divine being. And this Soul is able to do whatever she wills without loss of the gifts of Him who possesses His own being. Why would it not be so? His gifts are as great as He is Himself who has given this gift which transforms her by Him into Himself. This is Love Herself, and Love is able to do whatever She wills. And thus neither Fear, nor Discretion, nor Reason can say anything contrary to Love.

This [Soul] sees the fullness of her intellect; but God sees it in her without impediment from her, and thus the Virtues have nothing with which to shame her, which is why she speaks thus to Him:

Chapter 96: Here the Soul speaks to the Trinity.

[*Soul*]: Ah, Lord, who can do all things; ah, Master, who knows all things; ah, Lover, who is worthy of all things, do whatever you will. Sweet Father, I can do nothing. Sweet Son, I know nothing. Sweet Lover, I am worthy of nothing. And therefore I will nothing. Ah, for the sake of God! Let us not allow anything of ourselves or of another ever to enter within us for which it would be necessary that God place us outside His goodness!

Once upon a time, there was a mendicant creature, who for a long time sought God in creatureliness, in order to see if she would find Him thus as she willed Him, and as He Himself would be, if the creature allowed Him to work His divine works in her, without impediment from her. And she found nothing of Him, but instead remained hungry for what she sought. And when she saw that she found nothing, she pondered. And her thought about Him told her to seek Him, as she asked, at the depth of the core of the intellect of the purity of her sublime thought. And there this mendicant creature went to seek Him, and so she thought that she would describe God such as she desired to find Him in His creatures. And so this mendicant creature wrote what you hear. And she desired that her neighbors might find God in her, through writings and words; that is to say

170

and mean, that she wished that her neighbors become the perfect ones she described (at least all those to whom she desired to say this). And in doing this, and in saying this, and in willing this she remained, as you know, a beggar and encumbered with herself. And thus she would beg, because she willed to do this.

Chapter 97: How paradise is nothing other than to see God.

[*The Supreme Lady of Peace*]: This is sure, says the Supreme Lady of Peace, who lives by the life of glory, but not by glory itself which is in paradise only. Paradise is nothing other than to see God only. And thus was the thief in paradise, as soon as the soul was parted from his body, although Jesus Christ, the Son of God, did not ascend to heaven until the Ascension, but the thief was in paradise the same day as Good Friday. And how could this be? Certainly it had to be, since Jesus Christ had promised him. And it is true that he was in paradise the same day. Because he saw God, he was in paradise, for paradise is nothing other than to see God. And that is the truth about it, every and however many times one is unencumbered of oneself. But [this does] not happen gloriously, for the body of such a creature is too heavy. But the person is there divinely, for the interior is perfectly delivered from all creaturely things. Thus he lives, without a mediary, by the life of glory, and is in paradise, without being.

Gloss these words, if you want to grasp them, or you will grasp them poorly, for they have some appearance of contradiction for the one who does not attend to the core of the gloss. But appearance is not truth, but truth is, and not some other thing.

But what had this creature thought who made this book, who desired that one find God in her, in order to live what she said about God? It seems that she wanted to vindicate herself, that is, she desired that creatures beg from other creatures, as she had done!

Soul: Certainly, it is necessary to do it before one comes in all aspects to the state of freeness, I am completely certain of it. Yet even so, says this Soul who wrote this book, I was so foolish at the time when I wrote it; but Love did it for my sake and at my request, that I might undertake something which one could neither do, nor think, nor say, any more than someone could desire to enclose the sea in his eye, or carry the world on the end of a reed, or illumine the sun with a lantern or a torch. I was more foolish than the one who would want to do the other,

when I undertook a thing which one cannot say,
when I encumbered myself with the writing of these words.
But since I took my course
in order to come to my help,
to my final crown
of the being of which we speak
which is in perfection,

when the Soul remains in pure nothingness without thought, and not until then.

Chapter 98: Reason asks what those do who are in being above their thoughts.

[*Reason*]: Ah, for the sake of God, says Reason, what do those do who are in being above their thoughts?
Love: They are amazed by what is from the top of their mountain, and they are amazed by the same thing which is in the depth of their valley—by a thinking nothing which is shut away and sealed in the secret closure of the highest purity of such an excellent Soul. No one can open the closure, nor break the seal, nor close it when it is open, if the gentle Farnearness from very far and from very near does not close and open it, who alone has the keys to it, for no one else carries them, no one else could carry them.[86]

You ladies, to whom God has abundantly given this life by His divine goodness without withholding anything, and not only this life which we describe, but also the one of whom no human speaks, you will recognize your practice in this book. And those who are not of this kind, nor were, nor will be, will not feel this being, nor understand it. They cannot do it, nor will they do it. They are not, as you know, of the lineage of which we speak, no more than the angels of the first order are Seraphim, nor can they be, for God does not give them the being of Seraphim. But those who are not this now—but they are so in God, which is why they will be so—will understand this being and sense it, through the strength of the lineage from which they are and will be, more strongly indeed than those who have not understood it and sensed it. And such folk of whom we speak, who are this way and will be, will recognize, as soon as they hear it, their lineage from which they come.

Chapter 99: How such types, who are in such being, are in sovereignty in all things.

[*Love*]: Such souls, who are in being, are in sovereignty in all things. For their spirit is in the highest nobility of the orders of angels created and ordained. Thus folk such as these have, on account of this spirit, the highest mansion of all the orders and by nature the most gentle constitution. That is, because they are passionate or ardent, neither melancholy nor apathetic, so they have of the gifts of fortune the best portion, for all is theirs according to their will and their necessity, for themselves and for their neighbors, without reproach of Reason. Now you hear, through desire, the great perfection of the Annihilated Souls, of whom we speak!

Chapter 100: How great a difference there is among the angels, between one and another.

[*Love*]: It is said, says Love, and I say it myself, that there is as great a difference among the angels, between one and another by nature, as there is between men and beasts. This is easy to believe: so has the divine wisdom willed to work. No one asks why, if they do not wish to err, but it is believed, for it is true. And as much as there is to say about the angels, about one or another, as you have heard, so there is also as much to say, through grace, about the annihilated ones, of whom we speak to those who are not so. The one is very well born who is of such lineage. These are royal folk. They have hearts excellently noble and of great enterprise, for they would not do a work of little value, nor begin something which would not come to a good perfection. They are the smallest they can be and they must become the greatest by the witness of Jesus Christ Himself, who says that the smallest will be the greatest in the kingdom of heaven.[87] One ought to believe Him indeed; no one believes it who is not [the smallest]. For the one who is what he believes, believes truly. But whoever believes what he is not, it is because he does not live what he believes. Such a one does not believe truly, for the truth of belief is in being what one believes. Thus the one who believes this is the one who is [the smallest]. Such a one has nothing more to do with himself, or with another, or with God Himself, no more than if he were not; and so he is. Grasp the gloss. It is in his will that there is nothing belonging to himself for his own sake, no more than if he were not.

In these three words is fulfilled completely the perfection of the clear life. I call it clear, because it surpasses the blind annihilated life. The blind [life] sustains the feet [of the soul] here below.[88] The clear [life] is the most noble and the most gentle. It knows not what it is, whether God or human, for it is not. Only God knows about it, of Himself, in Himself, for its sake. Such a lady seeks God no more. She has no why, she has nothing to do with herself. Nothing is lacking to her, therefore why would she seek Him? Whoever seeks, he is "with" himself, and so he has himself, and so something is lacking to him since he sets about seeking.

Chapter 101: How this Soul does not will to do anything, and also how nothing is lacking to her, no more than to her Lover.

[*Soul*]: Ah, for the sake of God, why would I do something which my Lover does not do? Nothing is lacking to Him, why, therefore, would anything be lacking to me? Truly I would be wandering if anything were lacking to me, since nothing is lacking to Him. He lacks nothing, and therefore I lack nothing. And this point takes love of myself from me and gives me to Him, without a mediary and without holding back. I have said, says this Soul, that nothing is lacking to Him, why therefore would anything be lacking to me? He seeks nothing, why therefore would I seek? He ponders nothing, why therefore would I ponder?

Annihilated Soul: I will do nothing, Reason, says this Soul annihilated and clarified through the lack of love of herself; but you seek the one who does and you will do this, if I know you. But, thanks be to God, I am no longer wary of you.

I have done everything, says this Soul.

Reason: Since when? From what time? says Reason.

Soul: Since the time, says the Soul, that Love opened her book to me. For this book is of such a kind, that as soon as Love opened it, the Soul knew all things, and so possesses all things, and so every work of perfection is fulfilled in her through the opening of this book. This opening has made me see so clearly that it made me give back what is His and receive what is mine—that is, He is, and thus He possesses completely of Himself; and I am not, and so it is indeed right that I not possess myself. And the light from the opening of this book has made me find what is mine and remain in this. Thus I have only as

174

much being as He is able to be of Himself in me. Thus Righteousness, by righteousness, has given what is mine back to me, and shown nakedly that I am not. Therefore [Righteousness] wills, through righteousness, that I not possess myself. This righteousness is written in the marrow of the book of life. It is thus with this book and with me, says this Soul, as it was with God and with creatures when He created them. He willed it by His divine goodness, and all this was done in the same moment by His divine power, and all was ordained in this same hour by His divine wisdom.

Ah, for the sake of God, says this Soul, consider what He did, and what He does, and what He will do, and then you will have peace, both moderation and the height, and peace from peace, such overwhelming peace that the corruption of your constitution could never be the source of correction, if you remain in overwhelming peace. Ah, God, how these are beautiful and grand words to the one who grasps the truth of the glosses!

Chapter 102: Here the Intellect of the Annihilated Soul shows the pity there is when wretchedness has the victory over goodness.

[*Intellect of the Annihilated Soul*]: Ah, for God's sake! says Intellect of the Annihilated Soul, am I not still in the captivity of corruption, where I must be whether I want to or not, if I am not lodged in the prison of correction? Ah, God! what a pity it is, when wretchedness has the victory over goodness. And so it is with the body and with the spirit. The spirit has been created by God, and the body has been formed by God.[89] Now these two natures—joined together in corruption, by nature and by justice—are in the font of baptism without reproach.[90] Hence these two natures were good by the divine justice which has made these two natures. And when defect took over this constitution and this creation, who were made by the divine goodness, no piety united this creature, however small the defect might be. Therefore we are distressed in bitterness, and we strive to force against ourselves what this creature does not will. There is no such thing as a small defect; since any defect is not pleasing to the divine will, it must displease Him.

Understanding by Divine Light: Ah, God, says Understanding by Divine Light, who would dare to call this small? I maintain that whoever names it small was never well illumined, nor will he ever be, if he does not repent of it. And there is even greater difficulty for him, since he has placed the pleasure of his Lord in such nonchalance. There is much to say to him about the kind of servant who serves his Lord in all the ways he understands would best please the will of his Lord!

Chapter 103: Here is shown what it means that the just man falls seven times each day.

[*Soul*]: Now there are some, says this Soul, who are helped by what Scripture says, that the just man falls seven times each day.[91] But those are indeed donkeys who interpret this to be any course of correction. Correction occurs when one falls into defect by the consent of one's will. Corruption is the heaviness of the constitution of our body.

According to this account, it would seem that we would have no free will if it were necessary for us to sin against our will seven times each day. It is not so, says this Soul, thanks be to God! For God would not be God if virtue were taken from me in spite of myself! For no more than God can sin, who cannot will it, can I sin if my will does not will it. My Lover has given me such freeness by His goodness through love. And so if I will something, why would not He allow it? If He would not allow it, His power would take freeness from me. But His goodness could not allow that His power unfree me in anything; that is, no power takes my will from me, if my will does not will to assent to it. Now His goodness, through pure goodness, has given me free will through goodness. He has not given me any more of whatever He has made for my sake. The surplus He has prepared for me by His courtesy. If He takes it back, He does me no injustice. But He has freely given me my will, and thus He cannot repossess it if it does not please my will. The supreme height of Love has given me such nobility by her Goodness through love that she can never take from me the freeness of my will if I do not will it.

Chapter 104: Here the Soul tells how God has given her free will to her.

[*Soul*]: You see how He has freely given me my free will. I have said above, says the Soul, that He has given me nothing more. But in saying this, one could interpret this to mean that He had not given me all things, or that He has not given me anything except free will, or prepared the other things for me. Certainly this would be a bad interpretation, for He has given me all things. He could not have held anything back from me. And Love confirms this, who says that such a thing would not be love from a lover if it were so. For insofar as He has given me free will by His pure goodness, He has given me all things, if my will wills: He does not withhold otherwise, of this I am certain.

Fear: And how, for God's sake, Lady Soul, has He given you all things? says Fear.

Soul: In this, says the Soul, that I have freely given Him my will, nakedly, without holding anything back, for the sake of His goodness and for the sake of His will alone, in the same way He gave it to me by His divine will for the sake of my profit, by His divine goodness. Now I have said, says this Soul, that God would not be God if virtue is taken from me in spite of myself. This is true. There is no more certain thing than that God is, and no more untrue thing than that virtue is taken from me if my will does not will it. And this is far from what Scripture says, that the just man falls in the course of correction seven times each day.

Chapter 105: What it means that the just man falls seven times each day.

[*Truth*]: I will tell you what it means, says Truth, that the just man falls seven times each day. It means that insofar as the will of the just man is completely given over to the contemplation of the divine goodness without any impediment, the body is feeble and tends toward defect because of the nourishment of the sin of Adam and thus is inclined often to give attention to lesser things than the goodness of God. And Scripture calls this a fall, for so it is. But the will of the just man is kept from consenting to the defect, which could grow from such an inclination. So such a fall, by which the just man falls through the above said inclination, is more virtuous for him than vice, because of his will, which remains free through the refusal of all defect, as has been said. Now you can see how the just man falls so low from so high, and how this fall, however low it might be, is more virtuous than vice.

Now pay attention. Since the just man falls seven times each day, it is necessary that he be lifted seven times, else he could not fall seven times. That one is blessed who often falls, for it follows that he came from the place where no one goes if he does not have, by righteousness, the name of "just." However, the one is the most blessed who always remains there. No one is able to always be there as long as the soul is accompanied by this wretched body in this world; but this fall does not cause the loss of peace through guilt or remorse of conscience, for the Soul lives by the peace of the gifts given to her above the Virtues—not contrary to the Virtues, but above. If this could not be, then God would be subject to His Virtues, and the Virtues would be contrary to the Soul, [Virtues] who have their being from their Lord, for the sake of the profit of [the Soul].

Chapter 106:   How the Soul states the goal of her petitions.

[*Soul*]: Now, says this Soul, I will state the goal of my petitions; in such petitions the request would be to accomplish the goal. Not, says this Soul, for the purpose of something which I might know how to ask for, or which I might wish to ask for, for none of the orders of angels, or any of the men or women saints who are in these orders, know how to ask for it. Therefore neither would the tenth state, which is in glory without being in any of the other nine orders, know how to ask for it, since those orders do not know it either.

Reason: And so what do you know, Lady Soul? says Reason.

Soul: God does it!

Love: She is able to know it well, says Love, through the divine nature of the drawing power of her love, which forms her petitions in her, without her knowing it. And her petitions are beyond any country where the creature can have understanding.

Soul: What marvel is this? says this Soul. Why would anyone know it except Him *whose I am or of whom I am, who is Himself in me?*[92] This is secret Love, who is beyond peace; there my love is established without myself. His goodness makes this drawing power for my sake, which daily gives me new love. But about what He is of Himself in me for my sake, or about what I ask, without asking of myself, about the drawing power of His pure nature I can know nothing, says this Soul. None of those in glory do this except for One alone who is one in Deity and three in Persons.

Love: But, says Love, in this she has said that she will say what is the goal of her petitions, that is, she will say what it is that she has. In truth, she has what no one can say or ponder except God, who always works His work in her, without her work, by His divine goodness, that is, without the work of the Soul.

Chapter 107:   Here begin the petitions of the Soul.

[*The First Petition*]: The first thing which she asks is that she see herself always (if she is to see anything) where she was when God made all things from nothing, so that she might be certain that she is not other than this[93]—when she is of herself—nor will she be eternally [other than this] because she had rebelled against the divine goodness.

The Second Petition: The second petition is that she see what she has done with her free will, which God has given to her, so that she might see that she has removed her will from God Himself in one sole moment of consent to sin. This means that God hates all sin, and whoever consents to do sin removes his will from God. This is true, for he does what God does not will and what is against His divine goodness.

Chapter 108:   A good consideration to avoid sin.

Now must the Soul consider the debt of one sole sin, in order to see how much she owes for two sins if she falls two times.

The Light of the Soul: Two times? says the Light of the Soul. Truly, no more than one could number how many times I have taken a breath, no more, or rather even less, could anyone number how many times I have removed my will from God. As long as I have had will, I have not stopped [removing it] until I lost will completely and I have given it back nakedly to Him who has given it freely to me by His goodness. For, whoever does well, should he see a greater good which he can do, if it is asked of him and he does not do it, he sins. Consider then what you owe from one of your defects and you will find that you owe as much to God for one of your defects as His will is worth which you have taken from Him in doing your will.

Now consider, to grasp it better, what kind of thing is the will of God. It is the whole Trinity, who is one will. Thus the will of God is one divine nature in Trinity. All this the Soul owes to God from one sole defect.

We will make a kind of parallel for bestial intellects. We maintain that this Soul who is nothing was once as rich as God is. If she willed to be freed of her debt which she owes, and to pay God neither more nor less than what she owes Him for one sole defect, this Soul would have remained completely nothing. Thus she would have remained in nothingness, because of herself she was not nothing, but instead she would have had of her nature what God has, except that she willed to carry out one sin. Nothing would remain in her inwardly since it was necessary through the power of judgment and righteousness that she be returned to nothingness before she would be freed from her defect, and so satisfy the rigor of justice.

And what could Truth then say, if she wished to speak rightly, if she wished to speak of other sins which are numberless as one could speak about one alone? And it is necessary to speak, for [Truth] herself is righteousness, and nothing other than righteousness.

Soul: Ah, Soul, says this Soul to herself, if you had everything which is described here, still you would give nothing to Him, instead it would be His through debt before you were freed of it. And how much do I owe therefore, says this Soul, from the other [defects] when there is no one who knows how to count them, except Justice and Truth? Alas, says this Soul, I owe such a debt, and will owe without end and without counting. For before I could owe nothing, I would have to have nothing, this you know and see. And God gave me will to do His will, to gain Him from Himself. Alas, I have added to my poverty, the great poverty of sin, but sins no one knows except for Truth alone.

Chapter 109: How the Soul is distressed that she cannot sufficiently satisfy the debts of her defects.

[*Soul*]: Ah, ah, God! says this Soul, who am I now, since I was nothing before I owed something? Who am I, since I was no thing before I owed to my God some thing, through the work of my own will. And I would have to be no thing again, if I had what this book says, where it speaks of the parallel which you have heard, before I would be acquitted of one of my defects, and not until! not until! not until! But now I have in myself neither [what is described], nor anything else, nor can I have it. And if I had it, you would see who I would be if I were acquitted from one sin. Never have I possessed something nor am I able to gain anything by myself, nor can anyone give me anything to pay my debts.

Ah, Truth, says this Soul, who am I? I pray you to tell me.
Truth: You were nothing, says Truth, as long as you had abandoned nothing of what I gave to you. Now you are another thing, for you are less than nothing by however many times, says Truth, you have willed something other than my will.
Soul: This is true, says this Soul. Truth of truth. Some other thing am I, I know well, and I receive it from you, Truth, says this Soul. I know no other thing better than this. If it could be that God would demand righteousness from one of my sins, without mercy, I would not suffer less eternal torment than He has power. But if you are righteous Truth, says this sin-filled Soul, and Justice firm and rigorous, yet Kindness[94] and Mercy, your blood-sisters sweet and courteous, remain on my side opposing you for the sake of all my debts, and in this, says this Soul, I calm myself. Whichever of these sisters aids me, whether Justice, or Mercy, or Truth, or Kindness, it does not matter to me, this is fully my will. It does not matter to me on which side of these two I fall,[95] all is one to me, and without joy and without fear.

Why without joy and without fear? Because one does not increase in justice in what one might take from me, nor in mercy in what one might do for me. And so also for me. I have no joy from the one, no anxiety from the other. Since my Lover neither loses nor gains in this, all is one to me from the one who alone is One. This point makes me one, and otherwise I would be two, as soon as it might concern me, for I would be with myself. The Son of God the Father is my mirror of this, for God the Father gave to us His Son in saving us. He had no other concern in giving this gift to us than the concern of our salvation alone. And the Son ransomed us in dying, in accomplishing obedience to His Father. He had no other concern in doing this than the will of God His Father alone. And the Son of God is exemplar for us, and thus we ought to follow Him in this regard, for we ought to will in all things only the divine will. And so we will be sons of God the Father according to the exemplar of Jesus Christ His Son.

Ah, God, how this is a sweet consideration! He has, by doing this, placed us in possession: not that it would be impossible that I could sin if I will; but that it is impossible that I sin, if my will does not will it. Thus we are in full possession by His full will, if He remains in us without seeking. Whoever seeks what He has, this is a defect of understanding; such a one has not the skill which gives such knowledge.

Chapter 110: How a skill in a creature is a subtle ability which is in the substance of the Soul.

[*The Seeker*]: What, then, is a skill in a creature?

Love: It is a subtle natural ability[96] from which intellect is born, which gives understanding in the Soul to interpret what someone says more perfectly than the one who says it himself, even though the speaker understands what he says. Why? Because intelligence reposes, and speaking labors; and understanding cannot undertake labor lest she be less noble.

This skill is nimble and tends by nature to attain the fullness of its enterprise, and its enterprise is nothing more than the righteous will of God. This subtle ability is the substance of the Soul; *and the intellect is the operation of the soul*[97]; and the understanding is the height of the Soul; and such understanding is from substance and from intellect.

This [Soul] dwells in a complete life of good habits. Thus Love, who gives her this being, remains in her and she remains in nothingness, but not in love.[98] For as long as the Soul is with herself, she remains in love. Such love made her prideful and charmed, as long as she remained in it. For Nature is on the side of such love, and often has the means to give and take in such a stage in which the Soul is dominated and impenetrable. In such a stage, she has perceptions and meditations, for this is the stage of contemplation which retains Thought with her in her service. Now [the Soul] remains in nothingness, for Love remains in her, and thus she is at such a stage without herself. Thus nothing remains of herself which might make her melancholy or charmed: Thought has no more lordship in her. She has lost the use of her senses—not her senses, but the use.[99] For Love has carried her from the place where she was, in leaving her senses in peace, and so has seized their use. This is the completion of her pilgrimage, and the annihilation by her rendering of her will, which is dissolved in [Love]. This is the captivity of the high sea, for she lives without her will and so she is in being above her deliberation. Otherwise she would be reproached by the sovereign who places her there without herself, and so she would have war against Love, who is the Holy Spirit, and she would be reproached by the Father, and judged by the Son.

Chapter 111: The difference between the sweetness of peace and the war which creates reproach or guilt of conscience.

[*Love*]: There is a great difference between the sweetness of peace, which surpasses all senses [and] which remains in the delights of full sufficiency the Lover gives through the juncture of love, and the war which creates reproach. One who remains in will is often in such a war, whatever good works his will might do. But that one has peace who remains in willing nothing where he was before he had will. The divine goodness has no reason to reproach him.

Soul: Ah, God, how this is well said! says the Unencumbered Soul. But it is necessary that He do this without me, just as He created me without myself by His divine goodness. Now am I, says this Soul, a soul created by Him without myself for the purpose of working between Him and me the difficult works of the Virtues, He for my sake and I for His sake, as long as I take refuge in Him. And I cannot be in Him unless He places me there of Himself without myself, just as when He made me by Himself without myself. This is Uncreated Goodness, who loves the goodness which she has created. Now Uncreated Goodness possesses properly of herself free will, and she gives us free will also by her goodness, free will beyond her power, without any why except for our sakes that we might be of her goodness.

Therefore we have will, departing from her goodness and outside her power, in order for us to be even more free, although [God] has will outside our power by His own proper freedom. Now the Divine Goodness saw that we might go the way of pestilence and perdition by the free will which He gave us and which departs from His goodness. And this goodness is given to us through Goodness. Thus He joins human nature to Divine Goodness in the person of the Son in order to pay the debt which we had committed by our unrighteous will.

Unrighteous Will: Now I cannot be, says Unrighteous Will, what I ought to be until I return to where I was before I departed from Him, where I was as naked as He is who is; to be as naked as I was when I was who was not. And it is necessary that I have this, if I wish to receive what is mine. Otherwise I will not have it.

Gloss this if you wish, or if you can. If you cannot, you are not of this kind; but if you are of this kind, it will be opened to you. You would already be profoundly annihilated if you had the means by which you could hear it, for otherwise I would not say it. If His goodness has taken from you the hearing, I do not disavow it.

Chapter 112: Concerning the eternal goodness which is eternal love.[100]

He is One Eternal Goodness who is Eternal Love, which tends, by the nature of charity, to give and overflow His total goodness. Such eternal goodness begets pleasing goodness, and from this eternal goodness and pleasing goodness the loving Love of the Lover is in the Beloved. The Beloved regards the Lover forever by this loving Love.[101]

Chapter 113: How thinking about the passion of Jesus Christ makes us have victory over ourselves.

I will help those who will hear this book to grasp that it is necessary for us to retreat within ourselves—through thoughts of devotion, through works of perfection, through petitions of Reason—our whole life, by our power, which Jesus Christ did and which He preached to us. For He says, as it has been said: "Whoever will believe in me, he will do such works as I do, and still even greater works will he do."[102] And it is necessary for us to do this before we have victory over ourselves. If we were to do this by our power, we would arrive at the point where we would possess all this, in placing outside of ourselves all thoughts of devotion and all works of perfection and all the petitions of Reason, for we would not have anything more to do with those. And then the Deity would work His divine works in us, for our sakes, without us. He is who is, because He is what He is of Himself: Lover, Loved, Love.[103] And therefore we are nothing because we have nothing of our own. *May you see this complete naked nothing by hiding or veiling, and then you would have Him who is his true being in us.*[104]

Chapter 114: If the human creature can remain in life and be forever "without" herself.

I ask the blind, or the clarified ones who see better than do the former, if the human creature can remain in life and be forever "without" herself? If these two do not say it to me, no one will say it to me, for no one knows it if one is not of this lineage.

Truth: Truth says yes for her, and Love declares it, who says that the Annihilated Soul is "without" herself when she has no feeling of nature, no work, nor any interior work, neither shame nor honor, nor any fear of anything which might happen, nor any affection in the divine goodness; nor does she know any longer any indwelling of will, but instead [she] is without will at all moments. Thus she is annihilated, "without" herself, whatever thing God might suffer from her. Thus she does all things without herself, and so she leaves all things without herself. This is no marvel: she is no longer "for" her own sake, for she lives by divine substance.

Chapter 115: Here is described the eternal substance, and how Love generates the Trinity in the Soul.

He is one eternal substance, one pleasing fruition, one loving conjunction. The Father is eternal substance; the Son is pleasing fruition; the Holy Spirit is loving conjunction. This loving conjunction is from eternal substance and from pleasing fruition through the divine love.[105]

Soul: Ah, Unity, says the Soul grasped by Divine Goodness, you generate unity, and unity reflects its ardor in unity. Divine love of unity generates in the Annihilated Soul, in the Unencumbered Soul, in the Transparent Soul, eternal substance, pleasing fruition, loving conjunction. From the eternal substance the memory possesses the power of the Father. From the pleasing fruition the intellect possesses the wisdom of the Son. From the loving conjunction the will possesses the goodness of the Holy Spirit. This goodness of the Holy Spirit conjoins it [the will] in the love of the Father and of the Son.[106] This conjunction places the Soul in being without being which is Being. Such Being is the Holy Spirit Himself, who is Love from the Father and from the Son. Such Love from the Holy Spirit flows into the Soul and she is enlarged from the abundance of delights from a very lofty gift, which is given by a spark and majestic juncture from the sovereign Lover, who gives Himself simple, *and makes Himself a simple One.*[107] And because He gives Himself simple, He shows that there is nothing except Him from Whom all things have being. And so nothing is except Him in love of light, of union, of praise: one will, one love, and one work in two natures. One sole goodness, through conjunction of the transforming power of love from my Lover, says this Soul who is at rest without obstructing the outpouring of divine Love. By such divine Love, the divine Will works in me, for me and without my possession.

Chapter 116: How the Soul is delighted by the suffering of her neighbors.

This [Soul] sees in her Lover a full perfect love, and so she seeks no occasion to have His assistance, but instead she takes what is His as her own. Within her highest part this Soul is delighted many times, without her knowledge and willingly or not, by the sufferings of her neighbors, for she discerns within his[108] spirit and knows without her own knowledge, that this is the way by which they will arrive at the gate of their salvation. She discerns her light in the highest place where she is united, and so she is pleased by the pleasure of Him to whom she is united, for His pleasure is the salvation of creatures. This [Soul] is united here to His will, and thus she has joy by His goodness, on account of the concord by which His goodness has thus united her, without the knowledge of Reason.

And so it is now, that this causes Reason to discern that she is delighted and so [Reason] tells her that she has sinned by this, because she is delighted in the suffering of her neighbor. Reason always judges according to what she knows, for she wishes always to do the work which is fitting for her to do. But in this case she is one-eyed, and so she cannot see the high things, and thus she makes her complaint to the Soul. Reason is one-eyed, and this no one can deny, for no one can see high things unless he exist eternally. And rightly Reason cannot see this for it is necessary that her being faint away.

Chapter 117: How this Soul shows that she is an exemplar of the salvation of every creature.

Now speaks the exalted Spirit who is no longer in the dominion of Reason: God has nowhere to place His goodness, it says, if He places it not in me, nor has He a dwelling place which might be appropriate for Him, nor can there be a place where He might completely place Himself, if it is not in me. And through this I am an exemplar of salvation, and even more, the salvation itself of every creature and the glory of God. And I will tell you how, why, and in what. First, because I am the height of all evil, for I contain of my own nature what is wretched, and therefore am I total wretchedness. And He who is the height of all goodness contains in Himself, by His own nature, all goodness, and therefore is He total goodness. Thus I am total wretchedness and He is total goodness, and one must give alms to the poorest lest one take from them what is theirs by right. Now God cannot do what is unjust, for then He would destroy Himself.[109] Thus His goodness is mine by reason of my necessity and by reason of the righteousness of His pure goodness. Since I am total wretchedness and He is total goodness, it is necessary for me to have the totality of His goodness before my wretchedness can be terminated. My poverty cannot be overcome with less. And His goodness could not allow me to beg, since His goodness is powerful and most worthy. But I would be forced to beg if He did not give me the totality of His goodness, for I am total wretchedness; for anything less than the totality of the abundance of all His goodness could not fill the abyss of the depth of my own wretchedness. And so in this way I have in me, by His pure goodness through goodness, the totality of His divine goodness, which I have had without beginning and will have without end. Thus He knows completely this need, and through [this need] have I possessed completely [His goodness] by the knowledge of His divine wisdom, by the will of His divine goodness, by the work of His divine power, *because otherwise I would faint away if He were not continuously of such use to me. And therefore I say that I am the salvation of every creature and the glory of God. As Christ by His death is the redemption of the people and the praise of God the Father, so I am by reason of my wretchedness the salvation of the human race and the glory of God the Father.*[110] For God the Father has given to His Son the totality of His goodness, which goodness of God the human race comes to understand through the death of Jesus Christ His Son, who is the eternal praise of the Father and the ransom of the human creature.

[*Soul*]: Similarly I tell you, says this Soul, that God the Father has given and poured out in me the totality of His goodness. Such Goodness of God the human race comes to understand by means of my wretchedness. Thus it appears clearly that I am the eternal praise of God and the salvation of the human creature. For the salvation of every creature is nothing other than the understanding of the goodness of God. Thus, since all will have understanding through me of the goodness of God, which goodness of God creates such goodness in me, this goodness will be understood by them through me. Nothing was ever understood if not my wretchedness. Since the divine goodness is understood by them through my wretchedness, and their salvation is nothing other than understanding the divine goodness, therefore I am the cause of the salvation of every creature, for the goodness of God is understood by them through me. And since the goodness of God is understood through me, I am His sole glory and His sole praise. For His glory and His praise is nothing other than the understanding of His goodness. Our salvation is founded in nothing other, by His total will, than in understanding His divine goodness, and I am the cause of this. For the goodness of His pure nature is understood through the wretchedness of my crude nature. I have no possibility of possessing His goodness other than by reason of my wretchedness.

Thus I can never lose His goodness, for I cannot lose my wretchedness, and in this point He has assured me about His goodness. The nature of my wretchedness alone has adorned me with such a gift, and not any good work which I might ever do, which no one could do. A good work gives me neither comfort nor hope, but only my wretchedness, for I have by it this certainty.

Now you have seen—and you can see it if there is any light in you—how, in what, and why I am the salvation of every creature, and the glory of God. And since I possess His total goodness, thus I am the same that He is through the transformation of love. For the stronger transforms the weaker into itself.

This transformation is most delicious, as those know who have tasted it. There is not a pupil of the eye which is so impenetrable, whatever thing one places within it, be it fire, or iron, or stone— which is the death of the pupil of the eye[111]—as is divine love if one does something contrary to it [love], and if one is not always in the perfect fullness of her pure will.

Now you can perceive how my wretchedness is the source of possessing His goodness, on account of the occasion of my necessity. For sometimes God allows some evil to be done for the sake of a greater good which must be birthed from it afterward. All those who are planted as seeds from the Father and are come into this world, have descended from the perfect into the imperfect, in order to attain to the most perfect. And there the wound is opened in order to heal those who are wounded without their knowledge. Such folk are humble of themselves. They have carried the cross of Jesus Christ, through the work of goodness, or they carry their own.

Chapter 118: Of the seven stages of the pious Soul, which are elsewhere called states.

Soul: I have promised, says this Soul, ever since Love has over-powered me, to say something about the seven stages we call states, for so they are. And these are the degrees by which one ascends from the valley to the height of the mountain, which is so isolated that one sees nothing save God. Each degree of being has its own level.

The first state, or degree, is that the Soul, who is touched by God through grace and stripped of her power of sin, intends to keep for the rest of her life, that is until death, the commandments of God which He commands in the Law. And thus the Soul regards and considers, through great fear, that God has commanded her to love Him with all her heart, and also her neighbor as herself.[112] So it seems to this Soul to be labor enough for her to do all that she knows how to do. And it seems to her that, even if she lived a thousand years, her power would be fully occupied with maintaining and keeping the commandments.

Unencumbered Soul: At such a point and in such a stage I found myself once upon a time, says the Unencumbered Soul, and I was this. Now no one should be afraid to come higher. And one will not be afraid if he has a gentle heart and is full of noble courage within. But a petty heart dares not to undertake a great thing or to climb high, because of a lack of love. Such folk are so cowardly. But it is not surprising because they remain in sloth, which does not allow them to seek God whom they will never find if they do not diligently seek Him.

The Second Stage: The second state or degree is that the Soul considers that God counsels His special lovers to go beyond what He commands. That one is not a lover who can refrain from accomplishing all that he knows pleases his beloved. But the creature abandons self and strains self above all to do the counsels of men, in the work of mortification of nature, in despising riches, delights and honors, in order to accomplish the perfection of the evangelical counsel of which Jesus Christ is the exemplar. Thus [the Soul] fears neither the loss of possessions, nor people's words, nor the feebleness of the body, for her beloved does not fear them, and so neither can the Soul who is overtaken by Him.

The Third Stage: The third stage is when the Soul considers herself in the affection of the love of the work of perfection, by which her spirit is sharpened through a boiling desire of love in multiplying in herself such works. This is done by the subtlety of understanding of the intellect of her love, which does not know how to offer consolation to her beloved except in what He loves. For a gift is not prized in love other than to give to a lover the thing most loved.

So it is that the will of this creature loves only the works of goodness, through the rigor of great enterprises of all labors by which she can nourish her spirit. So it seems to her rightly to realize that she does not love anything except these works of goodness, and for this reason she does not know what to give love if she does not sacrifice this. For no death would be martyrdom to her except abstaining from the work she loves, which is the delight of her pleasure and the life of her will which is nourished by this. And thus she relinquishes such works from which she has such delight, and she puts the will to death which had life from this. In order to accomplish this martyrdom, she obliges herself to obey another will, in abstaining from work and from will, in fulfilling another will, in order to destroy her own will.[113] And this is more difficult, much more difficult than the other two stages were. For it is more difficult to conquer the works of the will of the spirit than it is to conquer the will of the body or to accomplish the will of the spirit. Thus it is necessary to be pulverized in breaking and bruising the self in order to enlarge the place where love would want to be, and to encumber the self by several stages in order to unencumber the self to attain one's being.

The Fourth Stage: The fourth stage is that the Soul is drawn by the height of love into the delight of thought through meditation. And she relinquishes all exterior labors and obedience to another through the height of contemplation. Then the Soul is so impenetrable, noble, and delicate that she cannot suffer any kind of touch except the touch of the pure delight of love, by which she is singularly joyful and charmed. [This love] makes her proud of the abundance of love, by which she is mistress of resplendence, that is, of the brightness of her soul, which makes her marvelously filled with love by great faith through the concord of union which places her in possession of its delights.

So the Soul believes that there is no higher life than to have this over which she has lordship. For love has so grandly satisfied her with delights that she does not believe that God has a greater gift to give to this Soul here below, which is such love as Love has poured out within her through love.

Ah, it is not strange if such a Soul is overtaken, for gracious love makes her completely inebriated, and so inebriated that it allows no perception except what she has through the power by which love delights her. And thus the Soul cannot value another state, for the great brightness of love has so totally dazzled her sight that she sees nothing beyond her love. And there she is deceived, for there are two other stages here below which God gives that are greater and more noble than this. But love has deceived many souls[114] by the sweetness of the pleasure of her love, which overtakes the Soul as soon as she comes near to it. Against such power none can prevail. This is known by the Soul whom Love has carried higher beyond herself, through Fine Love.

The Fifth Stage: The fifth stage is that the Soul considers that God is Who is, from whom all things are, and she is not if she is not of Him from whom all things are. These two considerations give her a marvelous amazement, and she sees that He is total goodness who has placed free will in her who is not, except in total wretchedness.

Now the Divine Goodness has placed free will within her by pure divine goodness. Thus enclosed within the one who is not except in wretchedness, who is therefore total wretchedness, is free will from the being of God who is Being, who wills that the one who has no being might have being according to such a gift from Himself. And thus the Divine Goodness pours out from [His] bosom one rapturous overflow of the movement of Divine Light. Such movement of Divine Light, which is poured into the Soul by light, shows to the will *of the Soul the rightness of what is and the understanding of what is not in order to move the will of the soul*[115] from the place where it now is, where it ought not to be, in order to dissolve it where it is not, whence it comes, where it ought to remain.

Now the will sees by the light from the overflow of Divine Light, which Light gives itself to such a will in order to dissolve this will into God, not being able to place itself there without such Light. [The will sees] that it cannot profit if it does not depart from its own will. For its nature is evil on account of the tendency of nothingness, toward which nature is inclined, and the will has placed her [the soul] in less than nothing.[116] Now the Soul sees this inclination and the loss of the nothingness of her nature and of her own will, and so she sees by Light that the will must will the Divine Will alone without any other will, and that for this purpose this will was given. And thus the Soul removes herself from this will, and the will is separated from the Soul and dissolves itself, and [the will] gives and renders itself to God, whence it was first taken, without retaining anything of its own in order to fulfill the perfect Divine Will, which cannot be fulfilled in the Soul without such a gift, so that the Soul might not have warfare or deficiency. Such a gift accomplishes this perfection in her and so transforms her into the nature of Love, who delights her with full peace and satisfies her with divine food. Thus she is no longer concerned with the war of nature, for her will is nakedly put in the place from where it was taken, and where by right it ought to be. And this Soul always had warfare as long as she retained the will within her outside of her being.

Now such a Soul is nothing, for she sees her nothingness by means of the abundance of divine Understanding, which makes her nothing and places her in nothingness. And so she is all things, for she sees by means of the depth of the understanding of her own wretchedness, which is so deep and so great that she finds there neither beginning nor middle nor end, only a bottomless abyss. There she finds herself, without finding and without bottom. One does not find oneself who cannot attain this. And the more one sees oneself in such understanding of wretchedness, the more one understands, through truth, that one cannot understand the wretchedness, not the least bit, by which this Soul is in the abyss of wretchedness, and in the chasm of such a resting place and of such defense. Such is the flood of sin which contains within it all perdition. This Soul sees herself as such, without seeing. And who makes her see herself? The depth of humility which seats her on the throne, who reigns without pride. There pride can no longer force entry since the Soul sees herself and so does not see herself. And this not-seeing makes her see herself perfectly.

Now this Soul is at rest in the bottomless depths, and the depths are the lowest. And this depth makes [the Soul] see very clearly the true Sun of the Highest Goodness, for she has nothing which would impede the vision. The Divine Goodness shows Himself to her through the goodness which draws her, transforms her and, through a joining of goodness, unites her into pure Divine Goodness, where goodness is the mistress. The understanding of these two natures, of which we have spoken, the Divine Goodness and [the Soul's] wretchedness, is the ability which has endowed her with such goodness.

Therefore she wills only one thing: the Spouse of her youth, who is only One. Mercy shaped with justice makes peace which has transformed such a Soul into His goodness. Now she is All, and so she is Nothing, for her Beloved makes her One.

Now this Soul has fallen from love into nothingness, and without such nothingness she cannot be All. The fall is so deep, she is so rightly fallen, that the Soul cannot lift herself from such an abyss. And also she ought not to do it, but instead she ought always to remain there. And there the Soul loses pride and youth, for the spirit has become old, which leaves her being neither enjoying nor charmed any longer, for her will has departed which used to make her, through the feeling of love, hard and prideful and impenetrable in the height of contemplation in the fourth stage. But the fifth stage has set her right, [something] which has shown the Soul to herself. Now she sees herself and understands the Divine Goodness, an understanding of Divine Goodness which makes her see herself again. And these two glimpses take away her will and desire and works of goodness. Thus she is completely in repose and placed in possession of free being, which gives her rest through excellent nobility of all things.

The Sixth Stage: The sixth stage is that the Soul does not see herself on account of such an abyss of humility which she has within her. Nor does she see God on account of the highest goodness which He has. But God sees Himself in her by His divine majesty, who clarifies this Soul with Himself, so that she sees only that there is nothing except God Himself Who is, from whom all things are. And He who is, is God Himself. And thus she does not see according to herself, for whoever sees the One who is does not see except God Himself, who sees Himself in this same Soul by His divine majesty. And so the Soul is at the sixth stage, freed, and pure and clarified from all things —but not at all glorified. For the glorification is at the seventh stage, which we will have in glory, of which none know how to speak. But this Soul, thus pure and clarified, sees neither God nor herself, but God sees Himself of Himself in her, for her, without her. God shows to her that there is nothing except Him. And thus this Soul understands nothing except Him, and so loves nothing except Him, praises nothing except Him, for there is nothing except Him. For whatever is, exists by His goodness, and God loves His Goodness whatever part He has given through goodness. And His goodness given is God Himself, and God cannot separate Himself from His goodness so that it would not remain in Him. Therefore He is what Goodness is, and Goodness is what God is. And thus Goodness sees itself by His goodness through divine light, at the sixth stage, by which the Soul is clarified. And so nothing is, except He who is, who sees Himself in such being by His Divine Majesty through the transformation of love by the goodness poured out and placed in her. And thus also He sees Himself of Himself in such a creature, without appropriating anything from the creature. All is properly His own, and His own proper Self. This is the sixth stage, which we have promised to say to the hearers, by the enterprise of Love. Love of herself through her high nobility has paid the debt.

The Seventh Stage: The seventh stage Love keeps within herself in order to give it to us in eternal glory, of which we will have no understanding until our soul has left our body.

Chapter 119: How the Soul who has caused this book to be written excuses herself in having made this book so long in words, which seems small and brief to the Souls who remain in nothingness and who are fallen from love into such being.

[*Soul*]: Ah, Ladies in no way known, says the Soul who causes this book to be written, you who are in being and established[117] without separating yourselves from the Being [which] is not known, truly you are in no way known, but this is in the land where Reason has lordship. I excuse myself, says this Soul, to all those who remain in nothingness and who are fallen from love into such being. For I have made this book very large through words, [though] it seems to you very small, insofar as I am able to understand you. Now please pardon me by your courtesy, for necessity has no law. I did not know to whom to speak my intention. Now I understand, on account of your peace and on account of the truth, that [this book] is of the lower life. Cowardice has guided [this book], which has given its perception over to Reason through the answers of Love to Reason's petitions. And so [this book] has been created by human knowledge and the human senses; and the human reason and the human senses know nothing about inner love, inner love from divine knowledge. My heart is drawn so high and fallen so low at the same time that I cannot complete [this book]. For everything one can say or write about God, or think about Him, God who is greater than what is ever said, [everything] is thus more like lying than speaking the truth.

I have said, says this Soul, that Love caused [the book] to be written through human knowledge and through willing it by the transformation of my intellect with which I was encumbered, as it appears in this book. For Love made the book in unencumbering my spirit by her three gifts, of which we have spoken. And thus I say that [the book] is of the lower life and very small, even though it seemed to be large at the beginning of the demonstration of this being.

Chapter 120:   How Truth praises such Souls.

Truth praises those who are such, and she says:

> O emerald and precious gem,
> True diamond, queen and empress,
> You give everything from your fine nobility,
> Without asking from Love her riches,
> Except the willing of her divine pleasure.
> Thus is this right by righteousness,
> For it is the true path
> of Fine Love, whoever wishes to remain on it.
> O deepest spring and fountain sealed,
> Where the sun is subtly hidden,
> You send your rays, says Truth, through divine knowledge;
> We know it through true Wisdom:
> Her splendor makes us completely luminous.

Soul:

> O Truth, says this Soul, for God's sake, do not say
> That of myself I might ever say something of Him,
> save through Him;
> And this is true, do not doubt it,
> I was never lady by myself in this.
> And if it pleases you to know whose I am,
> I will say it through pure courtesy:
> Love holds me so completely in her domain,
> That I have neither sense, nor will,
> Nor reason to do anything,
> Except through her, as you know.

Chapter 121: Holy Church praises this Soul.

[*Holy Church*]:

> Courteous and well taught lady, says Holy Church,
>   how this is wisely said.
> You are the true star,
>   who brings the dawn,
> And the pure sun without spot,
>   who receives no impurity,
> And the fullest moon,
>   who never wanes;
> And so you are the banner,
>   who goes before the King.
> You live completely by the kernel,
>   who no longer has will,
> And those live by straw and by chaff
>   and gross silage,
> Who have retained the practice
>   of human will.
> Such folk are servants of the law,
>   But this Soul is above the law,
> Not contrary to the law.
>   By the witness of Truth,
> She is satisfied and filled:
>   God is in her will.

Soul:

> Ah sweetest Love Divine,
>   who art within the Trinity,
> The hour is such that I marvel
>   how those can continue,
> Those who are governed by Reason and Fear,
>   Desire, Work, and Will,
> And who know not the grand nobility
>   of being ordered by nothingness.

The Holy Trinity:[118]

> O heavenly rock,
>   says the Holy Trinity,
> I pray you, dear daughter,
>   let this be.
> There is not so great a cleric in the world
>   who knows how to speak to you about it;
> You have been at my table,
>   and I have given you my feast,
> And you are so very well taught,
>   and you have savored my feast so fully,
> And my wines from the full barrel,
>   by which you are so filled,
> That the bouquet alone makes you inebriated,
>   and you will never be other.
>
> Now have you tasted my feast,
> And you have savored our wines,
> Says the Holy Trinity,
> No one but you knows how to speak of it,
> And thus you will not be able to give your heart
> In any other practice for any price.
> I pray you, dear daughter,
> My sister and my love,
> Through Love, if you will,
> That you no longer will to tell the secrets
> Which you know:
> The others will condemn themselves because of it,
> Where you will be saved,
> Since Reason and Desire govern them,
> And Fear and Will.
> Know, however, my chosen daughter,
> That paradise has been given to them.

The Chosen Soul: Paradise? says this chosen one, would you not accord them something else? Thus indeed murderers will have it, if they wish to cry for mercy! But in spite of this I will keep silence about it, since you wish it. And thus I will say a verse of song, with the leave of Fine Love.

Chapter 122:   Here the Soul begins her song.

[*Soul*]: [It is] in view of the ascent on high and the precious entry, and the worthy indwelling of human creation by the sweet humanity of the Son of God our savior [that] the Deity seated such humanity in highest possession in paradise, there to be elevated to the right hand of God the Father, joined to the Son for our sake, richly producing in it these graces and mercy, by which you are amazed. Thus, since that day, Fine Love separated me through courtesy. From whom? From myself, from my neighbors, and from the whole world, from the spirit of affection, and from the Virtues to whom I had been a servant through effort in the domination of Reason. Here I will tell you the truth about it:

> Such a beast I was,
> In the time that I served them,
> That I could not express it to you
> From my heart.
> And as long as I served them,
> And the better I accommodated them,
> Love caused me to hear tell of her
> Through joy.
> And in spite of all, as simple as I was,
> As much as I would consider it,
> So the will of Love held me in love.

And when Love saw me think about her, on account of the Virtues, she did not refuse me, but instead she freed me from their petty service and guided me to the divine school. There she retained me without my performing any service, there I was filled and satisfied by her.

> Thought is no longer of worth to me,
> Nor work, nor speech.
> Love draws me so high
> (Thought is no longer of worth to me)
> With her divine gaze,

That I have no intent.
Thought is no longer of worth to me,
Nor work, nor speech.

Love has made me find by nobility
These verses of a song.
It is [of] the Deity pure,
About whom Reason knows not how to speak,
And of a Lover,
Which I have without a mother,
Who is the issue
Of God the Father
And of God the Son also.
His name is Holy Spirit,
From whom I possess such joining in the heart,
That He causes joy to remain in me.
It is the peace of the nourishment
Which the Lover gives in loving.
I wish to ask nothing of Him,
To do so would be too wretched of me.
Instead I owe Him total faith
In loving such a Lover.

O Lover of gentle nature,[119]
You are to be much praised:
Generous, courteous without measure,
Sum of all goodness,
You do not will to do anything,
Lover, without my will.
And thus I must not hold silence
About your beauty and goodness.
Powerful you are for my sake, and wise;
Such I cannot hide.
Ah, but to whom will I say it?
Seraphim know not how to speak of it.

Lover, you have grasped me in your love,
To give me your great treasure,
That is, the gift of your own self,
Which is divine goodness.

THE MIRROR OF SIMPLE SOULS

Heart cannot express this,
But willing pure nothingness purifies [the heart],
Which makes me climb so high,
By union in concordance,
Which I ought never to reveal.

I used to be enclosed[120]
   in the servitude of captivity,
When desire imprisoned me
   in the will of affection.
There the light of ardor
   from divine love found me,
Who quickly killed my desire,
   my will and affection,
Which impeded in me the enterprise
   of the fullness of divine love.

Now has Divine Light
   delivered me from captivity,
And joined me by gentility
   to the divine will of Love,
There where the Trinity gives me
   the delight of His love.
This gift no human understands,
As long as he serves any Virtue whatever,
Or any feeling from nature,
   through practice of reason.

O my Lover, what will beguines say
   and religious types,
When they hear the excellence
   of your divine song?
Beguines say I err,
   priests, clerics, and Preachers,
Augustinians, Carmelites,
   and the Friars Minor,
Because I wrote about the being
   of the one purified by Love.
I do not make Reason safe for them,
   who makes them say this to me.

Desire, Will, and Fear
  surely take from them the understanding,
The out-flowing, and the union
  of the highest Light
Of the ardor
  of divine love.

Truth declares to my heart,
That I am loved by One alone,
And she says that it is without return
That He has given me His love.
This gift kills my thought
By the delight of His love,
Which delight
  lifts me and transforms me through union
Into the eternal joy
  of the being of divine Love.

And Divine Love tells me
  that she has entered within me,
And so she can do
  whatever she wills,
Such strength she has given me,
From One Lover whom I possess in love,
To whom I am betrothed,
Who wills what He loves,
And for this I will love Him.

I have said that I will love Him.
I lie, for I am not.
It is He alone who loves me:
He is, and I am not;
And nothing more is necessary to me
Than what He wills,
And that He is worthy.
He is fullness,
And by this am I impregnated.
This is the divine seed and Loyal Love.

EXPLICIT

HERE FOLLOW SOME CONSIDERATIONS FOR THOSE WHO ARE IN THE STAGE OF THE SAD ONES AND WHO ASK THE WAY TO THE LAND OF FREENESS.

Chapter 123:[121] The first consideration is about the Apostles.

I wish to speak about some considerations for the sad ones who ask the way to the land of freeness, considerations which indeed helped me at the time when I was one of the sad ones, when I lived from milk and pabulum, and when I was still ignorant.[122] And these considerations helped me to suffer and endure during the time when I was off the path, and then they helped me to find the path. For by questions one can wander very far, and by questions one is directed to the way; one returns after one has gone away from [the path].

I asked, first of all, in my thought, why Jesus Christ said to His Apostles: "It is necessary that I go away; and if I do not go away," He said, "you cannot truly receive the Holy Spirit." [123] And then I had an answer from Righteousness, who told me that Jesus Christ said this to them because they loved Him too tenderly according to human nature, and feebly according to His divine nature. And therefore He said: "It is necessary that I go away." This was grievous for them to hear, yet by this grief they were able to perceive that their love was natural and not divine. The truth of hearing this was both grievous and strange to them, for they were troubled in understanding, and rightly, for thus were they gross in their love. Nevertheless, they still possessed the sweet grace of God. For such love does not sever one from the grace of God, but rather by it one possesses His grace. But [such love] impedes the gifts of the Holy Spirit, [gifts] which can sustain only divine love, which is pure, without mingling from nature.

Chapter 124: The second consideration is about the Magdalene.

Next, I considered the sweet Magdalene, and what service she accomplished for the arrival of her guest Jesus Christ, who was often in the hospitality of Mary,[124] in the great company of His Apostles. But she did this for the sake of nothingness, for Mary was not motivated out of the need which those who are obligated must meet. And our savior Jesus Christ returned often completely barefoot, suffering in His blessed body, and He was completely thirsty and exhausted, refused by everyone, for He found no one who would give Him something to eat or drink—all this the Magdalene knew. Nevertheless, she was not moved on account of something which He might have needed in His body, and she allowed her sister Martha to attend Him, which was [Martha's] function. But to love Him was accorded only to [Mary].

I also considered Mary, when she sought Jesus Christ our savior at the tomb and did not find Him.[125] But she found there two angels who spoke to her, offering to comfort her. But Mary received no comfort, no more than if this had been the shadow of two angels who had offered [comfort] to her. Mary sought the true Sun who created the angels, and thus she could not receive comfort from the angels.

Ah, Mary! Who were you when you sought and loved humanly through the affection of the tender grasp of your own spirit? Who were you, beloved, when you no longer sought but were united in the divine love without affection of your spirit?

Next I considered Mary, how she cultivated the earth of her Lord which He had left to her. For she sowed wheat there, without mingling anything, wheat which was joined to this tilled earth, and afterward her master made this bear fruit one hundredfold.[126] But this was not until Mary had done what she could and had to do. And when she had done what she could and what she had to do for God who demanded this of her, and who for this had created her of Himself for her sake, then Mary rested without doing any work of herself, and God accomplished His part gently in Mary, for Mary's sake, without Mary. For Mary had done her part and she held on to nothing more except the Master who had given her such earth to till.

Here I will say how this is so for the sake of the children; I do not say it for the sake of the wise ones.

When a man possesses a piece of land, and he must from necessity make his living from this land, he tills and plows and hoes this earth in the manner that he thinks and believes would be most valuable in order to harvest the wheat which one must sow in it. In this way one lives who has worked the earth and placed the wheat there. These two things he must do by his own strength before the man can have produce from his land for a living. But when the wise laborer has plowed and hoed the earth and placed the wheat in it, all his power cannot do any more. Instead he must leave the rest completely to God's good pleasure if he wishes to have happiness from his labor, for of himself he cannot do any more, and this you can see through the sense of nature. Now it is important that the wheat decay in the earth before there can be any new fruit from it by which the laborer can have sustenance, no matter how much work he has done. How the grain decays, how it revives by which it yields fruit one hundred-fold though great multiplying, no one knows but God who alone does this work; but this happens only after the laborer has done his work and not before.

Similarly, I speak to you truly about Mary. The earth which Mary worked was her body, which she punished through excesses and marvelous operations of ardent desires. She made these desires flow through her "earth," tilling it though works of goodness, by which she worked the earth of herself in all that she knew would be valuable for her earth, in order to yield the true seed of God's grace. For one good work alone does not engender the virtues, but many good works truly attest to them, and virtue makes the works perfect. Thus it was necessary that Mary have many works before the virtues were perfected in her.

Now you have heard how Mary worked by tilling the land which God had given to her to cultivate. Now I will tell you about the wheat without mingling which Mary sowed in her labor. Truly [the wheat] was the pure intention which she had directed toward God. When the intention is truly for the sake of the love of God, it is very difficult for it not to yield some fruit, unless the work be evil. She had such an intention in everything she did, for her affection was always in God for the sake of the love by which she tilled and sowed her earth which He had given to her to cultivate. She had such cultivation [to do] through the sin of deficiency, and in this way were the great sores taken from her.[127]

Now you might ask how this can be, that a work of goodness through true intent can be in the soul through the sin of deficiency. This is not on account of [the sin], nor was the sin always truly in all places where it had been. If [the sin] was in Jesus Christ, this was because of the sin of the human race,[128] and if it is in us, it is through our own sin truly, although the blind call such a life true perfection. And one calls it thus for those who do not see, who truly will not be able to perceive it. Those who have two eyes call it the sin of deficiency, and thus it is, without doubt. For it is necessary that an infant possess in him and accomplish the works of infancy before he is a perfect man; so also it is necessary that a man be ignorant and foolish through his human works before he possess the true seed of the being of freeness, which is worked in the soul by divine practice, without her work. And this divine practice stops and ceases to be worked in us certainly through our sin, whether in works of goodness or works of wretchedness.[129]

Now you have heard that a work of goodness is the sin of deficiency; now I will tell you why. It is because the least is in the place of the greatest, and through our sin of deficiency the least has its necessary being there, the least which makes us lose the gentle divine being. For insofar as we have in us works of goodness, which is the least, we cannot have along with it the gentle divine being, for He cannot dwell with this; He is too great to have a strange guest dwell with Him. And to have it was necessary for Mary, through the sin which you have heard. She possessed so ardently such work of goodness and she was so possessed by it and so strongly encumbered that the very encumbrance truly unencumbered her from herself. Now Mary has tilled and sowed her earth: the tilling is the difficult works of perfection, and the sowing is the pure intention. These two works we must do because of our sin of deficiency, but beyond this our labor cannot penetrate, and thus it is necessary that God do the rest. And so He does, as it appears clearly in Mary. For Mary was unencumbered of herself after her labor, when she had accomplished what was in her to do. And thus it is necessary that God do the rest without her, for her sake, in her. Since she had done what she had to do, she left the rest completely up to God's good pleasure in her when she had accomplished what was in her. Likewise ought we to do. But how her labor and tilling profited in her, and how Mary possessed this life from which she possessed fruit one hundred-fold through great multiplication, this no one knows but God who alone accomplishes this multiplication. Such working He accomplished in Mary in the desert, of Mary when Mary reposed from herself,[130] not when she sought after Him of herself, but when the divine goodness reposed in Mary. And this goodness reposes Mary from herself, without Mary, for Mary's sake.

Then Mary lived from new fruit which came by the work of God alone. Thus she accomplished the labor and undertook the tilling and the sowing, but not the fruit. Mary thus attained the course of her being not when she was speaking and seeking, but when she was silent and at rest.

Chapter 125: The third consideration is about Saint John the Baptist.

Next I considered the supreme saint, that is the very sweet Baptist, and how he was sanctified in the womb of his mother, though it was not of concern to him. And I pondered in my amazement why it was that he showed Jesus Christ to two of his disciples so that they might follow him, and yet he remained completely quiet. One cannot find that Saint John left the desert to go see Jesus Christ in human nature. This was sufficient to his status without his seeking Him. Divine Goodness accomplished Her works in him, Goodness who satisfied him without impeding him by seeking the humanity [of Christ].

And after this, I thought about when Jesus Christ went to see [John] in the desert, how John kept himself from holding onto Jesus Christ in his human person, and from following him. Afterward, I considered that he preached about our Lord Jesus Christ, and it is said that Jesus Christ sat down and gave attention to the sermon of the very sweet Baptist, but the Baptist did not deviate from his intention, no more than he had before, so much had the divinity taken over his intention.[131]

Then I thought about when he baptized Jesus Christ, and in doing this he held God the Son, and so he heard the voice of the Father and so he saw also the Holy Spirit. To whom did he show this? Did he not hide it? Did he take pride in himself in this? Not at all. He had no concern about it except to please the One who accomplished such a work by His goodness.

Chapter 126: The fourth consideration is about the Virgin Mary.

Next I pondered the sweet Virgin Mary, who was so perfectly sanctified. To whom did she show it, or reveal it, or [from whom did she] hide it? No one. She had no concern on account of such a work, nor did she hold on to it.

Then I pondered concerning her virginity; but I maintain about her that if the whole world were to be saved by her mediation in return for her withdrawing from her status of virginity, she would never consent to it in one sole thought, since Jesus Christ could accomplish [saving the world] by His goodness through the mediation of His death.

Then I pondered how she conceived the Son of God Jesus Christ by the power of the Holy Spirit. I say truly that she had in this moment more understanding and love and praise of the divine Trinity than all those who are in glory, except her. Ah, Lady, why would not this be so? I say of the good Baptist, who is only a thornbush compared to you, Lady, who are a nutmeg tree, that he was more perfectly filled with divine light in the womb of his mother than were the twelve Apostles on the day of Pentecost, when they received the abundance of the gifts of the Holy Spirit. Ah, adorned Lady, he was still more in need than you. For I say of the Son of God that if He had found in you any kind of deficiency, . . .[132] He would never have made you His mother. Lady, He could only be what you were, and so He could not be what you were not.

Then I pondered this lady at the cross, in the presence of the death of her child, there where the Jews crucified him completely naked before her face. Alas, such piety! Did anyone know better than this lady the righteousness which Jesus Christ possessed? And did she not know well that by injustice they caused Him to die? And was she not a mother in such knowledge? Lady, what evil would your thought desire for them for this? Lady, what would you owe them for the cruelty of this? Lady, what would you do with the forfeiture which they committed? Lady, truly, if there were need of it, you would have in this hour given your life so that they would have had pardon from God for this evil deed. But there was no necessity for it, for Jesus Christ accomplished this accord so abundantly and in such anguish that it suffices for all. Why so abundantly? Because the amount of His blessed blood which one could put on the point of a pin would have been sufficient for redeeming one hundred thousand worlds, if there were so many; yet nevertheless He gave it in so great abundance that none remained in Him. And this consideration made me depart from myself, so that it might make me live by divine pleasure. I said also that this accord was accomplished in such anguish. Why such anguish? Because I say that if all the sufferings, and deaths, and other torments, whatever they might have been, or are, or will be, from the time of Adam up until the time of the Antichrist, and if all the sufferings above said were gathered as one, truly this still would not be but one point of suffering compared to the suffering which Jesus Christ had, who had it in His precious and worthy body, from grief and being pierced, on account of the delicate tenderness of His purity.

Chapter 127: The fifth consideration is how divine nature is joined to human nature in the person of the Son.

After this, I pondered how the divine nature is joined for our sake to human nature in the person of God the Son. O true God, who is the one who could sufficiently ponder this? Who is so audacious to dare to ask or to seek it if His goodness itself had not accomplished it?[133] If Jesus Christ was poor and despised and tormented for our sakes, this is not a marvel. He could not be held by it, having received the overpowering love by which He loved us, since He had the humanity by which He could do this. But to say that divine nature took on human nature in joining it in the person of the Son, who is the one who would dare to ask for such an excess? In this there is enough to ponder in order to be eternally unencumbered of ourselves, if we would allow Righteousness to work in us. Alas, I have not left this work for Him [to do]! For if I had allowed Him to do what was pleasing to Him, He would have freed me as soon as He gave me this thought about Himself. But I did not wish that He heal the fear of such a loss [of myself]. My thoughts have made me follow many false steps: I think to find Him by my works, but I will not accomplish it, nor do I accomplish it, except through loss.

Chapter 128: The sixth consideration is how the humanity of the Son of God was tormented for our sake.

After this, I pondered how He who was God and man was shamefully despised on earth for my sake, and [I pondered] the great poverty in which He placed Himself for my sake and the cruel death He suffered for my sake. In these three facts and points are all His deeds contained without comprehension. O Truth, Way, and Life,[134] how is one to ponder this about you? It is a greater thing to inflame our hearts in love for you, in pondering only one of the benefits you have accomplished for our sake, than it would be if the whole world, heaven, and earth were engulfed in fire in order to destroy one body.

And then I pondered the purity of the Truth, who told me that I will not see the divine Trinity until my soul is without stain of sin, like [the soul] of Jesus Christ, which was glorified at the same point when she was created by the divine Trinity and joined to the mortal body and divine nature in the person of the Son. In the same moment that [the soul of Jesus Christ] was created and joined to these two natures, she was as perfect as she is now. It could not be otherwise: since the soul was joined to divine nature, the body, which was mortal, could not create any impediment to her.

Then I pondered who it is who will ascend to heaven. And Truth told me that no one will ascend there except the one who descended from there, that is, the Son of God Himself.[135] This means that no one can ascend there except only those who are sons of God through divine grace. And thus Jesus Christ Himself said that my brother, my sister, and my mother is the one who does the will of God my Father.[136]

Chapter 129: The seventh consideration, which is about the Seraphim, and how they are united to the divine will.

Next, I considered the Seraphim, and I asked of them what thing it was about the works which Charity accomplished for them through the mystery of the Incarnation in the humanity of Jesus Christ; whether it was that the divine Trinity created them; or whether [the Trinity] will do eternally whatever [work] in the creature by [divine] goodness for the sake of the creature. But Love told me that none of these was theirs except for one thing, and this thing is for the purpose of the divine willing of the divine will by the whole Trinity. And this is a sweet consideration, and profitable, which can unencumber the self in drawing near to the being which one ought to be.

Now we have seven considerations, which are fitting for those who are sad. The first is concerning the Apostles, the second concerns the Magdalene, the third is about the Baptist, the fourth concerns the Virgin Mary. The fifth is how divine nature is joined to human nature in the person of the Son. The sixth consideration is how the Humanity was tormented for our sake. The seventh concerns the Seraphim, how they are one in the divine will.

Chapter 130: Here the Soul speaks of three beautiful considerations, and how she does not understand the divine power, wisdom and goodness, except as she understands her own weakness, ignorance, and wretchedness.

Now I will tell you the considerations which I had in such a life, named above, that is, in the sad life, the time when I knew not how to restrain myself or how to endure. First I considered myself, and then I considered God, and I pondered how I willed great desires for His sake. I praised and delighted in these three things above all the others, and these considerations gave me the means to restrain myself and to endure.

And so I pondered and said: "Lord God, I do not know whence you are, for only your supreme divine eternal power comprehends this. Lord, I do not know what you are, for only your supreme divine eternal wisdom knows this. Lord, I do not know who you are, for only supreme divine and eternal goodness comprehends this."

Similarly I said thus of myself: "I do not know whence I am; your power comprehends this. I do not know what I am; your wisdom knows this. I do not know who I am; your goodness comprehends this."

Then I said: "Lord, I know not whence you are, for I know nothing of your supreme eternal power. I know not what you are, for I know nothing of your supreme eternal wisdom. I know not who you are, for I know nothing of your supreme eternal goodness."

Similarly I said also of myself: "Lord I know not whence I am, for I know nothing of my excessive weakness. Lord, I know not what I am, for I know nothing of my excessive ignorance. Lord, I know not who I am, for I know nothing of my excessive wretchedness.

Lord, you are One Goodness, through overflowing goodness, and all in yourself. And I am One Wretchedness, through overflowing wretchedness, and all in myself.

Lord you are, and thus everything is perfected through you, and nothing is made without you. And I am not, and thus everything is made without me, and nothing is made through me.

Lord, you are all power, all wisdom, and all goodness, without beginning, without being contained, and without end. And I am all weakness, all ignorance, and all wretchedness, without beginning, without being contained, and without end.

Lord, you are one sole God in three persons, Father, Son, and Holy Spirit. And I am one sole enemy, in three miseries, that is, weakness, ignorance, and wretchedness.

Lord, how much do I comprehend of your power, your wisdom, or your goodness? Only as much as I comprehend of my weakness, my ignorance, and my wretchedness.

Lord, how much do I comprehend my weakness, my ignorance, and my wretchedness? Only as much as I comprehend your power, your wisdom, and your goodness. And if I could comprehend one of these two natures, I would comprehend them both. For if I could comprehend your goodness, I would comprehend my wretchedness; and if I could comprehend my wretchedness, I would comprehend your goodness: this is the proportion for it. And as I understand nothing of my wretchedness, compared to what it is in itself, so I understand nothing of your goodness, compared to what it is in itself. And as little as I understand, Lord, of your goodness, it gives me what understanding I have of my wretchedness. And as little, Lord, as I understand of my wretchedness, it gives me what understanding I have of your goodness. And yet truly, Lord, this is so little that one could say better that this is nothing compared to what remains than that it is something compared to what remains. And thus you are all: your Truth confirms it in me, and so I understand it.

Chapter 131: Here the Soul states that she wills only the will of God.

After this, I pondered, in light of my wretchedness and in light of His goodness, what I could do to calm myself about Him. And I placed myself in meditation by the pondering of a comparison with the consent of my will without turning back.[137] And so I said that if it were possible that I never had existed, so that I never would have done evil against His will, if this would please Him, it would be my pleasure.

211

And then again I said to Him that if it were possible that He could give me as great torments as He is great in power to avenge Himself of me and of my sins, if it would please Him, it would be pleasing to me.[138]

Then I said to Him that if it could be that I had existed for as long as He is, and that I existed without any deficiency, and that I might suffer as much poverty, rejection, and torments as He has goodness, wisdom, and power in Him, so that for eternity I would never do evil against His will, if this would please Him, it would be my pleasure.

After this I said that if it could be that I might return to nothingness, as I came from nothingness, so that He would be avenged of me, if this would please Him, it would be my pleasure.

Next I said that if I could have of myself as much worthiness as He has of Himself, so that one could neither take it from me nor diminish it unless I alone would will it, I would place everything in Him, and I would sooner return to nothingness than try or will to keep something which did not come from Him. And even beyond this, if it could be that I might have without end what has been named above, I would not be able, nor would I will to do any other thing.

And then, even more, I said that if I might have by my proper condition what was said above, that is, as much worthiness as He has of Himself, I would love better that all things should return to nothingness without recovery *than if I should have something which came not from Him.*[139] And if I should have as great torments from Him as He has power, still I would love better such torments if I had them from Him, than I would whatever eternal glory I might have of myself.

Then in my meditations I said that before I would do anything which might be contrary to His pleasure, I would prefer that the humanity of Jesus Christ suffer again as many torments as it had suffered for my sake, rather than something I do be displeasing to Him.

After this I said that if I knew and it would be so that everything He created from nothing, both myself as well as other things—that is, all things—must return to nothingness, if I should do evil against His will, I would rather that all things said above would quickly proceed toward nothingness, than that I do evil or will to do it.

Then I said that if I knew that I ought to have as many eternal torments as He has goodness, even if I did no evil against His will, I would rather suffer them eternally than do something which I knew could be displeasing to His will.

Again, I said to Him that if it could be that He could and would give to me eternally as much goodness as He had worthiness, I would not love the goodness except for His sake. And if I should lose such a gift, it would not matter to me except for His sake. And if He should give it to me again after such a loss, I would not take it except for His sake. And if it could be that it would please Him better that I return to nothingness, I would rather no longer have any being than have such a gift from Him. I would love it better that I remain in nothingness. And if it could be that I possess the same as what He possesses of Himself, as well as He possesses it, without anything lacking to me, and if I knew that it would please Him more that I have as many torments as He has goodness, I would love it better that it be so.

And then I said that if I knew that the sweet humanity of Jesus Christ and the Virgin Mary and the whole court of heaven could not bear that I have such eternal torments and that I not receive the being from which I had departed; and then should God perceive in them this pity and this desire, and should He then say to me, "If you desire, I will return to you that from which you departed on account of my will, and I will remove you from such torments because my friends in my court desire it, for if it were not their will, I would not return it to you, and you would be in eternal torments; but because of their love I return such a gift to you, if you wish to take it." If it were thus, I would refuse forever and remain in the torments rather than take the gift, since I would not have it by His will alone, but instead I would receive it through the prayers of the humanity of Jesus Christ and the Virgin Mary and the saints. For I could not tolerate it if I did not have the gift from the pure love which He has for me of Himself, from His pure goodness, from His will alone, as a lover has for his beloved.

And afterward, I considered in my pondering, as if He Himself were asking me, how I would fare if I knew that He could be better pleased that I should love another better than Him. At this my sense failed me, and I knew not how to answer, nor what to will, nor what to deny; but I responded that I would ponder it.

And then He asked me how I would fare if it could be that He could love another better than me. And at this my sense failed me, and I knew not what to answer, or will, or deny.

Yet again, He asked me what I would do and how I would fare if it could be that He would will that someone other love me better than He. And again my sense failed, and I knew not what to respond, no more than before, but still I said that I would ponder it. And this I did, and I told Him of my thoughts. I told Him that these three things were far more difficult than what had been said before. And I was in distress of thinking how it could happen that I might love another better than Him, that He might love another better than me, that another might love me better than He. And there I fainted. For I could respond nothing to these three things, nor refuse, nor deny. Again and again He assailed me for a response. For as long as I was at ease and loved my self along "with" Him, there was nothing I could do for myself, nor could I have calm in myself. I was held in bondage, and I could not move. No one knows this if he has not been tested in this way. So I could have no peace until He had my response. I loved myself so much along "with" Him that thus I could not respond from loyalty. If I had not loved being "with" Him, my answer would have been immediate and loyal. And suddenly He demanded my answer, if I did not wish to lose both myself and Him, on account of which my heart suffered great distress.

Now I will tell you my answer. I said to Him that He willed to test me in all points. Alas, what do I say? Certainly I have never spoken a word about it. The heart alone has this battle. It is the heart who responds in the anguish of death that it would wish to depart from its love, by which it has lived, if it thought that by so doing it could live longer. But in order for this to be so, it could will this only by willing its own will. And so I answered and said to Him:

Response to the three questions stated above: "Lord, if it were possible that the things said above, which are in question, ought to be so eternally as well as in truth of fact, I will say to you, by you, and for your sake, what I would will for the sake of your love.

If I have the same as you have with the creation which you have given me, thus would I be equal to you except in this point, that I can exchange my will for another—which you would not do—since you would will these three things which have been so grievous for me to bear and swear. And I would know without doubt that your will would will it without diminishing your divine goodness, and I would will this without ever willing anything further. And thus, Lord, my will has ended in saying this; my will is martyred, and my love is martyred: You have guided these to martyrdom. To think about them is disaster. My heart formerly always thought about living by love through the desire of a good will. Now are these two things dead in me, I who have departed from my infancy."

Chapter 132: How Justice and Mercy and Love come to the Soul when she has departed from her infancy.

Then appeared the Land of Freeness, and there Justice came to me, and asked me what sort of clemency I wished from her. And I answered her, such as I was, that I wished no clemency from her, nor from anything which could torment me. Then came Mercy, who asked what help I wished from her. I responded immediately, as I was, that I wished no aid from her nor from anything which could be a blessing for me.

Then to me came Love, filled with goodness, who had so many times set me outside of my mind, and in the end gave me the death about which you have already heard. And she said to me:

Beloved, what do you wish from Me?
I contain all things which were,
And are, and shall be,
I am filled by all things.
Take from me all which pleases you:
If you desire from me all things, I will not deny.
Say, beloved, what do you wish from me?
I am Love, filled with the goodness of all things:
What you will, we will.
Beloved, tell us plainly your will.

Then I responded quickly that I was Pure Nothingness. Alas, what would I will? Pure Nothingness never had any will at all, and I will nothing. There is nothing of me in the goodness of Love, there is nothing of me of all things which are hers. She is of herself truly filled. She is; nothing is if it is not of her. And so I say that this satisfies me completely, and so it suffices me.

Then I began to depart from my infancy and my spirit began to become old when my will died and my works finished and my love ended which made me charming. For the overflowing of the divine Love, which showed itself to me through divine Light by a Spark piercing me from the height, revealed suddenly Him and me; that is,

He the Most High, and I so low that I cannot raise myself ever so little or help myself. And there was born my good.

If you do not understand, I cannot help you. This is a miraculous work, of which one can tell you nothing, unless it is a lie.

Chapter 133: **Here the Soul says that the considerations noted above are for the sad ones, and she shows again who are the sad, and how these considerations are in the life of the spirit.**

[*Soul*]: Now you have heard some considerations, says this Soul, which I contemplated in order to unencumber myself and find the way. Such is what I contemplated when I was sad, for all those who are sad possess affection of spirit. And these considerations are in the life of the spirit, through affection of the tenderness of the love which the Soul possesses toward herself. But she thinks that she possesses this love toward God, by whom she is wounded; but, to be sure, it is herself whom she loves, without her knowing it and without her perceiving it. And there they are deceived who love through the tenderness which they have by affection, which does not allow them to arrive at understanding. And thus they remain as children in the works of children, so they remain as long as they have affection of the spirit.

Here Divine Love speaks: Ah, God, says Divine Love, who reposes in the Annihilated Soul, how long a road it is and a great distance from such a sad life to the life of freeness, for over such a life of freeness, Willing-Nothing has lordship! And this Willing-Nothing sows the divine seed, which is taken from the heart of divine will. Such a seed can never fail, but so few folk are disposed to receive such a seed. I have found many who are lost in the affection of the spirit by means of the works of the virtues in the desires of a good will, but I have found few of the gentle sad ones. And even fewer have I found who are free, that is, who live the life of freeness, who are such as this book describes, who have one sole will which Fine Love makes them have. For Fine Love makes one have one love and one will, and thus my will has become one Willing-Nothing. And such Love is from Him who is singularly fine [and is] established by divine work. Such a Soul is naked and so she does not fear, in such nudity, that the serpent might bite her.[140] Since God cannot increase His joy, similarly [the joy] of this Soul cannot be moved nor increase from His work, unless He did it by His own work. If [the Soul] were moved by her work, she would be there for herself; but if she is naked, this cannot be.

And since His goodness cannot be diminished, anxiety cannot grow in her from His work; and thus she does not grow there from her work. For if she grew from her work, she would be there for her own sake; but if she is naked, this cannot be.

Unencumbered Soul: This is true, says the Unencumbered Soul, I am at such a point through relinquishing perfectly myself; miracles are subservient to Faith, and such miracles give me true knowledge of the divine gifts: Faith is the cause of this.

Chapter 134: How the Soul is in perfection of being when she does not take Holy Church as exemplar in her life.

[*Love*]: Such a Soul, says Love, is in the greatest perfection of being, and she is closest to the Farnearness, when she no longer takes Holy Church as exemplar in her life. The Soul is thus under the work of Humility, and so is beyond the work of Poverty and above the work of Charity. She is so far from the work of the Virtues that she cannot understand their language. But the works of the Virtues, who obey the Soul without contradiction, are completely enclosed within such a Soul, and because of this enclosure, Holy Church does not know how to understand her. Holy Church singularly praises Fear of God, for saintly Fear of God is one of the gifts of the Holy Spirit. Still, Fear of God would destroy the being of freeness if she could penetrate such being. But perfect freeness possesses no why. The Soul has survived the thrust of the sword in killing the pleasures of the body and in putting to death the desires of the spirit. She has placed all her love beneath her feet, and she is concerned with herself no more than if she were not. The greater part has delivered her from the debts which she owed to Jesus Christ and therefore[141] *she owes Him nothing, however much she may have been obligated. The more, or the greater part shows itself to her, because it frees her from the lesser. Indeed the more, or the greater part, wills to have total possession without any mediary within her. And the great sense of nature, by which the deceived are permitted to govern themselves through the affection of the life of the spirit in struggling with themselves about themselves, destroys the depth*

217

within the deceived, because they are not able to understand the naked-
ness of this depth, nor to believe the goodness of God generously given for
their sakes. Therefore they remain in their works.

Chapter 135:[142]

Oh, how greatly they are deceived who remain content to struggle
with themselves in this! Because whatever a creature can do of the works
of goodness, it is nothing in the presence of divine wisdom. Therefore,
divine goodness does not give its goodness to the soul on account of this,
but only for the sake of His own goodness. And one sole encounter or one
meeting with that ultimate eternal ancient and ever-new goodness is
more worthy than anything a creature might do, or even the whole Holy
Church, in a hundred thousand years. His farness is greater nearness,[143]
because, from nearby, in itself, it better knows what is far, which [know-
ing] always makes her [the Soul] to be in union by his will, without the
interference of any other thing which may happen to her. All things are
one for her, without a why, and she is nothing in a One of this sort. Thus
the Soul has nothing more to do for God than God does for her. Why?
Because He is, and she is not. She retains nothing more of herself in
nothingness, because He is sufficient of Himself, that is, because He is
and she is not. Thus she is stripped of all things because she is without
existence, where she was before she was. Thus she has from God what He
has, and she is what God is through the transformation of love, in that
point in which she was, before she flowed from the Goodness of God.

Chapter 136:

There she does not pray, no more than she did before she was. She
receives what she has from divine goodness by the seed of His love, from
that noble Farnearness. This does not disturb her, for what she loved the
most she hates the more. This is the way. She has no greater part, nor
middle, nor lesser part in His love; therefore she is not saddened by
anything, whatever happens. She has no bottom, therefore she has no
place; if she has no place, therefore she has no love. Whatever is said, all
work is prohibited to her in the simple existence of divinity, as had been
formerly commanded by Christ, Son of God the Father. One arrives at
such a goal who has not the means by which to do good works, and it
follows also that such a one has not the means by which to do evil works.
Thus Love gives all things to the Soul, and now gives her repose in the
presence of her neighbors.

It is just, says this Soul, that all things be subordinate to me, because all things are made for my sake. Therefore I receive all things as mine, without prohibition. Why would I not? You have loved me, you do and you will do with all your power as Father. You have loved me, you do and you will do with all your wisdom as Brother. You have loved me, you do and you will do with all your goodness as Lover. Nor have you ever been other than this, sweet Father, sweet Brother, sweet Lover, even in one instant or in a blink of an eye, that I might not be thus loved by you. Therefore I can indeed say that you love no one more than me. For as little as your goodness can tolerate that your humanity and its mother, and the angels and the saints not have glory by your infinite eternal goodness beyond their merits, so little could your infinite eternal goodness tolerate that I have the torments which I merit. Therefore I receive as much of your never-ending mercy as you have of power in respect to what I suffer.

Chapter 137: [How this Soul is in her professed religion, and how she has kept its rule well.][144]

Such is she in her professed religion, and she has fulfilled its rule. What is its rule? It is that she is dissolved by annihilation into that prior existence where Love has received her. Now she has passed the trial of her testing, and she has overcome the opposition of all powers.[145] But the above was exceedingly difficult for her. This is not a marvel. For there is no graver opposition than the opposition of friends: whoever puts them to death must pass through sword points. Then all ability is carried off, without recovery, and she is given the healing of all her infirmities. Oh, what great pity[146] it is in the death of the friends who would assist the Soul to conquer her enemies, and in the end she must put them to death! What kind of marvel is this? God does blessings of Himself as it is proper for Him to do, and so it is that this Soul no longer wishes to be in this place. Her thoughts, which placed her where God is, have been presumptuous;[147] but this is because she is beyond her being.

Chapter 138: How the Soul returns to her prior being.

Now this Soul is in the stage of her prior being,[148] and so has left three[149] and has made of two One. But in what does this One consist? This One is when the Soul is melted in the simple Deity, who is one simple Being of overflowing fruition, in fullness of knowledge, without feeling, above all thought. This simple Being does in the Soul through charity whatever the Soul does, for the will has become simple. Such a simple will has nothing to do in her, since it conquered the necessity of the two natures at the moment when the will was given up for the sake of simple being. And this simple will, which is divine will, places the Soul in divine being. No one can ascend any higher nor descend more deeply, *nor can anyone be more naked. Whoever wishes to attain this nakedness,*[150] must guard against the ways[151] of Nature, who lures in a subtle fashion as sun draws water from cloth. One cannot see it happen no matter how intently one stares. So Nature deceives herself without her knowing it if she does not pay attention with much great testing.

Chapter 139: How Nature is subtle in many ways.

Ah, God, how Nature is subtle in many ways, in demanding in the form of goodness and in the guise of her necessity what is not hers to have. Certainly what she demands often can be menacing: for with these deceits she receives often what is not hers, in pretending to disrobe herself of her power and vigor and by her apparent gentle manner. *I certainly have proved this to my great condemnation, but even more to my great good by surpassing or completing what I had to do on the basis of my own maliciousness in divine knowing, without my understanding. And this divine knowledge and that hiding of mine impeded me in the way of the homeland by covering me with matter in which I had to take on humility in order to attain what is mine. Thus in this case I lost what was mine, because it was not ever mine, what I had.*[152]

It is common most of the time that one would not find in a kingdom two persons who would be of one spirit. But when it happens by chance that these two find each other, they open themselves to each other, and cannot hide themselves from each other. And if they wish to do so, they cannot on account of the condition of their spirits and constitution, and on account of the practice of the life to which they are called, whether they want to or not. Such folk have a great need to be on their guard, if they have not attained the crown of the perfection of freeness.

And thus I say to you, in conclusion, as God has given you highest creation and excellent light and singular love, be fertile and increase this creation without deficiency, for His two eyes always see you. And so ponder and consider that this seeing makes the Soul Simple.

Deo gratias.

EXPLICIT

For the sake of the one who has written this book,
By the goodness of your heart, I pray you
That you pray the Father the Son and the Holy Spirit
And the Virgin Mary
That after this present life
In the company of the angels
They might render to her grace and praise.
Amen.

Chapter 140: [The Approval]¹⁵³

I [am] a creature from the creator by whose mediation the Creator made this book of Himself for those whom I do not know nor do I desire to know, because I ought not to desire this. It is sufficient for me if it is in the secret knowledge of divine wisdom and in hope. I greet them through love of the peace of charity in the highest Trinity, who deems them worthy of direction, by declaring in them the testimony of their life through the record of the clergy who heard this book.

The first of these was a Friar Minor of great fame, life, and sanctity who was called Brother John. This man said about the book, "we commend you through these words of love; therefore receive them with courtesy in love, because love bids you to the honor of God and His free servants and for the profit of those who are not yet this, who however, if it please God, still will be this." That Brother said that this book was truly made by the Holy Spirit, and that if all the clergy of the world heard only what they understood [of it], they would not know how to contradict it in any way. And he asked that it be well guarded for the sake of God and that few see it. And he said that it was so lofty that he himself could not understand it.

Afterward, a Cistercian monk named Dom Franco of the abbey of Villiers saw and read it. He said that he proved through Scripture that truth is what this book speaks.

221

Afterward, a certain Master of Theology named Godfrey of Fontaines read it. He said nothing unfavorable about the book, as little as the others did. But he did indeed counsel that not many should see it, because, as he said, they could set aside the life to which they were called in aspiring to the one at which they will never arrive. And so in this they could be deceived, because, as he said, the book is made from a spirit so strong and ardent that few or none are found to be like it. Nevertheless, he said, the soul is not able to arrive at divine life or divine practice until she arrives at the practice which this book describes. All other practices are inferior to this, said this Master, they are human practices; this alone is divine practice and nothing other than this.

This approval was made for the sake of the peace of the hearers, and for the sake of your peace as well we tell you about this that this seed might be made fruitful a hundredfold for those who will hear and are worthy. Amen.

NOTES TO THE MIRROR OF SIMPLE SOULS

1. Titles for chapters 135 and 136 do not appear in the text, although they do appear in the table of contents.

2. An exemplum is a story, which in this case contains the truth upon which Marguerite Porete intends to elaborate. Marguerite is employing here the well-known story of Candace and Alexander the Great, a favorite of medieval courtly writers. See *Version of Alexandre de Paris Text,* ed. E.C. Armstrong, D.L. Buffum, Bateman Edwards, L.F.H. Lowe, *The Medieval French "Roman d'Alexandre,"* Elliott Monographs 37 (Princeton: Princeton University Press, 1937), Branch 3, stanzas 246–47, pp. 242–43. For an introduction to the popularity of Alexander the Great in the twelfth and thirteenth centuries, see George Cary, *The Medieval Alexander,* ed. D.J.A. Ross (Cambridge: Cambridge University Press, 1956), Part B, "The Medieval Conception of Alexander the Great," pp. 77–273.

3. The image referred to here is the image of the Trinity within the soul, which is an important theme in Marguerite's thought.

4. Here Marguerite has presented the theme of farness and nearness of the soul's beloved which she will treat in depth with her concept of the Farnearness.

5. Matthew 19:20–21. The counsels of evangelical perfection, which informed the piety of the apostolic life (*vita apostolica*) movement, are based on this scriptural passage.

6. This is the first notice in *The Mirror* of the notion of Fine Love (*Fine Amour*), which for Marguerite Porete is divine, perfect love.

7. The religious life was viewed as having two aspects. Actives were those actively engaged in ministry in the world, e.g., priests not in monastic orders or those monks who were in the preaching orders. The other aspect was the contemplative life, which was most often a life lived in withdrawal from active engagement. The biblical symbols for each type were Martha for the actives and Mary for the contemplatives.

8. Song of Songs 1:5, 2:7, 3:5, etc.

9. Marguerite's idea of being "established" is similar to the notion of establishment to be found in the "Sister Catherine" Treatise. See Appendix, "The 'Sister Catherine' Treatise," trans. Elvira Borgstadt, *Meister Eckhart: Teacher and Preacher,* ed. Bernard McGinn, Classics of Western Spirituality (New York: Paulist Press, 1986).

10. This statement by the soul and what Love says in response is very obscure in the Old French.

11. The Old French is obscure. The Latin indicates that if the soul makes a personal demand on account of its own desire, the soul remains with itself in its own subjectivity.

12. Augustine, *In I Johannem* 7.8: "*Dilige et quod vis fac.*" [Love, and do what you will.]

13. There is no Latin text for this chapter, only Old French and Middle English.

14. A lacuna in the French, the Latin is added.

15. Bernard of Clairvaux, *On Loving God* 15.

16. The Latin reads: "*Sed qui talia dona vult habere, occidat desiderare et velle, quia aliter ipsa non habebit.*" [But the one who wishes to have such gifts kills desire and will, because otherwise he will not have them.]

17. The italicized sentence is a lacuna in the Old French, but appears in the Latin.

18. I John 4:16.

19. William of St-Thierry, *The Golden Epistle* 2.263. This phrase describes the transformative power of divine Love.

20. Ezekiel 17:3.

21. Perhaps Ruusbroec opposes Marguerite in his notion of the "common life"; see his *Little Book of Clarification*.

22. The italicized sentence is a lacuna in the Old French, but appears in the Latin.

23. This may refer to Jesus' valuing of the gift of the poor widow at the Temple; Mark 12:41–44, Luke 21:1–4.

24. A play on "where your treasure is, there will your heart be also"; Matthew 6:21.

25. The soul must attain the nothingness from which God created her.

26. The Latin is italicized and added here to indicate that Love is addressing God.

27. Word play: discretion = difference.

28. A phrase which probably refers to the traditional concept of spiritual progress, that reason and love are the two eyes of the soul; see William of St-Thierry, *Commentary on Song of Songs* 1:14.

29. A difficult passage. The Latin shows Love speaking, in which case the correct translation would be "such being must become our being"; namely, the soul must be transformed into divine

Love. Because the Old French shows Reason speaking, I have reversed it, since Marguerite's logic demands that Reason be set aside.

30. That is, the soul would not be dead to the world if she remains in will, lacking something, and therefore desiring it.

31. Even the author recognizes, on the basis of this remark, that this section is difficult and obscure. It remains so in both the Old French and the Latin.

32. Matthew 6:22: "If thine eye be single, thy whole body shall be full of light"; also Luke 11:34.

33. 2 Corinthians 12:1-4.

34. Esther, an allusion to Queen Esther, the Jewish queen of King Ahasuerus; see Esther 15:1-15.

35. The Old French word for pearl is *marguerite,* very likely a reference to the name of the author, and at the same time, a reference to the parable of the pearl, Matthew 13:45-46.

36. Matthew 8:22.

37. This reference comes out of the courtly tradition, where to be one-eyed is to be ugly to such an extent that one is incapable of true love. In Marguerite's schema to be one-eyed is to be incapable of the understanding Divine Love offers to the truly wise, in this case, the Sad Souls.

38. The theme of the highest stage of contemplation as a spark is as old as Gregory the Great, writing in the late sixth century. For a discussion of his thought see Cuthbert Butler, *Western Mysticism: The Teaching of SS. Augustine, Gregory and Bernard on Contemplation and the Contemplative Life,* 2d edition (London: Constable & Co., 1926), pp. 65-92.

39. A difficult passage, the sense of which seems to be that the soul who was carried up to the sixth stage would never be able to speak about the experience; the soul who does talk about it never had the experience and therefore demonstrates that her authority is lacking.

40. These sentences actually make one long and difficult sentence in the French.

41. This paragraph is extremely difficult to translate. The Latin is somewhat helpful, although the Latin translator seems to have "cleaned it up" significantly.

42. The Old French term is *abbit,* which I translate as dream, from the verb *abbire.* Alternatives could be, habit, as in clothing, or habitation. The Latin has *abyssus,* or abyss.

43. Old French, *erres;* Latin, *arras.* This is courtly terminology whereby the lover sends gifts to the beloved by means of an intermediary. In this case, the Farnearness acts as the intermediary and gives the gift of the image of the Trinity to the soul, which is the means by which the soul receives union with the Trinity.

44. The italicized phrase is added by the Latin and is the life referred to in the first line of Chapter 64.

45. The Old French term is *hostel,* a resting place appointed royalty when on a journey. For security, servants were often placed as guards outside the place.

46. Meister Eckhart used the same epithet for those who wanted to understand God in human terms; see German Sermon 52.

47. This is based on the Latin, which seems to make better sense of a difficult passage.

48. On being established, see above, chapter 11, and the "Sister Catherine Treatise."

49. Richard of St. Victor uses the same imagery in *The Twelve Patriarchs* 73.

50. Meister Eckhart makes a similar complaint in German Sermons 5b and 16b.

51. The Latin is helpful here: "Nothing is nothing; something is what is. Therefore I am not, if I am something, except that which God is."

52. This is the only place where Marguerite uses the term "jealous" to describe God. The term has an important courtly connotation which serves to reinforce the notion of distant and perfect love. For Andreas Capellanus, the term has a positive meaning whereby jealousy ennobles the heart of the lover; see *De amore* 378–79.

53. The reference of this pronoun is not clear. The Old French seems to intend the body with the masculine singular pronoun; the terms for soul and will are feminine nouns. The question was about the soul, however. The Latin reads "then a person [*homo*] is completely spiritual."

54. Perhaps an allusion to the parable of the wedding garment, Matthew 22:11–14.

55. A wordplay: the Old French term *surnom* means both surname and category.

56. A word play: Marie = Mary, marier = to marry; paisier = to make peaceful; to patriate or place in a region or country.

57. Matthew 17:1–9; Mark 9:2–9; Luke 9:28–36. Jesus tells the

disciples to remain silent in the Matthew and Mark accounts. Luke says only that the disciples told no one.

58. Luke 10:38–42. The Magdalene was a favorite among beguine writers, and she was believed to be Mary the sister of Martha, the woman taken in adultery, and the woman who washed Jesus' feet with her tears and dried them with her hair. For a modern translation of her "biography," see *The Life of Saint Mary Magdalene and of her Sister Saint Martha: A Medieval Biography,* trans. David Mycoff (Kalamazoo: Cistercian Publications, 1989).

59. Luke 8:2; for Marguerite's reflections about the Magdalene's importance, see chapter 124.

60. For Peter's denial of Christ, see Matthew 26:69–75, Mark 14:66–72, Luke 22:54–62, John 18:15–18, 25–27. For the healing power of Peter's shadow, see Acts 5:15.

61. Mark 14:51–52.

62. A difficult and important passage. God is God's gifts, therefore the gifts of grace are ineffable and incapable of human comprehension as is God himself. To receive gifts of grace is to receive God. Marguerite's radical understanding of this concept is crucial to her understanding of union.

63. The Latin indicates Love as the speaker.

64. Latin omits the relation between need and command.

65. The Old French has *reprendre,* to blame or accuse; the Latin, *purgare,* to cleanse or purify, makes more sense.

66. The image is a strong one. Love has offered her strong protection to the weak and needy soul, like a strong and just lord offers protection to a weaker and needier vassal. But the soul denies its weakness, refuses Love's offer, and Love leaves the weak soul to its own (blind, according to the Latin) protection.

67. This is another variation on a traditional image of union, sunlight in air.

68. The Latin makes more sense for this sentence.

69. Ezekiel 17:3. Traditionally applied to John the Evangelist's penetration of divine truth.

70. In Marguerite's thought the Farnearness is an expression of the reconciling love of the Trinity by which opposites are united. It plays a crucial role in her notion of union. See also chapter 61.

71. This is a variation on the drop of water in a vat of wine, a traditional image of union. Meister Eckhart uses a similar image of a drop of water in the sea in German Sermon 80. For an analysis of the

uses of this image in the Middle Ages, see Robert E. Lerner, "The Image of Mixed Liquids in Late Medieval Thought," *Church History* 40 (1971):397–411.

72. A truly courtly and gentle heart recognizes the largesse of a gift given with no concern for what might be received in return.

73. Song of Songs 3:4.

74. Richard of St. Victor has a similar notion in *The Twelve Patriarchs* 73 where Reason, symbolized by Rachel, must die before contemplation, symbolized by Benjamin, can be born.

75. The Old French is *"jusques a la gorge,"* a phrase used to describe the feeding of geese for fattening; also used for a glutton, that is, one who "gorges."

76. The concept of spiritual progress as a descent is reminiscent of Hadewijch's Vision I, the upside-down tree, where one begins at the top branches and climbs to the roots.

77. The divine seeing of the divine self here carries a strong similarity to Meister Eckhart's assertion that "the eye in which I see God is the same eye in which God sees me. My eye and God's eye are one and one seeing, one knowing and one loving" (German Sermon 12).

78. The Latin translator clearly thought this to be a reference to John 3:8: *"Spiritus sanctus ubi vult spirat."*

79. Italics follow the Latin, which seems more clear.

80. This is based on the Magdalene legend where Mary remained in the desert for thirty years; see *The Life of Saint Mary Magdalene and of her Sister Saint Martha: A Medieval Biography.* The desert imagery also was used by Meister Eckhart to indicate a union of indistinction; see German Sermon 48.

81. Word play: *marrie* = sad; *marie* = married; *Maria* = Mary, as in Mary Magdalene. Thus the sentence reads, "for she was *marrie*, but not *Maria*."

82. Neither the Old French nor the Latin is clear, but this seems to be the sense of this sentence.

83. John 14:12.

84. That is, the goal of the work of divine love is to restore the innocence of the soul before the Fall; see chapter 133.

85. Genesis 3:10.

86. See Revelation 3:7, and perhaps also 5:2–3.

87. Based on Matthew 18:3–4.

88. The sense is not clear here, especially when elsewhere the annihilated life is described as transparent or "clear."

89. Genesis 2:7.

90. The spiritual and corporeal natures are both subject to decay in which is no reproach; decay is distinguished from deficiency or defect, for which there is reproach.

91. Proverbs 24:16.

92. The italicized portion follows the Latin for clarity.

93. This refers to the virtual existence of the soul as the nothing from which all things were made at creation.

94. The Old French term is *Debonnaireté*, a courtly term that refers to gentleness of nature. The Latin has *pietas*.

95. The two sides are justice and truth on the one hand, and mercy and kindness on the other. See Ps. 84:11–12.

96. The Old French term is *engin*; the Latin term, *ingenium*, occurs in William of St-Thierry, *The Golden Epistle* 1.15, and Richard of St. Victor, *The Mystical Ark* 3.21. The concept can refer to intellectual acumen or heroic physical activity, or to the artifacts resulting from these achievements. The term in medieval writing is multivalent and points to the human capacity for shaping the environment for human advantage. See Robert W. Hanning, *The Individual in Twelfth-Century Romance* (New Haven, Conn.: Yale University Press, 1977).

97. The Latin includes this addition, which does not appear in the Old French and does not seem to be a lacuna, but may be either an addition by the Latin translator or an omission by the fourteenth-century French copyist. I include it in this translation because it clearly contributes to the trinitarian pattern of the faculties of the soul. See chapter 115.

98. This distinction between desirous, yearning love and Fine Love, or Divine Love, is important for Marguerite's schema. See below, chapter 118, the fourth stage.

99. The term *senses* (Old French, *sens*; Latin, *sensus*) refers to the given created intellectual nature of the sad soul. In this instance, Marguerite tells us that the human faculties remain, but the soul no longer makes use of them in a human way. William of St-Thierry offers a similar perspective; see *The Mirror of Faith* 15.27, and *Meditations* 3.8.

100. No "speaker" is indicated in this chapter or in chapter 113. *Truth* speaks in chapter 114. Whether or not this indicates that Marguerite is speaking in her own voice is difficult to determine.

101. This phrase describes the creative energy of divine love. The

self-diffusiveness of goodness comes from the Dionysian tradition; see Pseudo-Dionysius, *The Divine Names* 4.1, 4.4. The love relation within the Trinity is Augustinian; see Augustine, *De trinitate* 8.14; see chapter 113.

102. John 14:12.

103. Augustine, *De trinitate* 8.14. This phrase describes the divine love within the Trinity.

104. The Latin supplies this lacuna in the Old French.

105. This seems to parallel the description of intellect in chapter 110.

106. Neither the Old French nor the Latin is clear. "It" in this sentence could be the Holy Spirit, the goodness of the Holy Spirit, or the will. I have decided in favor of the will because it fits with Marguerite's notion of union. The role of the Holy Spirit is reminiscent of William of St-Thierry (e.g., *The Golden Epistle* 2.257) and Richard of St. Victor (e.g. *Mystical Ark* 5). The generation of the Trinity here also bears some similarity to the birth of the Word in the soul for Eckhart (e.g. German Sermon 2 and Sermon 6).

107. The italicized portion is from the Latin. For an important discussion on this notion, see Bernard McGinn, "Meister Eckhart on God as Absolute Unity," *Neoplatonism and Christian Thought*, ed. Dominic J. O'Meara (Albany, N.Y.: State University of New York Press, 1982).

108. The reference of the pronoun is not clear. I have chosen the masculine pronoun because the context indicates that the soul is at the stage where she possesses only the divine knowledge, where her knowing is the divine knowing. Therefore the masculine pronoun would convey the wisdom of the Holy Spirit.

109. Here Marguerite declares that the soul emptied of all will requires the divine filling because of the nature of the abyss of humility on the one hand, and the nature of divine goodness on the other. This view is very similar to Eckhart's perspective in his treatise *On Detachment*.

110. The italicized portion, a lacuna in the Old French, is supplied by the Latin.

111. This reference, peculiar to our modern view, is related to the medieval understanding about how vision happens. Put simply, something in the eye is changed into what is seen, and therefore something in the eye "dies" in seeing.

112. See Luke 10.27.

113. The point seems to be that the submission of the soul and the destruction of the will is accomplished by the soul's own will in obedience to the will of another, perhaps referring to a superior in a beguine community. This therefore is not annihilation, which occurs in the fifth stage.

114. This deceiving love is the yearning, desirous love that Marguerite distinguishes from Fine Love, or Divine Love. See above, chapter 110.

115. The italicized portion indicates the Latin, which supplies a lacuna in the Old French.

116. This is a difficult sentence, and neither the Old French nor the Latin is especially helpful. The translation reflects what is said elsewhere, that the goal of spiritual progress for the soul is to attain the nothingness she had at creation.

117. The term "established" is used to render the condition of the annihilated soul at the sixth stage; see also chapter 11.

118. The Latin stops here and picks up again in chapter 123; the Middle English includes this section.

119. There is neither Middle English nor Latin for the rest of this chapter.

120. This could refer to enclosure regulations prevalent at the time.

121. The Latin begins again.

122. 1 Corinthians 3:1–2.

123. John 16:7.

124. For the medieval view of Mary Magdalene, see above, chapter 76.

125. John 20:11–13.

126. This section may be based on the parable of the sower, Mark 4:3–8.

127. This may be a reference to the seven demons that had been cast out from the Magdalene (Luke 8:2). This does not appear in the Latin. See above, chapter 76.

128. An obscure passage. Marguerite seems to be suggesting that whatever sufferings or deficiencies in the sense of things lacking were found in Christ's life were the results of original sin.

129. The Latin helps somewhat here, but it still is not clear. The point may be that whatever works are accomplished before the soul attains annihilation, the works are still less than God, and therefore are deficient.

130. Mary's repose in the desert is a motif of mysticism echoed in Eckhart's German Sermon 48, where the desert is the metaphor for union of indistinction.

131. This is a difficult paragraph in both the Old French and the Latin. The sense seems to be that the Baptist's intention and understanding has been completely filled with the divinity of Christ so that he is not at all concerned about the humanity of Christ, a common theme of medieval writing.

132. The Old French contains a simile, not included in the Latin, which might be a colloquial expression and is not translatable: "... *comme estre en vain le ploy d'un petit meulequin qui est ung petit ver hors de necessité....*"

133. A statement indicating that the exemplar for the sort of union Marguerite is claiming is the joining of divine and human nature in Jesus Christ.

134. John 14:6.

135. Based on John 3:13.

136. Matthew 12:50; Mark 3:35.

137. What follows is Marguerite's version of the courtly "tests of love," whereby the quality of the lover's love for the beloved are tested for its purity. In Marguerite's schema these tests are the transformative moment for the soul.

138. A lacuna in the Old French, this paragraph is in the Latin text.

139. A lacuna in both the Old French and the Latin texts, the Middle English is followed for the italicized portion.

140. This refers to the restoration of the soul to the innocence before the Fall; see chapter 94.

141. The italicized portion which follows is a lacuna in the Old French; the translation here is from the Latin. The same portion is also preserved in the Middle English.

142. Chapters 135, 136, and part of 137 are missing in the Old French. They are preserved in the Latin, on which this translation is based, and the Middle English. Old French chapter titles appear in the Table of Contents, however.

143. This statement is Marguerite's crucial description of the Farnearness as God's immanent transcendence and God's transcendent immanence. The last sentence of this paragraph points to the concept of the virtual existence of all creation within the divine.

144. This chapter title is preserved in brackets in the Old French.

145. That is, the created powers of the soul which in the early stages of spiritual progress were her friends, assisting her along the spiritual path.

146. The italicized portion continued the Latin as was the case for chapters 135 and 136. The Old French picks up again at this point.

147. The Old French term is *oultrecuidez,* which may be a play on "oultre cuidiers" meaning "beyond thought." The Latin indicates the latter meaning (*ultra credentiae*).

148. That is, the being she had at creation, nothing.

149. A puzzling expression which may refer to the three deaths which were required in order to attain spiritual perfection.

150. The Latin is followed here for clarity.

151. The term is *engins,* which in this case, are the subtle ways that Nature can impede the progress of the soul toward spiritual perfection.

152. The italicized portion is obscure in the Old French and the Latin seems to help somewhat. This passage seems to be referring to the humans' hiding their nakedness in the garden in Genesis 3:8–11 and God's subsequent covering them with skin. Marguerite's interpretation of this event as a "clothing" with matter is an ancient Christian interpretation.

153. The approval has been preserved in the Latin, on which this translation is based, and the Middle English, and has been added here by the editors of the critical edition as the final chapter.

Bibliography

Primary Sources: *The Mirror of Simple Souls,*
by Marguerite Porete

MANUSCRIPTS

Old French:

Presumably three copies exist, but only one is accessible; late-15th C., owned by a nunnery at Orléans, preserved at Musée Condé, Chantilly, MS F XIV 26. Edited by Romana Guarnieri (see below).

All known medieval translations are accessible:

Four Latin:

Three in the Vatican Library; Vat. latino 4355, Rossiano 4, Chigiano C. IV. 85. 1 fragment in the Bodleian Library, Laud. lat. 46.

Three Italian:

One, 14th C. preserved at Florence; the other, late-14th C. found in manuscripts in Naples, Vienna, and Budapest. It is possible that thirty-six copies were circulating in Italy in the 15th C.

Three Middle English:

15th C. probably translated by Carthusians; British Museum, MS Add. 37790, Bodleian Library, MS 505, St. John's College, MS 71.

BIBLIOGRAPHY

A Carthusian monk, Richard Methley (1451–1528) translated from the Middle English to Latin, late-15th C., Pembroke College, MS 221.

EDITIONS

Doiron, Marilyn, ed. *Archivio Italiano per la Storia della Pietà* 5 (1968):242–355. Middle English.

Guarnieri, Romana, ed. *Archivio Italiano per la Storia della Pietà* 4 (1965):513–635. Old French.

Guarnieri, Romana, and Paul Verdeyen, eds. *Corpus Christianorum: Continuatio Mediaevalis* 69. Turnhout, Belgium: Brepols, 1986.

MODERN TRANSLATIONS

Crawford, Charles, ed. Anonymous, *A Mirror for Simple Souls*. New York: Crossroad Publishing Company, 1981. A partial translation from the Middle English.

Kirchberger, Clare, trans. *The Mirror of Simple Souls*. London, 1927. This was published under the auspices of the Downside Benedictines, before Marguerite's authorship was established in 1946 by Romana Guarnieri.

Longchamp, Max Huot de, trans. Marguerite Porete, *Le Miroir des âmes simples et anéanties*. Paris: Albin Michel Éditions, 1984.

TRANSLATIONS OF SELECTIONS

Petroff, Elizabeth A., ed. *Medieval Women's Visionary Literature*. Translated by Dom Eric Levine. New York, Oxford: Oxford University Press, 1986, pp. 294–98. The selection is Chapter 118, the seven stages of the soul.

Wilson, Katharina M., ed. *Medieval Women Writers*. Translated by Gwendolyn Bryant. Athens, Ga.: The University of Georgia Press, 1984, pp. 204–26. Selections are Prologue, Chapters 2–6, 11, 61, 118.

BIBLIOGRAPHY

Zum Brunn, E., and G. Epiney-Burgard, *Women Mystics in Medieval Europe*. Translated by Sheila Hughes. New York: Paragon House, 1989, pp. 143–75. Translation of various chapters.

Other Primary Sources

Armstrong, E.C., D.L. Buffum, B. Edwards, and L.F.H. Lowe, eds. *Version of Alexandre de Paris Text. The Medieval French "Roman d'Alexandre,"* vol 2. Elliott Monographs 37. Princeton: Princeton University Press, 1937.

Berkeley, Theodore, trans. *William of Saint-Thierry: The Golden Epistle, A Letter to the Brethren at Mont Dieu.* Cistercian Fathers Series 12. Kalamazoo, Mich.: Cistercian Publications, 1980.

Bossuat, Robert, ed. *Li Livres d'Amours de Drouart La Vache: texte établi d'après le manuscrit unique de la Bibliothèque de l'Arsenal.* Paris: Champion, 1926.

Christ, Karl, ed. *"Le Livre du paumier," Mittelalterliche Handschriften: Festgabe zum 60. Geburtstage von Hermann Degering.* Edited by Alois Bumer and Joachim Kirchner. Leipzig: n.p., 1926.

Christ, Karl, ed. *"La Regle des fins amans.* Eine Beginenregel aus dem Ende des XIII. Jahrhunderts," *Philologische Studien aus dem romanisch-germanischen Kulturkreise.* Halle: n.p., 1927.

Colledge, Edmund, and Bernard McGinn, eds. *Meister Eckhart: The Essential Sermons, Commentaries, Treatises, and Defense.* Classics of Western Spirituality. New York: Paulist Press, 1981.

Continuatio chronici Guillelmi de Nangiaco, in *Recueil des historiens des Gaules et de la France* 20. Paris: Welter, 1894.

Conway, M. Ambrose, trans. *Bernard of Clairvaux: Treatises II.* Cistercian Fathers Series 13. Kalamazoo, Mich.: Cistercian Publications, 1980.

Davis, Thomas X., trans. *William of St-Thierry: The Nature and Dignity of Love.* Cistercian Fathers Series 30. Kalamazoo, Mich.: Cistercian Publications, 1981.

Davis, Thomas X., trans. *William of St-Thierry: The Mirror of Faith.* Cistercian Fathers Series 15. Kalamazoo, Mich.: Cistercian Publications, 1979.

Déchanet, Jean, ed. *Guillaume de St-Thierry. Le Miroir de la foi.* Sources chrétiennes 301. Paris: Éditions du Cerf, 1982.

Déchanet, Jean, ed. *Guillaume de St-Thierry. Exposé sur le Cantique des Cantiques*. Sources chrétiennes 82. Paris: Éditions du Cerf, 1962.

Déchanet, Jean, ed. *Guillaume de St-Thierry. Lettre aux Frères du Mont-Dieu (Lettre d'or)*. Sources chrétiennes 223. Paris: Les Éditions du Cerf, 1985.

Dumeige, Gervais, ed. *Richard de St. Victoire. De IV gradibus violentae caritatis*. Paris: Vrin, 1955.

Dunn, Charles W., ed. *Le Roman de la rose*. Translated by Harry W. Robbins. New York: E.P. Dutton & Co., Inc., 1962.

Edmonds, Irene, trans. *Bernard of Clairvaux: On the Song of Songs*. Cistercian Fathers Series 40. Kalamazoo, Mich.: Cistercian Publications, 1980.

Fredericq, Paul. *Corpus documentorum inquisitionis haereticae pravitatis neerlandicae*, 2 vols. Ghent, 1889–1906.

Hanning, Robert, and Joan Ferrante, trans. *The Lais of Marie de France*. Durham, N.C.: Labyrinth Press, 1982.

Hart, Columba, trans. *William of St-Thierry. Exposition on the Song of Songs*. Cistercian Fathers Series 6. Spencer, Mass.: Cistercian Publications, 1970.

Hart, Columba, trans. *Hadewijch: The Complete Works*. Classics of Western Spirituality. New York: Paulist Press, 1980.

Hourlier, Jacques, ed. *Guillaume de Saint-Thierry: La Contemplation de Dieu*. Sources chrétiennes 61. Paris: Éditions du Cerf, 1968.

Hourlier, Jacques, ed. *Guillaume de Saint-Thierry: Oraisons méditatives*. Sources chrétiennes 324. Paris: Éditions du Cerf, 1985.

Leclercq, J., and H. M. Rochais, eds. *Sancti Bernardi Opera*, 3 vols. Rome: Editiones Cistercienses, 1957–77.

McGinn, Bernard, ed. *Meister Eckhart: Teacher and Preacher*. Classics of Western Spirituality. New York: Paulist Press, 1986.

Menzies, Lucy, trans. *Mechthilde of Magdeburg. The Flowing Light of the Godhead*. London, 1953.

Morel, Gall, ed. *Offenbarungen der Schwester Mechthild von Magdeburg oder Das fliessende Licht der Gottheit*. Darmstadt, 1963.

Mycoff, David, trans. *The Life of Saint Mary Magdalene and of her Sister Saint Martha: A Medieval Biography*. Cistercian Studies Series 108. Kalamazoo, Mich.: Cistercian Publications, 1989.

O'Donovan, Daniel, trans. *Bernard of Clairvaux: Treatises III*. Cistercian Fathers Series 19. Kalamazoo, Mich.: Cistercian Publications, 1977.

Paris, P. *Les Grandes chroniques de France*, vol. 5. Paris, 1837.

Pickford, Cedric E., ed. *The Song of Songs: A Twelfth-Century French Version*. New York: Oxford University Press, 1974.

Poirion, Daniel, ed. *Guillaume de Lorris et Jean de Meun: Le Roman de la Rose*. Paris: Garnier-Flammarion, 1974.

Quint, J., ed. *Die deutschen Werke*, vol. 2: *Meister Eckhart: Die deutschen und lateinischen Werke*. Stuttgart and Berlin: W. Kohlhammer, 1936–.

Richard of Saint Victor. *Opera omnia*. Edited by J.P. Migne. *Patrologiae cursus completus: Series latina* 196. Paris, 1844–64.

Richard of Saint Victor. *La Trinité*. Edited by Gaston Salet. Sources chrétiennes 63. Paris: Éditions du Cerf, 1959.

Rychner, Jean, ed. *Les Lais de Marie de France*. Les Classiques Français du Moyen Age. Paris: Champion, 1983.

Schweitzer, Franz-Josef. *Der Freiheitsbegriff der deutschen Mystik*. Frankfurt am Main: Peter Lang, 1981. "Schwester Katrei," pp. 322–70.

Sister Penelope, trans. *William of St-Thierry. Meditations*. Cistercian Fathers Series 3. Kalamazoo, Mich.: Cistercian Publications, 1977.

Walsh, Kilian, trans. *Bernard of Clairvaux: On the Song of Songs*. Cistercian Fathers Series 7. Kalamazoo, Mich.: Cistercian Publications, 1976.

Walsh, Kilian, trans. *Bernard of Clairvaux: On the Song of Songs*. Cistercian Fathers Series 4. Kalamazoo, Mich.: Cistercian Publications, 1979.

Walsh, Kilian, and Irene Edmonds, trans. *Bernard of Clairvaux: On the Song of Songs*. Cistercian Fathers Series 31. Kalamazoo, Mich.: Cistercian Publications, 1979.

Walsh, P. G., ed. *Andreas Capellanus on Love: De amore, English and Latin*. London: Duckworth & Co., 1982.

Walton, Robert, trans. *Bernard of Clairvaux: On Loving God. Treatises II*. Cistercian Fathers Series 13. Kalamazoo, Mich.: Cistercian Publications, 1980.

William of Saint-Thierry, *Natura et dignitas amorae*. Edited by J.P. Migne. *Patrologiae cursus completus: Series latina* 184. Paris, 1844–64.

Wiseman, James, ed. *John Ruusbroec: The Spiritual Espousals and Other Works.* Classics of Western Spirituality. New York: Paulist Press, 1985.

Zinn, Grover A., trans. *Richard of Saint Victor: The Twelve Patriarchs, The Mystical Ark, Book Three of The Trinity.* The Classics of Western Spirituality. New York: Paulist Press, 1979.

Secondary Sources

Barber, Malcolm. *The Trial of the Templars.* New York: Cambridge University Press, 1978.

Bell, David N. *The Image and Likeness: The Augustinian Spirituality of William of Saint-Thierry.* Cistercian Fathers Series 78. Kalamazoo, Mich.: Cistercian Publications, 1984.

Butler, Cuthbert. *Western Mysticism: The Teaching of SS. Augustine, Gregory and Bernard on Contemplation and the Contemplative Life,* 2d edition. London: Constable & Co., 1926.

Bynum, Carolyn Walker. "Did the Twelfth Century Discover the Individual?" *Jesus as Mother: Studies in the Spirituality of the High Middle Ages.* Los Angeles: University of California Press, 1984.

Cary, George. *The Medieval Alexander.* Edited by D.J.A. Ross. Cambridge: Cambridge University Press, 1956.

Chenu, M.-D. "Monks, Canons, and Laymen in Search of the Apostolic Life," "The Evangelical Awakening," *Nature, Man, and Society in the Twelfth Century: Essays on New Theological Perspectives in the Latin West.* Edited by Jerome Taylor and Lester K. Little. Chicago: University of Chicago Press, 1968.

Colledge, Edmund, and J. C. Marler, " 'Poverty of the Will': Ruusbroec, Eckhart and *The Mirror of Simple Souls," Jan van Ruusbroec: The Sources, Content and Sequels of His Mysticism.* Edited by P. Mommaers and N. de Paepe. Leuven: Leuven University Press, 1984.

Colledge, Edmund, and Romana Guarnieri. "The Glosses by 'M.N.' and Richard Methley to 'The Mirror of Simple Souls,' " *Archivio Italiano per la Storia della Pietà* 5 (1968):357–82.

Colledge, Edmund. "Liberty of Spirit: 'The Mirror of Simple Souls'," *Theology of Renewal* 2 (1968):100–117.

BIBLIOGRAPHY

Cropp, Glynnis M. *Le Vocabulaire courtois des troubadours de l'époque classique*. Geneva: Librairie Droz, 1975.

Dagens, J. "Le 'Miroir des simples ames' et Marguerite de Navarre," *La Mystique Rhénane*. Colloque de Strasbourg, 16–19 mai 1961. Paris: Presses universitaires de France, 1963.

Delmaire, Bernard. "Les Béguines dans le Nord de la France au premier siècle de leur histoire (vers 1230–vers 1350)," *Les Religieuses en France au xiiie siècle*. Edited by Michel Parisse. Table ronde organisée par l'Institut d'Etudes mediévales de l'Université de Nancy II et le C.E.R.C.O.M. Nancy: Presses Universitaires de Nancy, 1985.

Devlin, D. "Feminine Lay Piety in the High Middle Ages," *Distant Echoes*. Edited by John A. Nichols and Lillian Thomas Shank. *Medieval Religious Women*, vol. 1. Cistercian Studies Series 71. Kalamazoo, Mich.: Cistercian Publications, 1984.

Dronke, Peter. *Women Writers of the Middle Ages: A Critical Study of Texts from Perpetua (d. 203) to Marguerite Porete (d. 1310)*. New York: Cambridge University Press, 1985.

Gilson, Etienne. *La Théologie mystique de Saint Bernard*. Paris: Vrin, 1947.

Grundmann, Herbert. *Religiöse Bewegungen im Mittelalter: Untersuchungen über die geschichtlichen Zusammenhangen zwischen der Ketzerei, den Bettelorden und der religiösen Frauenbewegung im 12. und 13. Jahrhundert und die geschichtlichen Grundlagen der deutschen Mystik*. Berlin: n.p., 1935; reprint, Hildesheim: Georg Olms, 1961.

Guarnieri, Romana. "Frères du Libre Esprit," *Dictionnaire de Spiritualité* 5:1241–68. Paris: Beauchesne, 1964.

Hallam, Elizabeth M. *Capetian France, 987–1328*. London: Longman House, 1985.

Hanning, Robert W. *The Individual in Twelfth-Century Romance*. New Haven, Conn.: Yale University Press, 1977.

Heid, Ulrich, "Studien zu Marguerite Porete und ihrem 'Miroir des simples âmes'," in *Religiöse Frauenbewegung und mystische Frömmigkeit im Mittelalter*, edited by P. Dinzelbacher and D.R. Bauer, pp. 185–214. Cologne, 1988.

Kelly, Douglas. *Medieval Imagination*. Madison, Wis.: University of Wisconsin Press, 1978.

Kieckhefer, Richard. *Repression of Heresy in Medieval Germany*. Philadelphia: University of Pennsylvania Press, 1979.

BIBLIOGRAPHY

Lambert, Malcolm. *Medieval Heresy: Popular Movements from Bogo-mil to Hus.* New York: Holmes & Meier Publishers, Inc., 1977.

Le Grand, Léon. "Les Béguines de Paris," *Mémoires de la société de l'histoire de Paris et de l'Ile-de-France* 20:295–357. Paris: Champion, 1893.

Lea, Henry C. *A History of the Inquisition in the Middle Ages,* 2 vols. New York: n.p., 1887.

Leff, Gordon. *Heresy in the Later Middle Ages: The Relation of Heterodoxy to Dissent, c. 1250-c. 1450,* 2 vols. New York: Barnes & Noble, Inc., 1967.

Lerner, Robert E. "An Angel of Philadelphia in the Reign of Phillip the Fair: The Case of Guiard of Cressonessart," *Order and Innovation in the Middle Ages: Essays in Honor of Joseph R. Strayer.* Edited by William C. Jordan, Bruce McNab, and Teofilo F. Ruiz. Princeton: Princeton University Press, 1976.

Lerner, Robert E. *The Heresy of the Free Spirit in the Later Middle Ages.* Los Angeles: University of California Press, 1972.

Lerner, Robert E. "The Image of Mixed Liquids in Late Medieval Thought," *Church History* 40:397–411.

Little, Lester K. *Religious Poverty and the Profit Economy in Medieval Europe.* Ithaca, N.Y.: Cornell University Press, 1983.

Malvern, Marjorie M. *Venus in Sackcloth: The Magdalen's Origins and Metamorphoses.* Carbondale, Ill.: Southern Illinois University Press, 1975.

McDonnell, E. W. *The Beguines and Beghards in Medieval Culture, with Special Emphasis on the Belgian Scene.* New Brunswick, N.J.: Rutgers University Press, 1954.

McGinn, Bernard. "The God beyond God: Theology and Mysticism in the Thought of Meister Eckhart," *Journal of Religion* 61:1–19.

McGinn, Bernard. "Love, Knowledge, and *Unio Mystica* in the Western Christian Tradition," *Mysticism and Monotheistic Faith: An Ecumenical Dialogue.* Edited by Moshe Idel, and Bernard McGinn. New York: Macmillan Publishing Co., 1989.

McGinn, Bernard. "Donne mistiche ed autorità esoterica nel XIV secolo" ("Women Mystics and Esoteric Authority in the Fourteenth Century"), to appear in *Poteri carismatici e informale.* Edited by Agostino Paravicini. Bari, 1992.

McLaughlin, E. C. "The Heresy of the Free Spirit and Late Medieval Mysticism," *Medievalia et Humanistica* n.s. 4 (1973):37–54.

BIBLIOGRAPHY

Mierlo, J. van. "Béguins, béguines, béguinages," *Dictionnaire de spiritualité* 1:1341-52. Paris: Beauchesne, 1937.

Mommaers, Paul. Introduction, *Jan van Ruusbroec: Opera omnia I, Boecsken der verclaringhe.* Edited by G. De Baere. Leiden: E.J. Brill, 1981.

Newman, F. X., ed. *Meaning of Courtly Love.* Papers of the first annual conference of the Center for Medieval and Early Renaissance Studies, State University of New York at Binghamton, March 17-18, 1967. Albany, N.Y.: State University of New York Press, 1968.

Orcibal, J. " 'Le Miroir des simples ames' et la 'secte' du Libre Esprit." *Revue de l'Histoire des Religions* 175 (1969):35-60.

Partner, Peter. *The Murdered Magicians: The Templars and Their Myth.* Rochester, Vt.: Thorsons Publishing Group, 1987.

Patchovsky, A. "Freiheit der Ketzer," in *Die abendländische Freiheit vom 10. zum 14. Jahrhundert,* pp. 265-86. Edited by Johannes Fried. Sigmaringen, 1991.

Pépin, Jean. " 'Stilla aquae modica multo infusa vino, ferrum ignitum, luce perfusus aer.' L'Origine de trois comparaisons familières á la théologie mystique médiévale," *Miscellanea André Combes (Divinitas 11).* Rome: n.p., 1967.

Peters, Ursula. *Religiöse Erfahrung als literarisches Factum: Zur Vorgeschichte und Genese frauenmystischer Texte des 13. und 14. Jahrhunderts.* Tübingen, 1988.

Ruh, Kurt. " 'Le Miroir des Simples Ames' der Marguerite Porete." *Verbum et Signum.* Edited by H. Fromm, W. Harms, and U. Ruberg. Munich: W. Fink, 1975.

Ruh, Kurt. "Beginenmystik: Hadewijch, Mechthild von Magdeburg, Marguerite Porete." *Zeitschrift für deutsches Altertum und deutsche Literatur* 106 (1977):265-77.

Ruh, Kurt. "Gottesliebe bei Hadewijch, Mechthild von Magdeburg und Marguerite Porete," in *Romanische Literaturbeziehungen im 19. und 20. Jahrhundert. Festschrift für Franz Rauhut zum 85. Geburtstag,* pp. 243-54. Edited by A. San Miguel, et al. Tübingen, 1985.

Ruh, Kurt. *Meister Eckhart: Theologe, Prediger, Mystiker.* Munich: C.H. Beck, 1985.

Schmitt, Jean-Claude. *Mort d'une hérésie: L'Église et les clercs face aux béguines et aux béghards du Rhin supérieur du xive au xve siècle.*

Civilisations et Sociétés 56. Paris: École des Hautes Études en Sciences Sociales, 1978.

Schulenburg, Jane Tibbetts. "Strict Active Enclosure and Its Effect on the Female Monastic Experience (ca. 500–1100)," *Distant Echoes*. Edited by John A. Nichols and Lillian Thomas Shank. *Medieval Religious Women*, vol. 1. Cistercian Studies Series 71. Kalamazoo, Mich.: Cistercian Publications, 1984.

Strayer, Joseph R. "Philip the Fair: A 'Constitutional' King," "France, the Holy Land, the Chosen People, and the Most Christian King," *Medieval Statecraft and the Perspectives of History: Essays by Joseph R. Strayer*. Princeton: Princeton University Press, 1971.

Strayer, Joseph R. *On the Medieval Origins of the Modern State*. Princeton: Princeton University Press, 1970.

Strayer, Joseph R. *The Reign of Philip the Fair*. Princeton: Princeton University Press, 1980.

Summers, Janet I. " 'The Violent Shall Take It by Force': The First Century of Cistercian Nuns, 1125–1228." Unpublished Ph.D. dissertation, University of Chicago, 1986.

Verdeyen, Paul. "Le Procès d'inquisition contre Marguerite Porete et Guiard de Cressonessart (1309–1310)," *Revue d'histoire ecclésiastique* 81 (1986):47–94.

Index to Introduction

INDEX TO INTRODUCTION

Index to Text

Other Volumes in this Series

John Climacus • THE LADDER OF DIVINE ASCENT
Francis and Clare • THE COMPLETE WORKS
Gregory Palamas • THE TRIADS
Pietists • SELECTED WRITINGS
The Shakers • TWO CENTURIES OF SPIRITUAL REFLECTION
Zohar • THE BOOK OF ENLIGHTENMENT
Luis de León • THE NAMES OF CHRIST
Quaker Spirituality • SELECTED WRITINGS
Emanuel Swedenborg • THE UNIVERSAL HUMAN AND SOUL-BODY INTERACTION
Augustine of Hippo • SELECTED WRITINGS
Safed Spirituality • RULES OF MYSTICAL PIETY, THE BEGINNING OF WISDOM
Maximus Confessor • SELECTED WRITINGS
John Cassian • CONFERENCES
Johannes Tauler • SERMONS
John Ruusbroec • THE SPIRITUAL ESPOUSALS AND OTHER WORKS
Ibn 'Abbād of Ronda • LETTERS ON THE SŪFĪ PATH
Angelus Silesius • THE CHERUBINIC WANDERER
The Early Kabbalah •
Meister Eckhart • TEACHER AND PREACHER
John of the Cross • SELECTED WRITINGS
Pseudo-Dionysius • THE COMPLETE WORKS
Bernard of Clairvaux • SELECTED WORKS
Devotio Moderna • BASIC WRITINGS
The Pursuit of Wisdom • AND OTHER WORKS BY THE AUTHOR OF THE
    CLOUD OF UNKNOWING
Richard Rolle • THE ENGLISH WRITINGS
Francis de Sales, Jane de Chantal • LETTERS OF SPIRITUAL DIRECTION
Albert and Thomas • SELECTED WRITINGS
Robert Bellarmine • SPIRITUAL WRITINGS
Nicodemos of the Holy Mountain • A HANDBOOK OF SPIRITUAL COUNSEL
Henry Suso • THE EXEMPLAR, WITH TWO GERMAN SERMONS
Bérulle and the French School • SELECTED WRITINGS
The Talmud • SELECTED WRITINGS
Ephrem the Syrian • HYMNS
Hildegard of Bingen • SCIVIAS
Birgitta of Sweden • LIFE AND SELECTED REVELATIONS
John Donne • SELECTIONS FROM *DIVINE POEMS*, SERMONS, *DEVOTIONS AND
    PRAYERS*
Jeremy Taylor • SELECTED WORKS
Walter Hilton • *SCALE OF PERFECTION*
Ignatius of Loyola • *SPIRITUAL EXERCISES* AND SELECTED WORKS
Anchoritic Spirituality • *ANCRENE WISSE* AND ASSOCIATED WORKS
Nizam ad-din Awliya • *MORALS FOR THE HEART*
Pseudo-Macarius • THE FIFTY SPIRITUAL HOMILIES AND THE *GREAT LETTER*
Gertrude of Helfta • *THE HERALD OF DIVINE LOVE*
Angela of Foligno • COMPLETE WORKS
Margaret Ebner • MAJOR WORKS